Captivating Stories
Intrigue Comedy & Adventure

A collection of amazing stories

Written by

Paul Mitch

Copyright © 2018 Paul Mitch

ISBN: 978-0-244-42766-5

All rights reserved, including the right to reproduce this book, or portions thereof in any form. No part of this text may be reproduced, transmitted, downloaded, decompiled, reverse engineered, or stored, in any form or introduced into any information storage and retrieval system, in any form or by any means, whether electronic or mechanical without the express written permission of the author.

Contents

The Journey of a Lifetime

The Naval Reunion

Strange Encounters of the Third Kind

The Highland Fling

The Lime Coloured Suit

Escape to the East

Good Morning Vicar

The Mystery of the Vanishing Inn

The Amazing Adventures of Freddie Frobisher

The Lost Treasure of the Nazis Gold

Esmeralda the Duck

Saved by Doctor Death

Schizophrenia in F Sharp Major

Harry the 'Hamster' Hillier

Hello Boyo

The Journey of a Lifetime

The story that is about to unfold is a true account of the extraordinary events that took place in my life in the year 1992. That was the year when my whole world fell apart. I can only describe the events that took place as being truly heartbreaking. Not by any stretch of the imagination could I have foreseen the tragic circumstances that was about to unfold. The first of these untimely events came about when my marriage had all but evaporated. The situation was made more complicated when I was made redundant several weeks later. These two things coming so close together had a profoundly unsettling effect on me. I would have thought my marriage was going rather well. I had a lovely wife with five beautiful children; even a house in the country to boast of, and everything seemed just rosy. Oh, but how very wrong I was.

The whole sorry business began when my wife suddenly decided to go away for a short break to the Isle of Wight, taking the children along, plus the dear old mother-in-law and leaving me behind to carry on regardless. I thought it rather strange because she never left me alone like this before, but come to think of it there were a few little niggily things that began to creep into our relationship. I had also noticed a slight change in her attitude towards me but I'm sure there was no cause for alarm.

Anyway, during the course of the week I received a letter from a firm of solicitors. They, on behalf of my wife were about to issue divorce proceedings against me with immediate effect. The situation was made more desperate when I was advised to vacate the house at the earliest possible opportunity. What the hell is going on I asked myself, and why oh why was this happening to me? What had I done to deserve all this? I was sick with worry.

In my attempt to clarify the situation I made frantic phone calls to my wife and her solicitors, but to no avail: both parties were adamant. The following week I took time off from work and set about the task of finding alternative accommodation. Therefore having scoured the estate agents and local newspapers I found nothing that was affordable. I thereby found myself running out of time. To cut a long story short I was forcibly removed from my home and thus thrown out and onto the streets, making me homeless and destitute. As luck would have it, the only thing I possessed in life was a beaten-up old van, so consequently, as a result of my misfortunes, I found myself living in the darned thing whilst the local council found me a proper place to live.

The sad thing was I hardly knew anyone. Most of my friends had either, moved on, died, or emigrated, so it looked as though I was very much on my own. I became deeply depressed with life and things in general. I felt I had lost everything that was dear to me. It seems like only yesterday when I sat in the comfort of my home, bouncing my children up and down on my knee, but now I found myself walking the streets a lonely depressed man. My situation began to look very bleak. I had absolutely no one to turn to for help. There I was a middle aged man with no home and nothing to show for my years of toil. Sadly, both my parents had passed away. I didn't even have a brother or sister to confide in. Summing up the situation I felt thoroughly gutted by the whole ghastly business. My fortunes however were about to change when the local council offered me the chance to go into sheltered accommodation. I at last began to buck up a bit and decided that my top priority in life was to establish new friendships again.

Anyway, I first registered for unemployment in August 1992 at the local Jobcentre shortly after being made redundant. The procedure was to sign on the dotted line every two weeks. This unfortunately, through no fault of my own, was going to be part of my life, for a very, very, long time. I filled in all the application forms to make my new claim and gave them back to the lady who was interviewing me.

"I see your last job was a Salesman/Estimator for an engineering company," she kindly informed me, "Why did you leave?"

"Well believe it or not I was made redundant due to the company going into receivership. More to the point I didn't receive a single penny from the proceeds and for this reason I am making a claim for unemployment benefit."

"Of course" she said, smiling back. "Look, I'll get your claim processed as quickly as possible, and will a bit of luck you should be hearing from us by the end of the week."

The following years were very turbulent really, mostly taken up with endless court hearings and social workers in regards to my children who I hardly saw anything of since divorcing. After this period had quietened down my life began to tick away at a nice gentle pace. I was still unemployed and sadly, still signing on the dotted line. But hey! I was really beginning to get the feel of this 'Rocking and Rolling thing'.

It was a Thursday morning and my day to sign on at the Jobcentre. I arrived as usual, spot on time, but to my dismay, I was informed that I was being put on a three month training course called Job Club. Apparently, the aim of the course was to find me a job, but more importantly to acquire better skills at preparing CV's and developing techniques at interviews etc. I was told to report to a Mr Pugh in two weeks time and all the necessary paperwork would be posted on to me.

I was simply horrified by the sheer thought of it all.

And so in August 1996, I arrived as requested at the Job Club Training Centre. Having found the appropriate building I made my way inside to find lots of people scurrying about with bits of paper and carrying folders – but to my surprise it looked rather nice. I was told to sit down and wait for the arrival of my course teacher. Five minutes later this guy turns up, smartly turned out in a grey-flannelled suit, accompanied with a big broad smile.

"Ah, you must be Paul?" he said reflectively.

"Yes, that's right, I am."

"Good, I'm you're course teacher Alan Pugh."

Alan pointed towards a stairway which led to the first floor of the building. Thereafter I was led into a brightly lit room that was festooned with bright florescent lights. Inside was a mixture of high-tech equipment that consisted of computers, fax machines and telephones, plus the necessary back-up to make my course go off with a bang. Seated down at well spaced out tables was a cross section of about thirty people from all races and nationalities who were busily engrossed in what they were doing.

I was then asked to pay attention. "Every time you enter or leave the building, you must sign in or out for fire regulations, is that clear," Alan said in a commanding voice. I was then instructed to grab myself a desk and load up with a pen and lots of writing material.

"To put you more in the picture I'll give you a run-down on the course and its main objectives," Alan began to explain. "Each and every day I want you to sift through the local newspapers and employment magazines and of course Yellow Pages. We also have a cross-section of jobs by courtesy of the Jobcentre service. I want you to study the jobs on display and if there is anything suitable, then by all means, phone up the said company and arrange an interview, which will hopefully lead to a job.

"I can't wait to get going," I said, trying to impress Alan with my eager spirit. Alan wondered off and left me with a pile of stationary, writing material and employment magazines to plough through. Giving my surroundings the once over I began to study the variety of faces on display, as one does in a strange place. They looked a decent enough bunch. A few oddballs scattered here and there but I'm sure there was nothing to worry about.

Just before our morning tea break Alan Pugh was trying to attract our attention by banging his ruler hard down on the table.

"Children, children! Can I please have your attention, oh and do please put your sweeties and Rupert Bear books away. I've have something to tell you all. We have a new member joining us today."

Standing next to Alan was a man who went by the name of Basil.

Alan asked. "Do pray tell us Basil what you've up to for the last couple of years?"

"Up to, up to. Well, I've been doing a bit of this and a bit of that - wheeling and dealing, ducking and diving," was Basil's reply.

"Oh, yeah!" Alan smiled, as if to say, I know what the buggers been up to. "Now come on, out with it Basil, let's have the true version. What prison were you in, my son?

"Bedford," Basil grinned.

Alan obviously assumed it was a remarkable achievement for a man who had recently appeared before Winchester Assizes.

"Say no more squire," Alan beamed, "oh and do feel free to have a browse through the Police Gazette. Cor blimey, I don't half get-em!" Alan sighed.

With the course finished for the day I made my way home before stopping off at my local newsagents where I treated myself to a newspaper plus a few luxuries like sweets and a bit of baccy. Flicking through the pages of a London newspaper a tiny advert appeared at the foot of the classified section to the effect that a brand new club was being formed, called The Travel Companions Club. The advert went on to say that the club wanted to attract people who were interested in making new friendships along with the possibility of forming travel groups. There was a London number to ring and a chap called Peter who apparently was the club organiser. With my enthusiasm levels reaching epic proportions, I decided to cut out the advert and thereby give it a try. On reflection though, I was a little apprehensive about the whole thing - but weighing up my options I decided to get in touch with the person in question to basically get the low-down on this new club of his.

However, little did I know that the call I was about to make would change my life beyond my wildest dreams. Summing up nerves of steel I dialled up the number and waited for a response.

"Good evening," a voice said, "Peter here, how can I help you?"

"Yes, I do believe you can. My name's Paul and I'm making enquiries about your new club that's advertised in the newspaper."

"Ah, it's so nice to hear from you Paul and do let me explain what we're about. Well, the prime aim of the club is to bring together like-minded people who share the love and passion of travel, but more importantly, who would also like to explore the possibilities of making new friendships along with lots of travel throw in for good measure. Look, why don't you come along to our very first meeting next Sunday here in London? We have around twenty five to thirty people coming from all walks of life and cultures and you'll be most welcome to come along," Peter said.

"Why, yes, its sounds brilliant Peter, and yes, I would love to come along."

It so came about that while in the course of our conversation Peter went over the details of the venue, date, time and location etc. Saying our goodbyes I put the phone down and felt pretty chuffed with myself. Perhaps this could be the start of something truly exciting and I began to wonder what might come from it?

The following Sunday I was on my way to the bright lights of London and immediately homed in at one of London's plushest hotels called the Imperial. Upon reaching the reception area I stood there for a moment in a confused state of indecision and wondered where I was supposed to go. Thankfully, a notice at reception gave listings of the evenings events. It confirmed that the meeting place for The Travel Companions Club would take place in suite 202. Moments later I was poking my head round a door. Inside was a mixture of around thirty people, busily chatting away and deeply engrossed in what they were doing. A biggish chap rose from his chair and thrust out his hand to greet me.

"Let me guess now, you must be Paul?"

"That's right I am."

"Ah, it's so nice to meet you, Paul. Look, I'm Peter, the club organiser. Sit yourself down and mingle and I'll get you a drink."

No sooner than I had downed my drink when the proceedings began. Peter, the club organiser, sat at the head of a large oval table who gave me the impression he was the Chairman of a well known consortium group that was about to charge up a high-level board meeting, which led up to Peter delivering his spiel.

"Ladies and gentlemen, can I first say I am so pleased you were able to make it here tonight and I welcome you to the very first meeting of the newly formed Travel Companions Club. I am sure in the course of the evening we will have lots to talk about. The prime aim for starting such a club was an overwhelming desire to bring together like minded people who share the love and passion of travel but at the same time would like to explore the possibilities of making new friendships, together with the intention of forming travel groups, sharing ideas, experiences and costs etc. Whether we travel in small groups or team up as a pair, it's entirely up to you. But tonight folks, I would like you to come up with a barnstormer of an idea for a thundering good trailblazer of a trip to anywhere in the world.

Suddenly there was a mad rush for briefcases. Click, click, click they went, as they opened up with a sense of urgency. People began pulling out maps, charts and compasses etc. There was hardly any room to move. One chap was engulfed with a map that languished daintily on his head. People began shouting at Peter, trying to gain his attention.

"Hey, Peter, what about Borneo," was the cry from someone.

Another man stood up and suggested the great outback of Australia. Others begged Peter to try places like Norway, Chile, and South Africa: each called out with great passion. One elderly gentleman got up and snapped his fingers, totally convinced he had found the answer.

"Peter, I've got it, what about Bridlington?" he said.

We unashamedly burst out laughing at his crazy suggestion. As I sat there taking in the enormous potential the club had to offer I couldn't help absorbing the tremendous humour and indeed the fantastic sense of comradeship that had brought me here tonight. I therefore made an instant decision to join up that very evening, totally convinced; this was definitely the club for me and had no hesitation in parting with my money for a shiny new membership card. We talked and talked as the night grew shorter and people were getting swept away with Peter's exciting plans, but sadly our meeting was coming to an end. Peter stood up and said his final piece.

"Ladies and gentlemen, I would like to say before we all go home, you are indeed a super group of people, and I would like to take the this opportunity to thank you all for coming. One thing before we go home," Peter asked, "Could we please exchange names and addresses plus phone numbers so we can keep in touch."

We did as Peter asked and slowly left the hotel in dribs and drab but not before shaking everyone's hand in deep appreciation of their fantastic company. As I made my way back home I began to ponder over the evenings events. In effect: I was so glad I made the effort to come tonight and who knows what might come from it?"

Precisely three days after the club meeting in London, I was sitting at home watching the television when the phone rang. Who could that be I wondered? Down the line came a man's voice and a rather posh one at that, almost to the point, it had an almost apologetic manner attached to it.

"Hello, could I please speak with Paul?" the voice asked.

"Yes, speaking."

"Oh, that's great. Look, its David here. We met last Sunday at the club meeting in London."

"Ah, yes, I remember, you were sitting next to me and don't you come from the Reading, Berkshire area?"

"Yes, indeed I do. Look, regarding travel. I've got some really super ideas for a forthcoming trip, so I'll come straight to the point. I was wondering if you would like to team up with me and perhaps join me for a short weekend break."

I hesitated for a moment and of course my first reaction was understandably to say no.

"You see it's like this Paul. I've been looking for a travel buddy for some time now. What I'm offering you is the hand of friendship with lots of travel thrown in."

I sat there for a few worrying moments and tried to take in what he had said, for I was somewhat taken aback by his offer. But then I thought, why not, what the hell had I got to lose, so my final answer was yes.

"Listen, Paul, it would be really great if you could get yourself down to Reading this coming weekend, you can stay at my place for the night so we can get better acquainted. And so, after much discussion and deliberation I therefore decided to make the necessary arrangements with my new-found buddy who gave me precise instructions for a place to rendezvous.

The following Saturday I arrived at Reading as planned, coming in on the ten thirty train from Paddington, London. However, my immediate concern was whether this chap would actually turn up or not, or was he some demented crackpot who got his kicks from playing practical jokes on people. Playing it safe I decided to give him a call from the station call box at the same time keeping my fingers crossed he'd be in.

To my horror the phone rang and rang. "Is that David," I inquired with a concerned voice. "Look its Paul here, I've just arrived in Reading, where would you like to meet up?"

For a few worrying seconds there was a deadly silence. Then a voice sprung into action at the other end.

"Oh, I'm so glad you were able to make it, Paul. Look I'll pick you up at the front of the station near the taxi rank, shall we say in fifteen minutes."

"Yes, that's fine." Phew what a relief.

It was sometime later when I noticed a blue Peugeot car swing sharply into the forecourt area of the station, and from it, emerged a stout, well-built man of middle-age, who proudly donned a balding head, wore a shabby beige coloured Mac which had obviously seen better days. His face, I must point out, suggested a kindly nature, although a bit on the eccentric side. Finally, he then greeted me with a welcoming smile. However, it had come to my attention that the person in question gave me the impression he showed all the characteristics of a highly respected clergymen. My suspicions were truly justified, for it came to pass on meeting this man, I was gripped by the growing menace of something sinister that was afoot. It then transpired the would-be vicar thus bowed his head and then had the Gaul to address me in true clergy fashion.

"Good morning my son, are you of the faith?" He politely asked.

"Er, erm." I replied with a confused stutter.

"Come, come, my child, don't be shy." The bogus clergyman replied.

"Good morning your reverence," I replied back, and likewise bowed my head.

I was consumed by the impetuous urge to do a runner, but decided otherwise.

And that ladies and gentlemen was the beginning of a remarkable friendship with an odd ball of a character called David – and not by any stretch of the imagination could I have foreseen the unbelievable circumstances that would later develop from our meeting. Standing there shaking hands, I had the distant feeling we were definitely not strangers but very close friends, almost to the point as if I had known the chap for some considerable time, and in keeping with the true British tradition, our first topic of conversation was a good old moan about the weather.

"I say, it's turned out a bit cloudy again," says he, looking up at the sky. "Trouble is they forecast rain again, there's definitely a cold front on the way."

"Yes, I do believe there's a storm brewing up, nor-b-nor east, I shouldn't wonder, but never mind we might just miss the worse of it," says I.

Having emerged from my harrowing ordeal we proceeded accordingly and set forth on with our travel plans. David pointed towards the car and said. "Brr, by Jupiter, it's a bit nippy out here, shall we take a pew in the car."

With my luggage in place we left the urban sprawl of Reading and headed for the dizzy heights of Pangbourne. Thereafter, the road carved out an opening which revealed a setting of open rural countryside, amidst beautiful, charming villages. Narrow winding roads that led down leafy country lanes that were lined with neatly trimmed hedgerows. Then, arising from the early morning mist, a tiny hamlet appeared that was shrouded in serene isolation which totalled twenty houses in all. Big lavish looking properties that were set well back from the road. The more expensive ones had electronic gates to keep intruders out – and probably owned by a few of the filthy rich if I wasn't mistaken and built in a style fit for a king.

"That's my place," David said, as he pointed towards a rambling old period cottage. Soon the car was making its way up a gravel drive and as it did so I could hear the exquisite sound of tiny stones that were being grated and crunched as the car made its way up the drive. It soon became quite apparent that David's financial status was that of a very wealthy man. So imagine my surprise when I peeked in at a half-open garage and there sitting in all its glory was a beautiful old Bentley car, half covered up with dustsheets.

My word, I thought to myself, this is billionaire's row, and by George, I think I've struck it lucky, here.

In no time at all I was doing a grand tour of the old boy's home. However, my immediate attention was drawn to the enormity of the place. No less than four king-size bedrooms, an enormous L shaped lounge, together with an up-to-the-minute kitchen. And then, to make my day truly complete I caught sight of three toilets, glistening out with pride from each of the rooms.

"Struth! I am going to like it here," I thought.

David placed my luggage in one of the bedrooms and said. "This will be your room Paul. Look, make yourself comfortable and I'll go and make us a pot of tea."

So there I was sitting in the lounge when my host duly arrived back with the tea and biscuits. As he poured the tea out he slowly but surely began to open up and give me a detailed account of his life's precarious journey.

"Well, here goes," David began. "First of all I was born in a place called Bushey, just outside of the town of Watford. My educational upbringing was at a school in Pinner, Middlesex. To further my education I signed on at the Cassiobury College in Watford. My career choice, funnily enough, was electronics. In fact I managed to get myself straight into the Royal Air Force at the tender age of eighteen. Many years later I parted company with the RAF and then joined the Merchant Navy as a Communications Officer. I sailed under many a flag and a variety of different companies. In all I spent over thirty years at sea. Anyway, this year two separate situations came about that shook me to the very core. Firstly, my mother passed away after a long illness, and secondly I was made redundant due to company cutbacks. This chain of events had a devastating effect on me. I became deeply depressed, suicidal in fact. Somehow I managed to pull myself out of it and that's when I said, enough is enough. I therefore made a decision to do something about the situation so I decided to join up with The Travel Companions Club in London. My hope was to meet people and perhaps make a friend or two. I strongly believe that our paths were meant to cross. Call it destiny if you like, for I knew I was going to meet you, even before I stepped inside that hotel. As I've explained to you, I was at sea for all those years and visited many a port, but rarely staying on shore leave for maybe a day or two at most. Unfortunately, I never got the chance to explore the interior of a country, and that's what I would like to start doing now that I've got all this time on my hands. You see Paul; my greatest ambition is to voyage round the world on the QE2 luxury liner. I once saw her in port in Los Angeles and fell madly in love with her. I could if I so wish get a huge discount off the price of a voyage due to my naval connections. Anyway, that's enough about me. The plan I would like to put forward for our short weekend break is to pay a visit to the town of Tenby in Wales and there stop for one night. The following day with your permission I intend to head up to Aberystwyth via a brief look at Snowdonia, thus ending the day with a visit to Anglesey. I could if you so wish, drop you off back home in Bedfordshire. How does it sound? I hope it's to your liking."

"Why yes, it sounds brilliant David, you've certainly done your homework on the planning side of things, and yes, I'm really looking forward to it - can't wait to get going."

David looked at his watch in deep thought. "Look, it's getting rather late, what say we retire for the night so we can get an early start in the morning."

As we made our way to our respective bedrooms I lay there on my bed and my thoughts were of David. He seemed to be such a warm and genuine guy, together with an immense knowledge of the world in general. The chemistry between us I must point out was most commendable. I also savoured the fact we got on like a house on fire.

The next morning I was up at the crack of dawn and most eager to begin my trip to Wales. I decided to make myself a bit of breakfast, and, with my host in mind I thought I'd take him in some tea and toast. I knocked on his bedroom door but there was no answer. That's funny, I thought, his room was empty. I used my best detective skills and searched the house in its entirety but he was nowhere to be found. The situation was made clearer when the back door suddenly burst open. There to my astonishment was David, scantily dressed in a string vest and beholding a bright pair of boxer shorts, huffing and puffing away like mad. It was my host covered in sweat.

"Sorry I'm late old boy, been for a jog round the golf club, do it every morning." David immediately disappeared into his bedroom, only to reappear then minutes later, now fully dressed and raring to go.

In no time at all the Bentley was whizzing up the drive, heading west to join up with the M4 motorway at the Calcot intersection - destination Wales. Nestling in the southwest corner of Wales, lies the rugged coastline of Pembrokeshire which is blessed with broad sandy beaches, sheltered coves, tall cliffs and hidden caves. It was here in the small seaside town of Tenby that David had pre-booked us into a modest guesthouse for the night. During the course of the evening our desires took the shape of liquid refreshment, and so decided to call in at the Bull and Bush pub. As we sat there noshing away on a packet of crisps together with a pint of beer we sat back to enjoy the pub's atmosphere and notably with each other's company. This moment of relaxation gave us the golden opportunity to truly test each other out. But before I could get a word in I was asked this question. What would be top of my shopping list for a future holiday? That's easy to explain away. I told David; ever since I was young lad I had this insatiable urge to visit Arizona. In fact, I first became hooked on the very idea when I saw a programme on television that featured a scene from an old western movie. I was thereby hooked.

David completely changed the subject and told me he had the great pleasure of visiting Vancouver in Canada.

"I once sailed there and got stuck in port for a week. So what I did to relieve the boredom I took a passage on an old whaling ship that went up to Alaska by way of the Inland Passage. It was an incredible journey, a little hazardous perhaps, however, very enjoyable. As our ship sailed steadily northwards I encountered these huge fjords, identical to the ones in Norway, it was really quite breathtaking. Look I'll take you there someday," David insisted.

The following morning we parted company from Tenby and then set a course heading due north, but first calling in at the coastal town of Aberystwyth via a brief visit to the Snowdonia National Park. Our day ended up on the Island of Anglesey. It was here in a tiny place called Lilangeni I was whisked into a handily placed guesthouse for the night. That evening over dinner David asked me my thoughts on our little trip. I at once rose from my chair and stood to attention at the same time clicking both the heels of my boots together. I couldn't resist the temptation to give the poor old sod a rousing good salute.

"Sir, it is with great honour and privilege that I would like to convey my most humble gratitude to you. Furthermore, I'd be most honoured to serve under you."

David's sea haggard face told the whole story. It beamed like a Cheshire cat and was obviously feeling that things had gone blissfully well.

"Welcome aboard," David smiled; as he threw his arms around me.

With our friendship firmly cemented our final duty was to pay a visit to the town of Chester with mission accomplished. On the return journey home David made a rather outlandish statement. "Listen, how about doing another trip, just like the one we've this weekend, say the Lake District, and if all goes well with that one then maybe I'll think about doing a real big-un. Yes, you and me on a trip round the world, who knows?"

"Now, steady on old boy," I smiled.

In November 1996 a large envelope arrived at my home upon which was worded Cunard. I studied the mysterious envelope with great endeavour and I burned with curiosity as to what was inside. Quickly opening it up the contents revealed a letter plus an invoice which read something like this............

We at Cunard would like congratulate on you excellent choice of holiday and we wish you the very best of luck and hope you have a fabulous time on board our luxury liner, QE2.

This has definitely got to be a mistake I thought, as I hadn't booked a luxury cruise with Cunard. I read on and there in black and white was David's name and address on the invoice. I sat there flabbergasted. Not for one moment did I think the crazy old sea dog would actually go ahead and book such a costly and lavish trip as this. He certainly kept this a big secret alright with not a word or clue to his intentions. I knew that sailing on the QE2 was his life's ambition, but wow, what a Christmas present this was going to be. Cunard's letter also included the full details for the journey. The sailing dates were from the 17th of December 1996 to the 23rd of December 1996, and, as part of the Cunard package, a first class rail ticket was enclosed from Bedfordshire, down to Southampton via Waterloo. The actual cruise was from Southampton to Fort Lauderdale via a six hour stopover at New York for a sightseeing tour of Manhattan, all thrown in by courtesy of Cunard. I must have sat there for hours, going over and over everything, but it seemed legitimate enough. Better give David a call to see if he's trying to pull a fast one?

"David! I've just received a letter from Cunard with confirmation of a cruise aboard the QE2 luxury liner. I just want to know if this is some silly prank of yours."

"Good lord, no. I wanted it to be a great surprise and indeed a smashing Christmas present for you."

"So it is true. David! I just don't know what to say. How can I ever begin to thank you?"

"The only thing you need to worry about is making damn sure you get yourself on board that ship, and don't ever think about letting me down. This trip has cost me an absolute fortune."

"Listen I'll be there rest assured, but there's just one thing that puzzles me, how on earth do we get back from Florida?"

"I'm glad you asked me that. I've managed to get us a one way air ticket from Orlando to Gatwick with Virgin Atlantic. This means Paul, after our QE2 voyage finishes we can still carry on touring for two more glorious weeks, so all that remains for me to say, is see you on board the QE2."

I put the phone down going dizzy with excitement and totally shell-shocked with my unexpected, but amazing news. Well, it looks as though I'll well and truly be sailing under him now.

(My diary reads) On a bitterly cold December morning in 1996 I was about to set forth on a journey into the great unknown. And such was my excitement that I could hardly contain myself. I must admit I was on the threshold of a great adventure. To put you more in the picture it's the start of my fabulous holiday to the United States of America by way of a cruise aboard the QE2 luxury liner. Yes, I did say the QE2; even I find it hard to believe. In fact I've had to pinch myself a couple of times to make sure it was really me that was going. It seems quite extraordinary, for there I was just three days ago signing on the dotted line down at the Jobcentre? But now I find myself about to embark on one of the most thrilling journeys of my life.

Anyway, my travel arrangements for the day were as follows. My plan was to catch a fast train from Luton Parkway Station down to

London Bridge. Alight, and then catch an inbound train to Waterloo, just a few short stops away. With the usual hiccups associated with rail travel I eventually arrived at London's biggest terminal, Waterloo, with little more than five or so minutes to spare. Making the necessary enquiries that was connected with my journey; a station porter kindly informed me that the train to Southampton was ready and waiting on platform ten. For the first time in my life I found myself in the envious position of acquiring a first-class rail ticket and wanted to use its deadly powers with unreserved determination.

Finding an empty first-class non smoking compartment, I quickly boarded and made myself comfortable. But just as I was getting ready for the big off, the door of my compartment unexpectedly opened. It revealed a most elegant looking woman who stood in the doorway. She was exquisitely dressed in a beautiful fur mink coat and grasped in her hand was a cigarette holder. Taking a closer look at her face, I guessed she must have been in her sixties or early seventies. Digging deeper, I began to wonder what she looked like in her early days. Bet she was a real stunner in her youth. Her face told the whole story. Yes, the lady had usual lines and wrinkles associated with aging, but underneath all the camouflage and make-up was a beautiful gracious lady.

"Oh darling!" the lady cried in a terrible proper, actually, actually, public school accent. "Am I on the right train to Southampton, you see I'm sailing on the QE2 and its impetrative that I join her?"

I assured the lady that she was definitely on the right train and that I myself was joining the ship, as well.

"Oh, that's absolutely marvellous, darling," she said graciously. "Oh, by the way luvvy, is that seat free over there," she pointed.

It most certainly is," I reassured her. "In fact madam it would be a great honour and privilege to have your company." This seemed to please her and I wondered if this could be the start of a wonderful whirlwind romance. Maybe I could be her new toy-boy? My dreams were shattered in two split seconds when the lady began to holler at someone down the corridor.

"In, here, porter!" she shouted in a commanding voice which clearly revealed expertise at giving orders to the working classes. A man dressed in a railway uniform deposited three heavy suitcases in our compartment to which she knew as Abdullah. A five pound note was then deposited into Abdullah's hand as his tip.

"Memsaab, damn fine nice woman," was the cry from Abdullah as he held out his hand for yet more money.

"Now bugger orf, my good man, before I get annoyed, you're not getting a single penny more," the lady bellowed in an angry tone.

Within seconds Abdullah had mysteriously escaped on to platform ten as he muttered a few swearwords under his garlic-ridden breath in a broken type of Bengali English.

With a sudden jerk and a whistle our Connex train slowly but surely crept its way out of Waterloo Station and proceeded to make its way to the south coast of England. My new-found carriage companion introduced herself as Mrs P. Barrington-Farquhar-Jones, "or just call me Patricia for now," she said. Within a matter of minutes we began to strike up a note of bright conversation which seemingly was to last all the way to Southampton. As we got to know each other on slightly better terms the lady began to reveal her innermost secrets. Patricia told me that for the better part of her life she had lived in the London Borough of Belgravia. Then, upon reaching the age of twenty five she married an actor chap called Nigel. It's quite ironic really for shortly after getting married; Patricia herself went into the acting profession. First starting off in reparatory theatre and then going on to bigger things like the movie business, starring mostly in "B" type movies throughout the 1940's and 50's era. Patricia retired from the film industry in her late forties and went back to a more relaxed way of life. Regrettably, Nigel, her husband, sadly died in his prime, so making her a widow. Patricia went on to tell me she has lived alone ever since and now finds herself with hardly any friends or family to fall back on. These unfortunate set of circumstances had caused her terrible hardship and loneliness. To compensate for her rather sad past Patricia found herself sailing on the QE2 for months at a time.

"You see, luvvy," Patricia began to explain. "I so adore the ballroom dancing they hold on board ship. The ladies would turn out in their beautiful sequinned gowns and the gentlemen immaculately presented in their jacket and tails, oh it's so divine. Oh, and the QE2 itself. The promenade, the health spas, the beauty salons and the endless cabaret shows they put on. They'll spoil you something rotten," the lady smiled. And what line of work are you in, my dear," Patricia inquisitively asked.

"Oh, er, um. I'm in local government, the Department of Health and Social Security, dealing with the unemployed, you know. God! What a ruddy shower they are, had to get time off work, you know, one can't spend too long away, can one," I said, tipping my head away in deep shame. If Patricia only knew I was on the dole.

Patricia's company made the journey pass by with remarkable speed, and, having passed through the towns of Basingstoke and Winchester; it wasn't long before we coasted our way into Southampton Central Station. Leaving the train, Patricia suggested sharing a taxi together which seemed like a remarkably good idea. But much to my annoyance I had the terrible misfortune of becoming the new Abdullah, having been lumbered with her three heavy suitcases.

"Come on, luvvy, chop chop, you know your work rate is absolutely appalling. You really need to put a bit more zip in your work if you want the job as my valet."

As luck would have it a nearby taxicab was on hand to get me out of trouble.

Her command, "QE2 please driver," proved all that was necessary to make the cabby fully aware of our destination, as if he knew it off by heart. Our black metropolitan taxicab threaded its way through the back streets of Southampton before finally entering the gates into the old dock area. Following the old quay road, I could see ship after ship moored up in their berths and having their cargoes removed by the giant overhead cranes. In the distance I could see the faint outline of a passenger ship that came into view with its distinctive blue and white colours.

"Look, there she is, my beautiful QE2," Patricia excitedly said as she pointed ahead and almost yanked my arm off in the process. Our taxi came to a halt, coming alongside an enormous vessel, better known throughout the world as the famous QE2. How magnificent she looked as she sat there in the cold winter sun. Her huge overpowering presence was not for the fainthearted I can assure you.

I became rooted to the spot as I eyed her up and down, from her bow to her stern and studying the splendour of her pristine paintwork. Come to think of it in a few minutes time I'll be standing on board the most prestigious ship in the world.

"Come on, darling, wakey, wakey!" Patricia hailed, "Let's go and get checked in, these people will take care of the luggage as she pointed towards another likely looking Abdullah.

Once the Cunard people had cleared us and clipped our tickets it was just a matter of making our way up a gangway that led directly into the heart of the ship. And sure enough, waiting there to greet us was the Captain along with his fellow officers. By Jove, it's such a wonderful feeling standing here, me on board the most famous ship in the world; if only people back home could see me now. A porter took hold of my luggage and said he would show me to my cabin. Patricia waved goodbye and gave a little smile, whilst saying, "see you at dinner darling, let's meet in the Mauritania Restaurant at eight, and don't you forget luvvy."

How could I possibly forget such a charming invitation from such a gracious and distinguished lady as Patricia? God, am I in love or something? Having started to unpack in my cabin, I looked at my watch with some concern because the time had reached four thirty. Where on earth has David got? He should have been here ages ago. The ship sails at five. Better phone the steward to see if he can throw some light on the situation. Just as I was about to make my call the cabin door burst open. Standing there in the doorway was a man who looked thoroughly dejected with himself, but thankfully, it was David. Though I must say his appearance was one of a scruffy nature. His head and shoulders were covered with bits of twigs and leaves.

"Where the hell have you been?" I bellowed. "It looks as though you've been dragged thought a hedge backwards. I've been frantic with worry."

"Damn confounded leaves on the line at Basingstoke. I stuck my great big head out of the window and got pelted with the ruddy stuff."

It was however, such a pleasing sight to see the likes of David, especially after his little mishap. Congratulating him on his arrival we soon forgot our troubles and began to shake each other's hand, among other things, discussing how our travel arrangements had gone for the day. Chatting away, David's voice abruptly stopped in its tracks. He immediately realised it was half past four. "Damn, I almost forgot, at the exact stroke of 17.00 hours there'll be a big send off for the QE2 as she leaves port: it's customary you know - and not only that there'll be a huge firework display together with a brass band to send us on our way.

Like bolts of lightning we hightailed it to the top deck. I stood there spellbound, quivering with excitement and not knowing what to expect next. At precisely seventeen hundred hours the QE2 slipped gently away from her moorings. She was now under her own steam and gave two blasts of her mighty horn. It was obviously a goodwill gesture to inform the good people of Southampton that we're on her way round the world. 'Bye, bye, folks, see you all in six months time.' The excitement continued with a deafening explosion of fireworks that lit up the blackness of the night sky. From the quayside a brass band sprang into action and I could distinctly hear the sound of a good old fashioned marching song. People began waving from the Cunard building, wishing us a happy and safe voyage. My emotions got carried away with me as I watched this truly amazing spectacle. I took a deep breath and gave a little sigh, overwhelmed by the whole wonderful experience, almost to the point of tears. Dreaming away, I thought to myself, what a truly lucky man I am to be standing here tonight, made possible by my good friend David.

"Well, me old shipmate," David smiled. "Next stop will be New York and after that we carry on cruising to sunny Florida. Come on, I'll give you a grand tour of the ship before dinner.

Our first stop was the Queen's Room, a magnificent ballroom that was used for dancing and other important functions. Positioned on the walls was a stunning display of oil portraits of the Royal Family from their early youth and up to the present. Carrying on, we came to a small shopping mall that consisted of well-known high street retailers. There was even a Harrods store to boast of. I was shown several swish restaurants, a theatre, a movie house, the ship's library, a sauna plus a gym, a nightclub plus a computer room. The list was endless. And to quench ones thirst there was an abundance of bars and watering holes to enjoy. Boy, are we going to have fun.

I returned to my cabin somewhat tired and a little leg-weary from the exhaustive journey down from Bedfordshire, but who cares, I'm having the thrill of a lifetime. Though I must point out that never in my life had I seen such splendour on a grand scale? But would I be able to cope with my new extravagant lifestyle, I asked myself.

Sometime later I was summoned to David's cabin to discuss the dinner arrangements. Apparently, I would be dinning out in some style tonight, so therefore I would have to look my best which meant putting on my tuxedo suit. As from now on I will be in the company of millionaires and people of high standing. David also advised not to mention a word to anyone that I was on the Rock and Roll. "It could be most embarrassing to both of us," he insisted. "If people knew you were on the dole we'd be thrown to the lions. Just tell everyone you're a big knob in the city, well not too big."

The Piano Bar was a sort of sub-tropical establishment which served up a variety of beers, cocktails and liqueurs. The decor was of huge towering plants that spilled over from enormous Grecian urns. Placed in the middle of this densely populated jungle was a guy playing the piano, most brilliantly I must point out, as though he was doing a recital at the Royal Albert Hall.

Up till now my financial outgoings was pretty much zero. The one thing about this cruise, I didn't have to fork out a single penny. David, in other words, had the great fortune of copping the entire bill. To be out on ones account, the Cunard people said, better known as the deadly tab. I must reiterate to you people out there before I go completely mad. I am at this precise moment living the life of a film star with millionaire status. It's true. Whatever I want, it comes instantaneously. Just a snap of the fingers brings an instant response. Things unimaginable were happening to me that I never before dreamt of. It was like being on another planet and in another dimension. In a few moments time I shall be mixing it with people from the high society of life, the rich and the famous - people with power and money and certainly not your average Joe Blogs down at the Jobcentre. Its mind boggling really when I think of it, for there I was just a few short years ago, homeless and destitute, but now I find myself sailing half way round the world on the QE2 luxury liner.

(The Mauritania Restaurant 8pm)

A waiter of Filipino extraction escorted us to table sixteen and, as I floated across the beautiful shag-pile carpet, I could hear the chink of wineglasses together with the smell of freshly lit cigars that was made more enjoyable by the joyous laughter from my fellow passengers. So imagine my delight when I took to my seat and looked on with idle curiosity at my fellow dinner guests who sat directly opposite, making up a party of six people in total and, I might add, looking a trifle regal.

Let me see now, there was Mr and Mrs Windrush. He a London banker, she, Mrs Windrush, claimed to be the backbone of British society. Apparently she was into flower arranging, the odd tea party here and there, and, of course, her precious croquet matches - all in all a thoroughly boring fart of a woman.

The Major, as he was known, had I must say an exemplary past. Through muck and bullets he came with two bits of shrapnel deeply imbedded in one of his legs. Of course the Major had the usual war-wounds, gammy leg and all that, but nice old chap the Major, and very much the stiff upper lip type apart from being a bit on the deaf side. "Umm, what was that you said, old boy, can't quite hear you," he would say. Apparently, he's known to everyone as the "Galloping Major". A result of which was his passion for riding a shagged-out old mare called Daphanie. And how could I forget Patricia, my new found love whom I had met on the train coming down from London. Checking in at only seventy five years, she was a pure snip.

(So the scene was set for fun and laughter)

"Come on, you lot, tuck into your caviar," Patricia announced.

"Ah, a drop of the engine oil never hurt anyone," the Major swooned.

"By the way, aren't you two chaps in conglomerates," Mr Windrush enquired, directing his attentions to David and I. "You know, I'm sure I've seen you both coming out of Fortescue, Fortescue and Fortescue, the city bankers in Threadneedle Street."

"Good Lord no," David replied. "We're with Ramsbottom, Ramsbottom and Ramsbottom the chartered accountants." David insisted as he tipped his head away with deep embarrassment.

"I knew it, Windrush exhaled," charmed to make your acquaintances, I'm sure, and welcome to the club, old boy."

"Major! Will you accompany me to the Grand Gala Ball this Wednesday evening," Patricia asked in a commanding voice.

""Umm, what was that you said, my dear," holding his hand to his ear.

"Balls, darling, balls!!"

"Umm."

"Balkans Major, Balkans!"

The Major's eyes widened in amazement, pursed his lips, took a deep breath and then let out a thundering raspberry. "Ah, ball-bearings! Well, why didn't you say so, my gal, haven't got any I'm afraid, bit hard on the old teeth, you know."

"Will someone, anyone, lend the Major a hearing aid and, whilst you're about it, stick a new brain in his head. Thank heavens the Major is being mummified next week by a party of short sighted Nigerian dentists." Patricia scornfully said.

"Ladies and gentlemen," Mr Windrush started off, by addressing his attention to us all. It has been suggested in certain quarters that it is required of me to wear my jacket and trousers at all times. I would like to point out that the whole thing is quite preposterous and totally unworkable. Therefore, I would much prefer to slip into a size fourteen dress, adorned with the prettiest of lace knickers and the kinkiest of ladies underwear."

The rest of Windrush's sentence was drowned out by his wife's intervention.

"Quite frankly, no darling, Mrs Windrush fumed. "It is totally out of the question; think what people would say and the scandal it would cause. No! You'll just have to be content with wearing your Y-fronts round the wrong way."

"Tell me David," Mrs Windrush inquired, "rumour has it you've had the great pleasure of singing with the church queers? I mean choirs."

"Ah, but, occasionally Madame, and when my back-side is facing in a north easterly direction, but making damn sure the queers have been fully defrocked and that their sceptres are pointing in a very stiff, but hard, throgmorton position, hence joining the choir?"

"I knew it! So you're either quime, quare or queer, I take it?"

"Rumour has it that Mrs Windrush has been smoking in the ladies toilets again," beamed the Major.

"Now, look here, me old windy bum of a wife." Mr Windrush fumed, "If you really must smoke in such disgusting places as toilets, then I beg you my darling. Will you please, please, please, take your drawers down more slowly?"

"I'd like to give a toast to the Major's old regiment," Patricia interrupted as she raised her glass in the air, "and, for the life of me I can't remember the ruddy name of it. Ah, but it all comes back to me, now. Here's to the Queens, very own, Benghazi Burpers, of her Majesties Foot and Mouth Battalion. It was with great courage and termination that the Major, single handily, fought off two hundred of our fuzzy wuzzy friends and drove the blighters back along the banks of Umbaah, Umbaah River near Khartoum, and all because the randy old Major wanted to get his stain choppers around the tenderised plums of the chief's wife, Missy Ohdununga."

"Umm, what was that you said me dear? Ah, the chiefs wife. Damn fine stout woman, shame about me false teeth, though."

"Major! Patricia bellowed. The waiter informs me that you've been on the Piste again. It seems to me you were well and truly Liszt."

"Can't keep a damn secret from you lot," the Major frowned. "Well if you really must know, after downing three stiff Vodkas, I found myself bombing down the south slope of the Matterhorn, preciously perched on me Toboggan, totally abbreviated with me trousers dangling down at half mast and singing to a chorus of Rule Britannia."

"To my fellow dinner guests, I say this to you." Windrush exhaled. "Tabernacles, fur-lined willy-warmers, dodgy circumcisions, gay bishops with pointed things on their heads, bent coppers, defrocked clergymen on a mission of filth and debauchery."

"I say, steady on old boy," The Major gasped, "Bit strong on the old willy-warmers thing, aren't we?"

"Upon my word, what's that disgusting object that's manifested itself on the Major's dinner plate?"

"Good gawd, its dirty great Snorker," Windrush gasped.

"What on the QE2. Never!"

"Filthy things!"

"Outrageous!"

"The chef should be shot at dawn!"

Windrush began licking his lips as if to indicate he savoured the taste of a freshly cooked sausage.

"Ah, you can't beat a good old snorker," beamed the Major as he proudly held up his sausage for everyone to see.

"Frightfully boring conversation," Patricia smiled.

"Yes, frightfully," David agreed.

"I must say you lot, you're behaving like absolute cads." Patricia said with a cynical smile.

"Well, everyone, are we all agreed? Patricia announced in an air of expectancy. Shall we all meet this coming Wednesday evening in the Queens Ballroom for the Grand Gala Ball? The Major will of course be accompanying me, God help me, and for the rest of you, you can slog it out with who is dancing with whom."

As the evening drew to a close I rose from my chair and gave a little burp, followed by an enormous grunt. The dinner, I must mention was first class and the company was most stimulating. Leaving the restaurant I was emphatically convinced that my fellow dinner guests were a pathetic bunch of self-righteous, dim-witted, stuffy, outrageously perverted baboons. But there again we can't all be perfect, can we?

A typical day on the QE2 consisted of early morning breakfast in the buffet bar, followed by a grand slam walk on the promenade deck. Keep-fit classes in the gym, followed by a quick delve into the shop's library to get the low down on the QE2's position and course. This was superseded by afternoon tea in the Queen's Ballroom. The evenings were laced with a stupendous choice of goodies, ranging from a classical concert, the theatre or a movie. Thrown in for good measure was a cabaret show, later followed by evening drinks in the cocktail bar. Topping that lot was yet more food in the midnight buffet restaurant, before sliding gracefully into a retiring mode for the night. Struth, what a truly exhausting life I lead.

The next morning, seizing the opportunity to explore the ship in greater detail I decided to have a further look round the ship, this time by myself. I once again made an entrance into the Queens Ballroom to get a much more detailed look at the beautiful portraits of the Royal Family. Carrying on, I came to the ship's library, where I found an abundance of wealth waiting inside. Positioned at the entrance to the library was a giant-sized map of the world. Cunard used this particular map to give us passengers some idea of what our course and position was as we sailed round the world. A tiny model of a ship, no bigger than ones thumb was pushed along each day on a piece of string. I came to the conclusion it was a fascinating piece of engineering and a brilliant novelty idea. Along with this the library supplied vital information regarding the ship's logistics. Apparently she carried a crew of 921 and has the capability to take on 1,500 passengers. Her total gross tonnage was 70,327 and her dimensions were as follows. Her length was 963ft (293.52m) Breadth: 105ft (32.07) Draft: 32ft. She had a choice of five restaurants, two cafeterias, three swimming pools, several pubs, along with a nightclub. There was also a 481 seated cinemas, a casino, a hospital and a beauty salon together with a shopping mall, including a well-known branch of Harrods. In addition to this a world cruise would last around eighty days while taking in a multitude of ports. Furthermore, the QE2 had a top speed of 32 knots with a regular cruising speed of 28 knots, which by far made her the fastest ship afloat.

Pressing on from the library, I came to a spiral staircase, somewhere towards the stern of the ship. With great endeavour I decided to climb steadily upwards and as I did so I found the walls crammed with photographs of famous people - the likes of well known film stars and politicians that had once graced the ship. As I reached the top of the staircase, I was somewhat lost. It then transpired I had reached the Penthouse Suites. The real surprise came when one of the cabin doors suddenly opened. A man then appeared wearing a multi-coloured dressing gown. Taking a closer look at this mysterious stranger I assumed he had all the attributes of a stinking rich toff. There he stood; cool as a cucumber, madly puffing away on a big cigar, one so big it looked like a rocket launcher. His wrinkled haggard face began to look at me with great suspicion and surprise as he continued puffing away on his cigar. Finally, he began to get some spiel out of his system, but bless my soul I distinctly heard a dialect more in keeping with a Cockney accent.

"Ere, you look a bit lost Harry, my old sunshine, how's ya norf and saff," he gingerly asked?

But why is he calling me Harry and what the hell is your norf and saff for gawds sake. Better not say anything or he might donk me one. It so came to light that this gamely character was known to the local gentry as Sid, or Sidney to give him his full title. Chatting away, Sid started off by telling me he once owned a demolition company in North London which by all accounts made him a vast fortune. Apparently, he has since sold on the company and retired so to speak. He then went on to tell me he spends ten months of the year on the QE2. "Lovely old girl," he beamed. "Ere, look squire, why you don't come in and meet the missus," he suggested. I was immediately led into his cabin which bore all the hallmarks of super duper affluence. Well can you beat that? There sitting at a dressing table was Sid's wife going about setting her hair in curlers, complete with a cigarette dangling from her mouth.

"Now where's that podgy little dumpling of a wife got to, Sid declared. "Oh there you are my lovely," Sid smiled, as he cast his eyes on his dearly beloved.

"Bleedin hair can't do a fing wivit," Sid's wife moaned.

"For Gord's sake woman, stick syrup on ya bonce. Now where's that one I bought ya in London."

"Now why the bleedin hell didn't I think of that?"

Sid and his wife seemed to be a funny old pair, but nevertheless very likeable.

"Ere, what are you doing tonight Harry? Fancy joining me and the missus for the cabaret show?"

"Well, to be quite honest with you Sid, I don't really know," I replied back with a confused look of indecision. "Well, alright then, but could I bring a friend along?"

"Yeah, all right, but is he Kosher?" Sid enquired.

"Why of course he is, my friend once worked at a Bagel factory in North London."

Having convinced Sid about my friend's authenticity, I rushed back to my cabin to tell David the good news about my chance meeting with my illustrious new friends.

(Twas the night of the cabaret show)

At precisely eight o'clock in the evening our party of four had taken to our seats for the cabaret show to begin. I must admit I was instantly repelled by a feeling of extreme excitement, and felt pretty sure it would be the climactic moment of the day. The curtains drew back. The band struck up and then the compare appeared. "Ladies and gentlemen," he began. "It gives me great pleasure to welcome you to tonight's show. From New York we have Dino Vincello a truly great comedian, and from London, please welcome Charles Dickinson, a first class pianist, together, ladies and gentlemen with our very own floor show."

The show began with the appearance of sexy girl dancers that were proactively kitted out in black see-through fishnet stockings. It was a true sight to behold. In fact it had us men feeling a bit hot under the collar I can tell you. We particularly liked the various arrangements of the dancers as they went about their business in the most professional manner. Sid leaned across and whispered sweet nothings in my ear at the same time wiping his forehead in nervous anticipation. "Cor, blimey Harry," Sid gasped as he pointed to one of the girls. "Do my eyes deceive me; Sid gasped "For they seem to be wearing skimpy see-through leotards that protrude out of dirty great enormous bottoms. And you realise my old son that my poor old pacemaker has been going like the clappers for the last ten minutes."

I smiled and then winked back at Sid, pretending not to hear, but finally nodding back in approval. After the show I returned to my cabin, so imagine my surprise when I discovered a note had been shoved under my door. It was an invitation from the Captain to join him and his fellow officers for the Grand Gala Ball. It was with immense pride and privilege I gladly accepted the Captain's invitation and made plans accordingly with my friend David to accompany me.

Precisely three days out to sea we were somewhere in the depths of the North Atlantic Ocean. There I was having a snooze at the time when the PA system began to blast out an urgent warning. A storm of force twelve magnitudes was heading our way, which by all accounts was pretty bad to say the least. So being curious and never having seen a storm at sea, I decided to a peek outside on the promenade deck. Yes, I know, everyone else thought I was completely mad, too. In the distance the sky had turned to a ghoulish black colour. Swirling gale force winds had whipped up the mighty ocean to a raging torrent that sent fifty foot waves crashing over the ship. It was like being on a precipice. Just as I was beginning to get the feel of things an officer appeared on deck. He demanded I return to the safely of the ship.

"Are you completely mad," he raged. You're not allowed on deck when there's a storm."

Do you remember that map I spoke of earlier on, the one positioned at the entrance to the library. Well, it has since come to my attention that the QE2 had a new bearing and course. My observations confirmed that we were somewhere due south of Newfoundland. Our actually position was forty-one degrees latitude and forty-three degrees longitude and thirty-five degrees north. However, more alarming was the fact, someone had pencilled in the word Titanic just below the model of the ship. To throw some light on this intriguing mystery, an American couple who were standing next to me enquired if the QE2 would be passing over the same spot to where the Titanic went down. According to one of the officers he told us that as a mark of respect, the QE2, along with all other ships, would steer a course one third of a mile away from where the famous liner went down. "In fact, if you wander over to the portside of the ship, look down, for somewhere in the murky waters, lies one of the greatest liners in the world," he said. A few of us wandered over to a viewing area and as we stood there gazing out to sea I sensed an overbearing feeling of great sadness. It was on a bitterly cold night on the 14th April 1912 when a terrible tragedy occurred. It was when

White Star liner Titanic was on her maiden voyage to America when she encountered a huge iceberg and thereby sank, taking 1,523 poor souls down with her.

My first sight of land was on the morning of the 21st December 1996 at precisely 06.50am, Eastern Standard Time. While still dark outside I decided to have a peek outside through my porthole window. I could just about make out the faint outline of land and realised that New York was just a breath away. Thank goodness for that after spending days looking at the never-ending greyness of the North Atlantic Ocean. In fact New York would be our first port of call. A steward knocked on my cabin door and informed me we would be docking in thirty minutes. He strongly advised me to put some warm clothes on as the temperature was close to freezing outside. Having got myself washed and dressed I scrambled myself to the forward section of the ship to get a better look of our approach to the magnificence of the New York skyline. Above me was the monkey house as it's called by the seafaring community. On most ships it usual sits above the wheelhouse. Meanwhile, our floating palace continued to make good headway. To my portside was the magnificent lady in all her glory - The Statue of Liberty.

A sea rating explained to me that the Statue of Liberty was made from copper sheets and was assembled on a framework of steel. It arrived here in America around 1885 as a gift from the people of France to the American people. To my starboard side was Governors Island with the faintest glimpse of Brooklyn and Yonkers in the background. To my left was Staten Island. We continued to journey up the Hudson River. Coming into view was the magnificent sight of the huge skyscrapers that dominated Manhattan. I decided to venture out to the promenade deck to get a better look. It was bitterly cold with a strong head wind at around ten knots. David suddenly emerged from his pit, still dressed in his pyjamas, moaning and groaning about the weather. Well we are British, after all.

"By George, its bloody cold out here," he groaned, shivering away.

Pier 52 beckoned ahead and with aid of the tugs it wasn't long before we tied up and everything was made ready for us to proceed ashore. Cunard had generously laid on a sightseeing tour of

Manhattan and I couldn't wait to get ashore, along with the other passengers.

Having disembarked, I can't tell you how thrilled I was to be standing on American soil for the very first time. I didn't know whether to the kiss the ground like the Pope does or shout from the top of my voice. You see, I desperately wanted to tell the good people of New York I had finally arrived in their wonderful city. In heaven's name, it was me folks, Mr Rock and Roll himself, in person and doing a rip-roaring tour of your dazzling city. But where are all the screaming girls to greet me along with the media machine and the hoards of autograph hunters? Surely there'd be some reception for me - but alas no, just a long line of coaches to take us on our way.

It was one of those razor-sharp bitterly cold wintry mornings with the temperature well below zero. A cold blustery wind was coming in from the Hudson River, turning the harbour area to a blanket of frost. Having left pier 52 we headed for the stunning magnificence of the Lower Manhattan skyline. We twisted and turned down long winding avenues that led into busy bustling streets and where mighty structures loomed up to form dark satanic canyons.

Geologically speaking, Manhattan sits on bedrock of granite and marble and so safe are the foundations that they went and built the famous skyscrapers. Our tour guide for the day was a guy called Wayne who diligently informed us that thousands of books and millions of words had been written about this ennobled rock called Manhattan, but he said. "There is nothing like seeing it for real." Wayne continued. "When people think of New York City, Manhattan is often the first place they picture in their mind. For no wonder: the borough is home to such fabulous places as Central Park, Times Square, The Empire State Building, Broadway, and not forgetting Grand Central Station. However, there's more to the borough than just the sights. Manhattan also claims fame to its charming neighbourhoods."

Up ahead the more fashionable districts came into being: the likes of huge department stores sprung up before our very eyes. Macy's would you believe, followed by Bloomingdale's and then Tiffany's. From downtown to uptown we journeyed through a landscape of epic wonders, and for long periods we jounced our way through numerous streets that thronged to the sound of car horns, along with the street vendors that sold everything from hot-dogs to ice cream. I saw frail old ladies being escorted across the road by a very helpful New York cop.

"Hey, isn't that the famous Waldorf-Astoria," a lady passengers inquired.

"It sure is ma'am," someone pointed out.

Wayne informed us that the next scheduled stop on the agenda would be Times Square. My first impressions of Times Square were a place dominated by the constant noise of hustle and bustle. The abundance of colour and vibrancy that surrounds this place was truly wonderful. The whole place seemed to explode with a variation of amazing activity. Towering digital billboards displayed every conceivable commodity that one could imagine. It was indeed a truly magnificent sight to behold.

However, we didn't see shoot-outs or cop cars overturning, like you see in the movies. But what we did see however were the cops were wearing their black hats and capes, complete with a shooting piece by their side for any eventuality. So this is the Big Apple, the city that never sleeps. It's the very same city that has pumped my adrenalin levels up, almost to the point of explosion. Boy, what a place!!

With our tour reaching its halfway point we finally stopped for mid-day lunch at the Rockefeller Centre, situated on Sixth Avenue. The story behind this incredible building goes back to the 1930's. The building itself was named after a New York benefactor who paid a staggering fortune for the construction to be built. Another interesting point about the Rockefeller Centre is where the movie, "Gone with the Wind" had its movie premier. And such was the size of the cinemas screen: it's claimed to be the biggest in America. Recently the whole building had been thoroughly restored to its former art deco greatness. It was here we stopped for midday lunch.

Wayne our tour guide informed us that the restaurant was actually located on the sixty-fourth floor, which involved taking an elevator ride. Like a giant roller coaster we were whisked up to floor sixty-four.

"Siiiiiiiiixty fooooooouth flooooooor!!" The baby faced bellboy bellowed out.

Moments later we found ourselves sitting down to lunch and ready to start with proceedings. And so it so came to pass I'd been placed next to two Americans who I quickly discovered were a gay couple from Palm Springs, California. More to the point whose feminine gestures and hand movements just had to be seen, and with names like Arnie and Charlie, who the hell needs dogs. Arnie's hand slipped gently across the gleaming white tablecloth like a snake worming its way through the dense undergrowth. Arnie allowed himself to touch my hand with a squeeze. Combined with this very worrying development he then had the Gaul to ask me something quite suggestive. "Oh sweetie, he smiled, "I can't quite reach the salt. Could you pass it over to me honey?"

"Why, sure," I said, and being the nice chap as I am I started to sprinkle a little salt on his lunch.

"Oh, no, sweetie," he smiled, again touching my hand. "You see sugar; I always like to shake my own thing," he said, together with wink and a big smile that toothpaste manufactures would gladly sell their mothers for.

Hello, hello, hello, I thought, I certainly won't be sitting next to him at the cinema tonight, toothpaste or no toothpaste.

After lunch Wayne called us over to a viewing area to get a bird's eye view of the New York skyline. Through high-powered telescopes we were able to pick up images of the vast metropolis of this wonderful city. Looking down, I was able to pick out the tiny figures of the ice skaters in Central Park, and, across to my right I focused in on the feverish activity in Times Square.

By four in the afternoon our tour was all but over, so the necessary preparations were made ready to get back on board the QE2. With the help of the bellboy, we were whisked down to ground level once more and going down like a ton of bricks. Coming back through the Manhattan area, we came across the picturesque part of 14th Street to Houston Street, better known as Greenwich Village, plus the rare glimpse of the Chinese quarter of the Noho area. In the far off distance I could just about make out the enormous structure of the QE2 as she waited in her berth for our return. What a truly fabulous ship she looked as she sat there in the cold winter's sun and how proud I was to be sailing on the lovely old girl.

Having returned to my cabin after a wonderful days sightseeing tour of Manhattan I was being issued with fresh instructions from the high command, namely my sponsor David. He requested that I was to meet him at precisely 1800 hours. This, he informed me was for the customary celebrations in honour of the QE2 when she leaves port, just like it was at Southampton. Sometime later we managed to position ourselves on the main promenade deck to get the best panoramic views. Slowly but surely the enormous liner was being eased away from her moorings by the numerous number of tugs, placed alongside. Then all of a sudden and without any warning the whole night sky erupted into a blaze of colour. Rockets, firecrackers and flares crackled and popped across the New York skyline. Silently, the huge liner slipped away from her berth and into the darkness of the night and as she did so I sensed an overwhelming feeling of great sadness. The thought of leaving this wonderful city behind was too much to bear. I watched the flickering lights from skyscrapers as they gradually dwindled away into the distance.

David gave me a nudge, thinking I had fallen asleep. "Come on, me old hardy, let's have a drink before dinner," he asked.

"Yes, all right then," I replied back in a rather subdued voice.

"Come on, let's talk travel," David smiled. "Bugger it; let's talk big game reserve travel."

"You don't mean."

"That's right me old mucker, two weeks in the dense undergrowth of the Bognor Regis jungle!"

"By jingo, it'll be an absolute pleasure, old boy," and saluted him back in true naval fashion.

(Twas the night of the Grand Gala Ball)

So there I was heavenly scented and impeccably attired as I made my entrance into the Queen's Ballroom, only to find with great surprise I had landed into a world of gaiety and elegance and of rapturous music. Couples floated across the dance area like regal swans as the crystal chandeliers sparkled and glistened that formed an explosion of amazing colours. Back down to earth again I could see my friends waiting patiently for my arrival. Patricia's outstretched hand grasped mine as she pointed towards the dance floor. I was then into a series of highly sophisticated intricate patterns of footwork which included the waltz and foxtrot. "Slow-slow-quick-quick-slow" was the order of the day. Which brings me to the hilarious sight of our beloved friends the foxtrot dancers who were rigidly prancing about as though their head and shoulders had been encapsulated in plaster?

In the course of the evening I was introduced to the Captain, who I must point out was an extraordinary man of extraordinary character. And such was the popularity of the Captain, the poor chap had the terrible misfortune of doing the introductions as the guests arrived.

"Ladies and Gentlemen," the Captain hails, holding up his guest list. "It gives me great pleasure to introduce to you, Sir Charles and Lady Wilberforce from Windsor. Lord and Lady Upperton from Weybridge, Surrey. Mr and Mrs Pemberton from Henley on Thames. And please welcome our most distinguished guest with us here tonight. The right honourable Sir Charles Basil Braithwaite, Member of Parliament for the East Barnet constituency," says the Captain, giving me the nod of his head.

Had the Captain gone stark raving bonkers, for I am not the famous, Sir Charles Basil Braithwaite, but a poor innocent chap on the Rock and Roll? I had better not say anything or I might drop myself in it. "Thank you for those heart warming words Captain," says I. "I am simple overwhelmed by your kind thoughts and most magnificent introduction. I say this to you Captain. I will of course give you a mention in the House of Commons when I get round to proposing my forthcoming Bill on gay marriages. And, should you ever be tempted, dear Captain, I'm sure we could find you a big strapping hunk of a man.

I then overheard the Captain whisper something under his breath. "I wonder where the ruddy hell he whoofted in from?"

The ball was now in full swing: regal eyed and feverishly rat-arsed, we danced the night away to steps and tunes of a once forgotten age. Then, in one bout of uncontrollable madness, the men in our party began to rip their jackets off like bulls in a china shop. To the amazement of fellow passengers the gentlemen in question began flapping their arms about like regal swans that was about to take flight. David, the Major, along with Mr Windrush, together with the Captain and Petty Officer Phillips did the same. Our gang of five, feverishly rat-arsed men began racing round and round the ballroom like men possessed and it proved nothing could stop them from getting airborne.

"Pissed as ruddy farts, the lot of em," Sid's wife moaned.

Our new squadron of fighter pilots began operations with sorties that were more accustomed to night flying and awash with radio interference. Then, from out of the night sky came a sort of RAF come banter type thing.

The Major: "Spider leader here, is anyone receiving me? Zero one niner, I repeat, zero one niner, can anyone hear me?"

David: "Yes, Spider Leader, I can hear you, but number one engine's shot up, old boy. What shall I do? Roger and out."

Windrush: "For God's sake man, feather it back, you're engine!"

The Captain: "Captain to Mother Goose, where the hell are you?"

Mother Goose: "Fraid I'm in an over at the moment, gas mark 6."

The Captain: "Captain to Porky Pig. You've gone off the radar old boy."

Porky Pig: "Well, you're not going to believe this Captain but I'm also in an oven.

Petty Officer Phillips. "B for Bertie here, presently over North Sea."

Windrush: "Watch out B for Bertie, bogies high, I say bogies high."

"Umm"

"Bogies man, bogies."

David: "Parachute, I should say so, haven't had good jump in years."

Petty Officer Phillips: "I say, that chap who wanted to parachute. I'm afraid; it looks as though he's "Gone for a Burton."

Sid: "Pull it Major, the damn thing between your legs. Pull your stick; for God's sake man, get your nose up before it's too late."

The Major: Umm, what was that you said old boy. Did you say, come on jock, or was it, stick of rock?"

231 Squadron was about to indicate a very intricate move as they did their best to get their undercarriages and flaps down. The Major was still trying to get his end up when a mighty clash of heads accrued which resulted in a mid-air collision. Thus, 231 squadron was in complete disarray and had succumbed to free-fall. Their Spitfires and Lancaster's had been put to rest with their engines, well and truly feathered. The next day our brave band of fighter pilots was nursing sore heads and hangovers. However, Windrush was said to comment. "I say chaps, wasn't that a lovely day for flying."

The date is the 22st of December 1996, the day before we docked at Fort Lauderdale. David and I gathered all our friends together for a farewell meeting, just to say our goodbyes really. For tomorrow would be our very last day on the QE2, hence departing our separate ways. It was such a wrench to leave these lovely people behind, who for the last week had given us so much fun and laughter in our lives. With the usual handshakes and goodbye kisses, we exchanged names and addresses and then bade them farewell, wishing them lots of good luck as they voyaged round the world.

(Florida)
On the morning of the 23rd December 1996, the QE2 slipped gently into port. Our voyage was all but over. It was such a wrench leaving the lovely old girl behind, but like all good things in life they eventually come to an end. With the necessary documents at the ready, we wearily made our way through customs, before finally descending into the warmth of the Fort Lauderdale sunshine. The Florida climate was true to its word. The weather was hot and humid with wall-to-wall blue skies. The songbirds were singing and the flowers were still in full bloom, and funnily enough we were still in December.

An agreement had been reached between David and me. As from now on we'll be stopping anywhere along the line that took our fancy. So, having said that, our stay in Fort Lauderdale was just long enough to take in a hotel for the night, thereafter, the following day; we caught the first of a twice daily, Greyhound Coach Service to Laredo, Texas. Yes I did say Laredo. God knows what David was thinking of? Apparently, the intended journey would take in the entire West Coast of Florida, before eventually cutting into Texas via Tallahassee, Mobile and Baton Rouge.

The drive out of Fort Lauderdale was a pleasant enough affair as we journeyed through an endless scene of urbanisation. We went gate crashing down wide-lane avenues amid swaying palm trees, while meandering by fast food joints, retail parks and outer limit residential areas, leading to wide-open spaces, and ahead, a thundering great freeway called Alligator Alley.

For those of you not familiar with this part of the world, please allow me to explain the circumstances that led up its name. On both sides of the freeway are the Everglades, a marshy type swamp, and in these swamps live Alligators. Gazing out from my window seat I noticed a multitude of enormous brown logs that were floating about on top of the surface. Some of the logs were just laying there, half in the water while others were drifting merrily by. Heavens above, what was that I saw stir? Something moved from the undergrowth. Those so called logs I told you about were definitely on the move. I could actually see one of the logs moving at a rather sharpest pace. They weren't logs, but dirty great big Alligators. The odd few were just lying there by the riverbank, sunning themselves, while others were slithering down the embankment, probably on their way for their early morning dip. Some time ago the whole length of the freeway had been fenced in and made safe, thanks to the Florida authorities, spending millions of dollars and thus making sure the Alligators stayed behind closed doors. Before the fence was put up the Alligators were running wild across the road and thus causing chaos.

Naples the town is approximately two hundred and seventy eight miles as the crow flies from Fort Lauderdale and sits along the shores of the Gulf of Mexico bay. Naples tropical climate made a welcoming change from the never-ending swampland of the marshy Everglades. Trusty state highway 75 trundles all the way up the Florida coastline and offer some of the best scenery in the United States. Pushing our way further northwards, we coasted in and out of places with the sweetest of names, such as Bonita Springs, Fort Myers, Venice and Port Charlotte.

Towards dusk our final resting place for the day was the beautiful little seaside town of Clearwater which is located in the province of Pinellas County, northwest of Tampa and St Petersburg. To the west of Clearwater lies the Gulf of Mexico and to the southeast is Tampa Bay. After spending eight hours in the saddle riding shotgun it was decided that Clearwater was a good as place as any to spend the night. Installed at the coach depot was a conveniently placed cafeteria. Scattered amongst the debris of coffee cups and food was a selection of local newspapers. Scouring through one such paper, something caught our eye, for there tucked away in the classified section was a small advert which related to a property to let. The advert read something like this......

English family have at their disposal a luxurious bungalow to let in the Largo area, approximately three miles from central Clearwater. Long or short term is possible. Please contact Mr Benson for more details.

It suddenly dawned on us that perhaps a short stay in Clearwater, whether it is for one night or one week wouldn't be such a bad idea. Weighing up our options we decided to get in touch with the Benson's to get the low-down on their let?

"Mr Benson," David started off, as he put his shoved last quarter in the phone. "We've just read your ad in the local newspaper regarding a luxury bungalow to let. The thing is, is it still available?"

"Why, yes, it is, how long do you want it for?" A man's voice said.

"Well, it's quite possible; it could be for one week or even two. I can assure you Mr Benson big bucks are forthcoming."

"Yes, that'll be fine," was the reply. "Look, grab yourselves a taxi and I'll meet you on your arrival."

The next thing we knew was our taxi pulling up at the Bensons home with the whole family waiting there to greet us. Moments later we were to be given a grand tour of the place. I must admit, the most striking aspect of the property was how thoroughly delightful and accommodating it appeared. In fact it looked devilishly luxurious. However, our attention had turned to the enormity of the place. No less than four king-size bedrooms, an enormous kitchen, including all the latest gadgetry. And there to keep us cool was a swimming pool. The bedrooms boasted full en-suite facilities and not only that there was satellite television to watch with well over a hundred channels to choose from. In addition to this mind boggling information there were two tropical fans to keep us nice and cool at night. "By George, I'm gonna love here, just love it. Well, one has to keep up appearances, hasn't one?"

David quickly settled up terms with the Benson's, paying for two weeks up front. Once we were settled in the Benson's asked us to join them for evening dinner, plus the chance to get better acquainted. Mrs Benson or Ann started the ball rolling when she began to fill us in about their life's precarious journey.

"Well, to begin with," Ann started off, "we first came Florida for a holiday in1982, and, having taken in the enormous potential Florida had to offer, we simply fell in love with the place. On our return to the UK, we both decided that we both wanted a better life for ourselves, so we sold up and came back here to Florida, first buying this present property, then adding an additional one. We were both very fortunate to obtain good jobs in administration. In the course of our marriage we had two children, both boys. What about yourselves?" Ann asked.

"Well, you're not going to believe this Ann," David smiled. "Paul here is running for the envious position as Minister for Unemployment. And I myself is about to embark on a career as an airline pilot, flying dirty great Jumbo jet around the globe."

David's silly bit of dialogue certainly broke the ice with the Benson's and as a result the whole family took to us like ducks to water. The one thing I kept stum about was with me being on the dole. What would the Benson's have said, having just stepped off the QE2 and being a member of the Rock and Roll community?

That night as I lay on my bed an overwhelming feeling of great sadness fell upon me. I began to reminisce about my time on the QE2, and my thoughts were of the friends I had left behind. The dear old Major, God bless him. Mr and Mrs Windrush. But not forgetting of course my beloved Patricia. How I truly miss them. Although I found their company a bit on the loony side, it was nevertheless invigorating to say the least. I miss their endless banter at dinner and the hilarious capers we got up to at functions, together with their naughty little pranks at Gala Balls. Things regrettably will never be the same again.

Unfortunately, because of David's business commitments, the poor chap had been recalled back to the UK to sort out a few urgent business problems that had cropped up. But lucky old me was booked in for two more glorious weeks. What was I doing? Playing silly buggers with the Carpenter's, the Benson's neighbours for a round of golf, where I was repeatedly being asked what my handicap was?

It was now approaching the 24th of December, and yes, Christmas time. Ann our host, said, there'll be two days of celebration with the usual fun and frolics associated with Christmas. The great thing about Florida, you had all this lovely sunshine, each and every day. You could do things like swimming, cycling and walking etc. For the next two weeks I had Florida all to myself. On most days I would usually take the bus and visit some of the amazing places along the Florida coastline where I discovered such wonderful places as Dunedin, Tarpon Springs, along with Treasure Island and New Port Richey. But much to my bitter disappointment my holiday had flown by with remarkable speed and unfortunately it was coming to an end. Therefore it was time to head back to dear old blighty. I burst out crying when Ann came into my room to collect my luggage.

"Come on, she said, "we've got to get you Orlando airport to catch your flight back home."

"But, Ann, I don't want to leave, you're like family to me, I'm so happy here."

The Benson's were such nice people and how I will truly miss them. Mr Benson looked at his watch in a state of panic. "Look, we really must set off now, Paul."

By late afternoon we had arrived at Orlando Airport with the whole family huddled together in tears, saying our goodbyes.

"Do please come back and see us," Ann insisted.

In tears I parted company from my dear friends and wearily made my for the Virgin Atlantic desk to proceed with the check-in arrangements. It was many hours and thousands of miles later when I eventually arrived back in dear old blighty, bumping down at Gatwick International Airport. I had on a number of occasions passed through Gatwick and caught the train. However, on this particular occasion I had been dispatched to the National Express coach depot in search of transport back to Bedfordshire. But what greeted me next, sank my heart to the lowest depths imaginable. Inside the coach station was a long line of coaches that hogged the loading bays. To my disgust, they were spewing out thick volumes of diesel fumes and in the process, choking me till I was hoarse. And how could I forget the horrible long miserable faces that came from my fellow countrymen with their heads hanging down, almost to the point of shame. So this is jolly old England, the England I had come back to. The one and only thing I wanted to do at this moment in time was to catch the next available flight back to the sun-kissed state of Florida. God, what a come-down this was. This was indeed back to hard reality.

Footnote: This is a true story and is based on the authors own personal experiences.

The Naval Reunion

Never let be said that when things get downright depressing, something always comes along to cheer us up - and sure enough such a surprise had arrived in the post. It was an invitation from a dear old friend of mine called Reggie who had kindly invited me to join him for his sixtieth birthday party. Not only that, I would have the great honour of cutting the birthday cake along with singing a few of the party songs: you know, the sort of songs that eccentrically minded lunatics like to sing, such as ring-a-ring-a-roses and playing silly little games like knock-down-ginger, oh and not forgetting, pass-the-parcel. However, my reaction to this mind boggling news was met with a feeling of fear and trepidation. Let's face it the man's a complete nut.

So there I was sitting in the lounge, rooted to my favourite chair, the recliner, and eagerly awaiting the start of a live soccer match. Anyway, during the commentators summing up of the match, who should walk in but my manservant friend called Bartholomew. Shush! But Wait for it, secretly disguised as a butler. In he walked, holding up a highly polished silver tray and bearing on it a beautiful birthday cake, together with a superb arrangement of sandwiches and biscuits, plus a beautiful china teapot - bought I believe for ten dollars at some obscure back street establishment in Hong Kong.

"Pray sir! For who did ringeth the bell, and does sir want his tea served in the east wing or will the master retire to the smoke room," my butler friend informed me in a rather shaky, old boy, public school accent.

"For God's sake Reggie, take that ridiculous butlers uniform off and give us the tray over here. I'm famished."

By gad, what a luck chap I am to have such an eccentric fiend for a friend as Reggie. Well, I did warn you people out there that the poor man's demented, or haven't I told you yet? Lowering his heavy-laden tray on to the table we both felt a good gorging session was high on the agenda.

With a cheeky little grin I turned to Reggie and said. "Look, shall I start pouring the tea out and cutting the birthday cake, I believe it's my turn to be mum again." And like all good mums I delighted him with a cup of his favourite tea, the Bay Jonk, as it's affectionately known. Which according to ancient traditions is the only tea on the planet that puts hair in places that's not only naughty but damn right embarrassing?

"Well, if you really insist on being mum," Reggie grumbled, ruddy well get down to the ablutions and give the thing a damn good clean."

"No thanks, I'd much prefer to pour the tea out. I'm not the least bit interested to start cleaning out bogs."

"Come on man, drink your tea up before it gets cold". I nagged at him.

Gently placing my cup down on the table, I had noticed a letter that was addressed to Reggie but still unopened, and being the nice chap as I am, I passed the letter over to him. With great care he opened it up and I could see by the look on his face he found the contents very much to his liking.

"Well I never, look at this, it's from one of my fellow naval officers I served with at sea and apparently there're holding a banquet in Oxford for next Friday - it's a sort of grand reunion get together. My friend has kindly enclosed two tickets and it says I can bring a friend along. I say, how about coming with me?" Reggie beamed with an air of excitement. "I can assure you, it'll be a fantastic evening with plenty of plonk and a first class meal thrown in for good measure. The only problem is the invitation states that one should be appropriately dressed. Now the thing is do you have a smart suit to wear?"

"Good grief no," I replied back. "I tend to dress in casual clothes."

"Look, I tell you what, we'll zap into town tomorrow morning and I'll get you fixed up with something suitable."

The following morning I was whisked into town and thereby taken to a huge department store, believed to be the finest store for miles around. Up and up we went in the elevator till it reached the fourth floor of the gent's outfitters department. Browsing through the hundreds of suits on display, I came across this nice little grey flannelled number, priced at a mere £135. On showing price ticket to Reggie he seemed not the slightest bit concerned.

"Stick it on my account," he proudly boasted to the shop floor assistant.

I must say Reggie looked hilariously funny in a silly sort of way. He reminded me of one those well-disciplined army officers who enjoyed giving stern orders to his men. He addressed the assistant like he was some sort of private in the army on his first day of joining up. Beckoning the assistant over with his little finger a most unpleasant barracking noise came from the vicinity of Reggie's mouth.

"Oi! Come here you horrible little bleeder and let's be having you my son. Atten-shon! Come on man, get those shoulders back, legs together, left right, left right, taarrrr-haarhaaar, left right, left, heeeyaaaaar," Reggie yelled.

"Oh, just coming, sir," the terrified assistant replied.

We left the store feeling like a couple of old grumpy squaddies who had just put some poor innocent bugger on a charge, and I couldn't help noting the look on Reggie's face, that smug sinister smile of his.

"You have to treat these civvies with a bit of cold steel." Reggie smiled.

So there I was all kitted out with a top-notch suit in readiness for the banquet, thanks to Reggie's, kind generosity.

The day of the banquet had drawn near and nigh. I had arranged to meet the old sea dog as per instructions, and, that was to rendezvous with him at precisely seven o'clock outside the famous Randolph Hotel in central Oxford. And so with this in mind I left my house around midday and caught the X2 bus to Bedford. Alighted, and then boarded another coach to Oxford. Quite a pleasant journey till I reached the town of Buckingham, when a most unpleasant character got on, drunk and refusing to pay his fare, thus putting ten minutes on my journey. As luck would have it I still managed to arrive in Oxford for six thirty.

Oxford is famous the world over for its universities and historic buildings and for centuries or more it has been the home to lecturers and scholars. Today, Oxford is a thriving city with a mixture of ancient and modern attractions. Away from the busy bustling streets is a concoction of narrow cobbled roads and back-lanes that led by half-timbered houses and magnificent colleges teeming with ramparts, pinnacles and gaping towers. I strolled past ye old tea rooms and shops selling souvenirs, and how could one forget the endless stream of students that go about their business in a most dignified manner. The whole atmosphere seemed to give an air of graciousness and character about the place.

By coincidence, I heard the town hall clock strike its chimes, dead on the stroke of seven. Even more incredible I found myself standing outside the famous Randolph Hotel. In fact I was somewhat honoured and privileged. The reason for my sentimentality was this: the Randolph Hotel had previously been the setting for that most enjoyable TV series called 'Inspector Morse'.

But who should come haring round the corner at the wheel of an old jalopy? You've guessed it – it was jolly old Reggie who slowly but surely trudged his way towards me. But it was with raised eyebrows I was about to witness a scene of pure farcical comedy. There is without doubt, no more gratifying scene then that of a man's trousers, leaving the framework of an enormous belly and then sliding gracefully down towards his ankles and so thus displaying a bright pair of union jack underpants and what looked like a rather mean version of a swashbuckling Lord Flashard. Worse was to come. He then had the audacity to break into one of his famous routines, the one and only and unmistakable, Ministerial Walks routine. I was particularly drawn to my friend's gigantic strides, though in fairness I must point out that his attempts to do wheelies and cartwheels were way beyond the poor fellow. Returning back to sanity he addressed me in his customary seaman's role.

"Hello, shipmate, Reggie saluted. "Are we away anchor yet, me hardy?"

"Aye Captain" I growled, "but will you first give me and the people of Oxford a couple of broadsides."

"It'll be an absolute pleasure, old boy. I am lightning blue touch paper, stand by to repel all borders."

"I say, old bean," as I stared towards Reggie's heavily stained uniform. "Looks like you've seen action in the kitchen again? Ready for the function, are we?"

"Cor blimey, not half," was his reply.

Making our way towards his car the first thing that hit me was the overpowering stench of mothballs which notably came from the vicinity of Reggie's uniform.

"I say old boy, what a disgusting smell?"

"Ah, well, that'll be my mothball repellent; you see I always douse myself in the stuff, before a big bang, so as to keep my fellow officers on their toes."

"Mmm," the perfect way to make new friends and acquaintances, I thought.

Just a short walk from George Street was the old town hall, the venue for tonight's bash. Waiting there to greet us was the usher, whom with charm and courtesy, politely asked for our invitation tickets?

"Ah, yes gentlemen, I'll show you to your table, but first I'll announce your arrival to the other guests. My lords, rear admirals and gentlemen, please welcome able seaman Reggie Bartholomew Brown. And gentlemen it also gives me great pleasure to introduce Mr Brown's companion, who unfortunately has never been to sea."

A loud cheer roared across the auditorium with just a small section of the audience, shouting..."Bloody Civvies!"

A waiter of Spanish origin escorted us to our table, and there placed on gleaming white tablecloths, were our names, encapsulated on tiny little badges. The mighty hall was packed to capacity with well two hundred guests or more, dressed to the hilt in full naval regalia. Dithery old codgers that boasted a dazzling display of medals that dangled precariously from their uniforms.

"By George," Reggie gasped. "Look over there, that chap in the rear admirals uniform has managed to get himself some scrambled egg on his hat. Damn lucky bounder".

The speaker requested that we take to our seats as dinner was now being served and afterwards, wine, cheese and coffee, followed by after dinner speeches. The meal I must mention was first-class as was the friendly atmosphere.

The PA system suddenly crackled into life.

"Fellow Naval Officers, your attention please," the speaker urged as he banged his gavel down as though he had just sold something of great value.

"Gentlemen, gentlemen, who'll be the first to come up give us an account of their time at sea?"

Hands were going up in eager anticipation and it was difficult to see whom the speaker would choose first.

"Yes, you sir, down there in the front row with the eye patch and the gammy leg, please step forward and join me," the speaker urged.

The first candidate rose from his chair and made his way towards the stage at the same time wiping his forehead in eager anticipation.

"Pray sir, could you please tell us what your position was about the time of the Second World War?"

"Good evening fellow officers my name is Captain Bentwater and I was the captain of a huge battleship throughout the Second World War." Captain Bentwater took hold of the microphone and began to reveal his salty tale. "I first want to say a big thank you to all my fellow officers who served with me on board HMS Henry, affectedly known as the old boiler. Ah yes, I can remember the occasion quite vividly that day on the 5th June 1942. There I was gentlemen, standing on the bridge of my ship when I had the terrible misfortune of smelling something quite ghastly. To my disgust it was the overbearing stench of enemy Fokkers. Gentlemen! There were Fokkers here and Fokkers there; in fact the Fokkers were everywhere."

"Oh, excuse me," a gentleman from the back row interrupted. "Precisely how many Fokkers was there, Captain Bentwater?"

"Let me see now, as I recall, there was a least two of the Fokkers if my memory serves me right." Anyway, I gave the order to open up with 6-inch guns and twenty five pounders, plus I ordered the boiler room to make as much smoke as possible. By gad, we gave the blighters a damn good pounding, didn't we lads."

Fellow naval officers in the auditorium began shaking their heads in disbelief, hissing under their breath in an unsavoury manner and angrily pointing their fingers at Captain Bentwater.

A gentleman from the audience stood up and said. "Captain Bentwater, if I remember, weren't you still tied up in Portsmouth Harbour at this so-called battle of yours. In fact Captain, if the truth be known, you were banged up in your cabin, playing gin-rummy with fellow officers, and for the rest of the war Captain you were serving out a one to two in a military prison, on a Court Marshall, I do believe."

"Oh, yes, well, we won't go in to that right now," a rather red-faced Captain replied.

Captain Bentwater left the rostrum to a chorus of boos, hisses and shouts of bloody scoundrel.

"But who else would like to take to the podium and give us an account of their time at sea?" the speaker urged, making a passionate plea for more volunteers. "Yes you sir in the middle row, please step forward and join me."

A biggish chap rose from his chair and made his way forward to the podium. He introduced himself as Midshipman Melrose, who told the audience he had served on board a destroyer in the Second World War. "There I was gentlemen," Mr Melrose started off. "As I recall I was somewhere in the North Sea, just off the coast of Denmark. I was in a group of ships that totalled sixteen merchants with six destroyers as cover, in other words a convoy. We received a signal from the admiralty on the morning in question, stating that a large formation of Stukas and Heinkels had been spotted some twenty miles away and, as usual the Luftwaffe were up to their old tricks and out in force. I can remember the occasion quite vividly. At the time I was doing look-out duties when through my binoculars I could see a large formation of enemy planes at ten-o-clock high. Tension mounted as the intrusive aircraft began to go into a dive. We gathered they were making their final run-in to attack our ship. I immediately jumped on an anti-aircraft gun and began to fire my gun with some vengeance. Through the smoke and chaos of the battle, bombs and bullets rained in from every angle. Suddenly there was a deafening explosion. A bomb had entered the forward section of the ship and had managed to pierce the ships infrastructure which had the desired effect of shaking the ship to its foundations. Lads it was terrible. The air had filled with black smoke and flying bits of debris were whizzing past my head. I could hear the sound of bullets ricocheting from the burning metal of the ship. My God! The poor chap next to me has been hit, and, by the look of him, he's bought it, I'm afraid. I jumped on his more powerful gun and took over. I immediately opened up as I did so I could the see the tracer bullets leaving my gun, travelling at speed towards Jerry. Rat, tat, tat, it went. I do hope I get me a Stuka before he gets me? Smoke appeared from a burning plane. I've got one; I've got me a Stuka, and another and another. Out of the sky they dropped like flies, one by one they went crashing into the sea. Across to my stern I could see smoke bellowing up from a burning tanker. She's been badly hit and fire crews were trying to put out the raging inferno. And so the battle raged on. Our destroyers managed to down twelve enemy aircraft with the rest hightailing back to Berlin with their legs between their tails. And that gentlemen ends my true story of how I served my time during the Second World War from 1939 to 1945 in the Royal navy."

"Let's give this very gallant gentleman a rousing good handclap," the speaker insisted. But who else would like to come forward and give an account of themselves. Yes, that gentleman down there with his hand up, please step forward and join me sir. Can you please tell the audience what your position was while serving your time at sea?"

"Good evening, fellow officers, my name Hargreaves and I served my time in the Royal Navy as a Petty Officer on board a first class frigate called HMS Sternfast from 1940 to 1945. It must have been around October time 1943, when the admiralty despatched our frigate to sail for Norway with orders to track down a wolf-type pack of U-boats. The admiralty concluded that any threat from the Luftwaffe was minimal. The biggest threat however was the heavy build-up of U-boats that were operating in the North Sea.

On arrival at our destination a force twelve storm was blowing up at the time and our visibility was down to nil. At this rate we'd be lucky to stay afloat as the ship was being thrown about like a rag doll. It was at this point my radio officer picked up a distinctive signal that came from a distance of some twenty miles away with an estimated speed of eighteen knots, and that gentleman is what we were looking for, U-boats, and lots of them. Our orders were to follow with caution and attack when conditions were more favourable. The next day on a lovely calm morning with the previous night's storm well behind us, we proceeded with great care to tail the U-boats. Dogged by a series a false alarms my radio officer handed me a message.

"Sir, I have just picked up a signal and it appears we are in direct contact with the U-boats."

"Then on the radar equipment we could hear the distinctive bleeping sound of a passing U-boat that was blasting out from the scanners."

B......yinnnnnnnnnnnnnnnnnnnnnnnnnning
B......yinnnnnnnnnnnnnnnnnnnnnnnnnning
B......yinnnnnnnnnnnnnnnnnnnnnnnnnninng
B......yinnnnnnnnnnnnnnnnnnnnnnnnnninng

"Gentlemen of the audience, have you any idea what that sounds means?" Mr Hargreaves politely asked.

"Yes, I know what it means," a heckler from the front row stood up and declared. "It meant you and your crew were near a Chinese take-away and you'd just ordered Chow Mein with Prawn Balls to follow."

"No, no, no, it meant there was a blasted U-boat right under the belly of the ship."

"There's one thing that really puzzles me, Mr Hargreaves," the speaker interrupted. "Where on earth were your Hedgehogs, man? A good officer's duty is to throw his Hedgehogs overboard before going into battle."

"Ah, yes, our dear friends the Hedgehogs. Bit of a prickly situation was that, but yes, we did manage to throw a few of the little perishers over the side."

"Please explain to the audience what a Hedgehog is," Mr Hargreaves, the speaker asked.

"Well, a Hedgehog is a naval term for a depth-charge."

"Anyway on with my story, action stations were sounded and my instructions to the crew were to drop depth-charges, immediately. The attack began and raged on for several hours or more. Just as things were hotting up I happened to look through my binoculars where I saw a thick oil slick floating on top of the surface. Horrified, I then saw something rise out of the water. I at once recognised it as a Class-1 V11C German submarine. I was just to give the order to open up with our 0.5 anti-aircraft guns, when I saw a German officer waving a white flag at us and thus surrendering. The result of this battle was two enemy subs were sunk, one captured, with two escaping, so all in all not a bad day's work. And so ends my true and hopeful, interesting story.

"Thank you so much Mr Hargreaves for that mouth-watering tale and an account of your gallant deeds. Let's give this gentleman a really big hand," the speaker insisted. "We've got time for just one more guest to say his piece," the speaker requested, as he looked round for a suitable candidate.

It would inconceivable if the speaker was to call out Reggie's name. But surprisingly, he did just that. He asked the old sea dog to step forward and give a true account of his time at sea. The realisation of Reggie's time at sea was indeed a sobering thought.

For reasons unknown, Reggie seemed deliriously happy as he took to the podium. He at once produced a battered old briefcase and from it he took out a number of documents to which he held up for everyone to see."

"Friends and fellow officers," Reggie began, "it gives me the greatest pleasure to inform you, that today, I have just received the most fantastic news from the admiralty. It would seem, because of my past naval record, the hierarchy have shouldered me with the responsibilities of becoming overall Commander-in-Chief of the entire Pacific Fleet."

The news of Reggie's appointment came as a complete bombshell to his fellow officers.

"Frightful cad – he'll never get away with it."

"Put the bugger in a straightjacket." Rear Admiral Ramsbottom said ungraciously.

"What does it all mean," a bewildered speaker asked?"

"It means my good man," Reggie smiled, "I'll be taking my beautiful, hand-built dreadnought down to the local serpentine and there I will unleash a devastating display of awesome fire-power. Furthermore, my intention is to sink anything that comes into sight with military like precision. In addition to my heroic objectives my plan is to obliterate any little fart of a schoolboy's boat and blow the thing to smithereens."

"I say, well done sir," the speaker saluted. "By Gove, that'll give the snotty little brats something to think about. Let's give this very courageous man a really good hand".

After many gallant speakers had come and gone and told their extraordinary tales, our function was sadly coming to an end.

Reggie leaned across and asked for my thoughts?

"It was absolutely brilliant. I've never enjoyed myself so much."

"Well," Reggie smiled. "There'll be plenty more functions like this one, as I get invited to lots of reunions."

Our last duty for the evening was to give a toast to all those brave and gallant men who gave their lives at sea during those terrible years of conflict from 1939 to 1945. So with that we said our goodbyes and made our way back to our respective homes, ending a most enjoyable day.

Strange Encounters of the Third Kind

The elements to this story are somewhat bizarre if not fantastic. But let me assure you, the story that is about to unfold is a true account of the extraordinary events that took place while in the depths and isolation of the New Mexico wilderness, and, as assumed; it has all the ingredients of an encounter of the Third Kind. The scariest thing about the story is its frightening implications. Word for word, the story was told to me by a respectable police officer whose sincerity I did not doubt.

Anyway, I'll start my epic saga from the very beginning. It must have been around 1999 when I was in the final stages of planning the holiday of a lifetime to the United States of America, accompanied by my good friend Geoff. The initial plan was cover the two states of Arizona and New Mexico in one fail swoop, which in mileage terms was just shy of three thousand miles.

And so, after months of meticulous planning my long awaited trip had dawned. As far back as I can remember I dreamed about this day and now it's finally coming true. It must have all started when as a young boy I began to watch a countless number of cowboy and Indian films. One can picture the scene. Galloping across the desert landscape was the magnificent sight of the US cavalry, being hotly pursued by a band of Indians and in the distance the awe-inspiring sight of Monument Valley with the spectacular and weird shapes of the mesas, bluffs and buttes. And that's when I began to think what a fantastic place, Arizona must be. Call it pulling power if you like for today I will be seeing it for real and these were my thoughts as I caught the early morning train to Gatwick International Airport.

Flight 2607 was eleven hours into its flight when the British Airways 747 began to gradually descend. Peering out from my window seat I could see the breathtaking sight of Bryce Canyon in the state of Utah. It was at this point when the PA system suddenly crackled into life. It was the Captain, asking passengers to fasten their seat belts as we were about to land.

The next thing I knew was the sound of wheels bumping down at Sky Harbour Airport, Phoenix, Arizona. Once through the rigmarole of immigration we finally stepped out to the bright brilliant sunshine of the day. Armed with our luggage we took a hike over to the next building to pick up our hired car which Geoff had pre-booked from his home in the UK. They gave us a four-door Chevrolet Metro in a pearl white colour - a really smashing little car. Geoff suggested that we stop the night at Apache Junction just east of Phoenix. This would enable us to get a good night's sleep and recuperate after such a long day.

The following morning we treated ourselves to an enormous breakfast to fortify ourselves for the long day's drive. After paying the bill we darted around the corner to Bernie's Convenient Store to pick a few supplies for our epic journey into the great unknown. All gassed up and raring to go we set a course heading east, along highway 60, known to the local gunslingers as the Old West Highway as it's romantically know, destination Silver City. Our true western adventure kicked off in style with a grand slam drive through the breath-taking Sonora Desert. I took a deep breath and gazed on in wonder at the awe inspiring scenery. The road carved out an opening that revealed a landscape of incredible contrasts. For mile after mile it was a mixture of a wild rolling desert that was painted in a red colour and awash with a shrub called Sagebrush that spread its greenery across the red sandy soil. Beyond the horizon the sky sparkled with an unbelievable explosion of colours that snowballed down to form a blue and green haziness effect, caused by the optical effects of the sun. Then towering up to sensational heights was the magnificent sight of the Saguaro cacti. Tagging alongside the huge cacti was the pleasing sight of the humming birds, brilliantly hovering and then darting in and out of the deadly-like spines for food. But it was the reality of the Sonora landscape that was quite something to witness in the crystal clear, blistering heat. To make our day truly complete, rolling lazily across the desert floor I caught sight of the Tumbleweed, better known as Brush that made its way majestically across the red sandy soil and getting bigger and bigger as it gathered pace. Even more sensational was the crazy sight of the Roadrunners that could be seen scooting across the desert landscape, and in the process, kicking up a trail of dust. My observations gave me the impression I had just witnessed a scene from an old western movie, but sadly there were no cowboy or Indians about to make it come true. We ventured high and low as the miles rattled on and on till finally we came to a roadside clearing with a border sign. It gave notice that New Mexico, Land of Enchantment, eagerly awaited us.

(My dairy reads) Silver City proved to be a sleepy little place as we soon discovered by driving through its deserted streets with not a flicker of life to be had. With the help of Geoff's guidebook we came across a listing for a place called the Palace Hotel that was situated two blocks away. Sometime later we thus found ourselves standing in the main lobby area of a hotel, only to find with great surprise we had descended into a wonderful world of fantasy and make believe. Positioned all around us was a mixture of antiquities, stuffed animals, military uniforms, guns and native Indian artefacts. I looked on in disbelief at the many fixtures and fittings that were hanging precariously on the walls. More startling, in the far corner sat this huge brown bear, snarling its teeth, somewhat ferociously - stuffed of course. However, the biggest surprise came when Geoff approached the gent's latrines and there sitting in an upright position was the sight of two dirty great cannons. No, not the clergy type, but two enormous blockbusters that were pointing up with dangerous intent.

"My word," Geoff gasped. "I don't believe it. That one if I'm not mistaken is a Whistling Dick accompanied by the mighty Big Bertha."

"Now come on Geoff, keep it down a bit, you're not in your local pub now you know, coming out with language like that."

"No honestly, I think these two little beauties were probably used in the American Civil War, maybe by the Confederates?" Geoff explained.

But what were two dirty great cannons doing sitting in the lobby area of a hotel we asked ourselves?

Geoff had the answer. "It wouldn't surprise me if the owners of the place were trying to get some sort of theme going so as to pull in the punters so to speak."

That evening over dinner I was being issued with precise instructions for tomorrow's journey at the same time I was to given an in-depth history lesson on a location known as the Gila Wilderness area. Geoff was eager to inform me that this whole region was once inhabited by the great Apache chief called Geronimo. He further went on to tell me that the land stretching from Silver City to the far north once belonged to the great Apache Nation.

"You see our expedition to Gila is of great importance to me. I've done a lot of research and fact-finding on the subject. In fact, I'm so excited to be going there, and hey, we might even see a Gila monster?" Geoff mused.

I inquired if the Gila monster was as rare as the Loch Ness monster which seemed to irritate Geoff quite a bit. The very fact I didn't know what a Gila monster looked like really got to the poor fellow.

Geoff continued. "So you see our journey for tomorrow is one of great significance. In conjunction with our monster activities I thought it would be nice to do a bit of hiking, time permitting of course. Then, later on in the day the general plan is to head up to Albuquerque for a one night stopover at the YMCA, situated on the old route 66. However, here comes the exciting bit. Instead of taking the fast freeway route I thought it might be more adventurous if we took the more scenic route by way of a back road. I think it could turn out to be quite exciting."

Geoff at this point was feeling quite chuffed with himself with his meticulous planning and knowledgeable logistics. But little did we know that a tortuous yet spectacular drive lay ahead of us, filled with danger and intrigue, and, by far, the most worrying aspect of our journey was its uncertainty.

The next morning I awoke to be greeted by brilliant sunshine and wall-to-wall blue skies, and just perfect for sightseeing. At seven thirty in the morning we said our goodbyes to Silver City and headed north to the dizzy heights of Albuquerque. The drive up from Silver City was as wonderful as our guidebooks had predicted. We found ourselves entering a landscape of startling beauty.

For me, New Mexico conjures up scenes of breath-taking awesomeness and, although Hollywood's interpretation of the Wild West can be sometimes exaggerated, to a large extent it can be a profound reality. For as we drove along I could visualise the scene from an old western movie as we drove north. In the distance a gang of desperados were fleeing from the long arm of the law. A posse of the sheriff's men were hunting down Billy the Kid. A gunfight takes place outside a saloon and on the horizon the Apache meet up with the Navajo to join forces and form raiding parties. All of which makes fascinating thinking.

The miles rattled and rolled on as our journey took us through the obscurity of a wild rolling wilderness area to a place or places unknown, and definitely not the sort of route any sane person would take. The road fell sharply away and climbed sheepishly and incessantly through a landscape littered with rocky outcrops, canyons and creeks. In the distance snow-capped peaks formed a breath-taking backdrop. Moseying along quite merrily we found ourselves plunging in and out of deep gorges and gullies that eventually led to a high plateau. Before me I witnessed a vast wilderness area that stretched as far as the eye could see. The sheer ruggedness of this place emphasised the enormity of it all. Geoff informed me that we were in the midst of some of the wildest and most desolate areas on the planet.

So there we were in the middle of nowhere, completely lost. It really is quite scary how one can get lost out here and couldn't help feeling that we were totally cut off from the rest of the world. Coupled with this thought, it's almost impossible to maintain one's bearings, amid a landscape of total isolation. In fact, a sense of abandonment had prevailed upon us. However the beauty of this place was mind-blowing. The first signs of civilisation came in the form of a welcoming sign which indicated that the town of Socorro was close at hand. With no time to lose we pressed on regardless.

It was by chance however that we came to pull-in cum picnic area, and surprisingly, the only other occupant was a Highway Patrol car. The officer didn't take much notice of us at first he seemed much more pre-occupied on his two-way radio. But like all good cops his suspicions were soon aroused, after all we were in the middle of nowhere.

Feeling tired and weary from our long drive we decided to stretch our legs and take in a little water. I could see by the look on the patrolman's face he was getting mighty curious by the minute as to whom we were. His eyes by now were focused on our every move. He decided to leave his patrol car and make his way towards us at the same time placing his hand on his gun for any eventuality. He requested that we show him proof of our identity. No sooner than we had showed him our passports when his face lit up with a look of euphoria.

"Well would you believe it, a couple of Limey's," he smiled, and hugged us like two long lost brothers. "What the hell are you guys doing out here in the middle of nowhere?" he asked. We told the officer we were heading up to Taos via Albuquerque, thereafter; our intention was to cut across to the Grand Canyon area in Arizona.

After a good old chinwag the officer told us that his name was Scott and said he lived just a few short miles down the road with his wife and son. In any event he said he was coming off duty in a short while and asked us if we'd like to come back with him for a coffee. Before we knew it we were driving up an unmade road which led to an open piece of ground, reminiscent of a smallholding. Waving franticly from the front porch was the sight Scott's wife and son.

"Hi Hun," Scott waved, "look what I've brought you, a couple of Limey's."

"Oh Scott, you shouldn't have," she smiled. "Come on you guys I've got the coffee on."

The company I must mention was truly heart-warming along with the coffee that flowed like a mountain stream. While in the course of our new found friendship it was I who started the ball rolling when I asked Scott if he had ever seen a UFO before, being we were in the hotbed for that sort of thing. Judging by the expression on the patrolman's face I must have touched on something quite sensitive by the intense look on his face. I could actually see a look of terror in his eyes. He neither spoke nor said a word. For reasons unknown Scott seemed spellbound by my comment. He just stared into his wife's eyes. She returned the compliment by looking even more edgy and terrified. I thought myself, what the hell have I said?

Gradually, Scott began to unwind and get some spiel out of his system.

"What I am about to tell you guys has haunted me for many years. In fact you're the first person to come along who has ever asked me about UFOs. My story is so strange, so horrific, and so unbelievable that it defies human comprehension. The answer to your question is yes, I have seen a UFO, so has my wife, and so has my son along with the countless number of other people in the area. Not only have I seen a UFO but I had the terrible misfortune of coming face-to-face with extraterrestrial beings called the Greys."

Apparently the chain of events which led up to Scott's experiences went something like this.

"I was sitting at home at the time and off duty," Scott began to explain, "but my freedom was to be short-lived. From out of the blue I received a phone call from a fellow colleague back at the precinct. Fellow Officer Brady apologised for the sudden intrusion and he went on to tell me that the precinct had been inundated with phone calls from people who had reported seeing strange pulsating lights coming up from the creek, just off the main highway. Anyway in the course of his conversation he said he would need to go and investigate the matter, although he was a bit apprehensive about going there by himself.

"So I wondered if you could possibly come along with me Scott," Officer Brady asked. "I realise you're off duty but I don't relish the thought of going up there by myself."

Scott said he would be only too happy to help. So with that Scott took his wife along together with their eighteen year old son called Toby. Scott continued.....

"Sometime later we all rendezvoused in two separate patrol cars and parked high on a ridge that overlooked a deep ravine. We must have sat there for well over twenty minutes or so. Nothing happened. We were just about to pack and go home up when something incredible happened. From out of the creek a disc shaped object appeared. Suddenly we found ourselves being bombarded with a mixture of bright pulsating lights that formed a combination of different colours. The object gained a height of about two hundred metres or so and then it abruptly stopped in mid-air. From the belly of the UFO came two balls of transparent lights. The bigger of the balls stood there hovering. The smaller one scoured the creek floor as though it was searching for something - when finally both balls disappeared inside the ship. Then in a flicker the UFO took off at tremendous speed and completely vanished into thin air. But there was far worse to come," Scott said. "In addition to our encounter, my son Toby found himself being projected to within the nerve centre of the UFO, and under extraordinary circumstances he had the terrible misfortune of being abducted. By telepathic communication the Greys were able to communicate with my son, telepathically.

The leader of the Greys told my son that in order to travel through the universe from galaxy to galaxy their craft went through a series of three-dimensional time-tunnels or black holes. More incredible was the fact that the UFO did not use any form of fuel. In addition to the Greys there were up eighteen different types of extraterrestrial beings. Some were like the Greys while others took on the form of reptiles. There was even a species that resembled earth's people."

Towards the end of his abduction Toby asked the Greys, "what shall I tell my parents when I return? They'll never believe my story."

"I say this to you Toby and all of mankind; while the human race is destroying the earth in its greedy ways I give you this warning. Before the century draws to a close there will be a visitation in the form of an extraterrestrial being. He will descend from the heavens and his purpose is to hold judgement on the entire human race. He has the power to destroy the earth many times over, and such is his wisdom he will judge each earthling on his or her merits. His final decision could spell the end for the entire human race. I say this to you Toby, if you have no God, find one, for very soon you and everyone on the planet earth are going to need one."

Toby was transported back to earth and found himself back inside the car with his parents looking on. As time passed by, Toby sadly left the family home and went to live in the Phoenix area. By any measure it must have been a truly terrifying ordeal for the young man. Over a period of time Toby's whole character and personality had become deeply affected. He became distant, reclusive and unbalanced.

"What I am about to reveal to you next will simply blow your minds away," Scott continued in a distraught voice. "The next incident that came about is even more terrifying than my previous encounter. In 1975 rumours buzzed throughout the precinct that I was up for promotion, therefore I will never forget the day when I was summoned into the chief's office which I presumed was to pick up my promotion. As I sat there waiting patiently for something to happen there was a few moments of awkward silence till finally a door opened. It revealed a well-built, smartly dressed man, thereabouts in his mid-forties and beholding a black briefcase. To my knowledge I had never seen this man before and thought it rather strange as to why a complete stranger was allowed to attend a private meeting? The man in question refused to disclose or give any information about himself as to why he was here? Anyway, while in the course of the meeting the chief did his best to explain the circumstances behind the mystery. All he told me was that the man worked for the Secret Service and was based in Washington DC. That was all I was to know. Furthermore, it was established by the powers that be I was to pick up a diplomat from Albuquerque Airport at precisely fourteen hundred hours the following Tuesday and take him to an undisclosed destination somewhere at a secret location in the desert. The diplomat in question would then contact me once I had reached the airport and apparently he had been thoroughly briefed about me.

I must admit I left the chief's office feeling a little apprehensive as to what I was getting myself into. After all counter intelligence. It seemed very cloak and dagger stuff to me.

The following Tuesday I turned up at Albuquerque Airport as requested. As I waited there in the main terminal building a man approached me. He was dressed in a black suit and wearing dark shades accompanied by a brown leather briefcase. Being the good cop as I am, the guy in question had all the characteristics of a fully-fledged undercover agent. He didn't say a word just showed me his secret service badge. He then pointed towards the exit door and out to where a blue compact car was parked on the drop-off bay. The mysterious man sat in the back of the car and it looked like I was doing the driving but still nothing was said or spoken. The diplomat or whoever he was then produced a map of New Mexico. There marked in red ink was a big X mark. Gathering the way he was poking me in the back it was where I was supposed to go.

Anyway, as we threaded our way through the complexities of Albuquerque we thus found ourselves in the proximity of an open desert terrain. Sometime later we reached what looked like some sort of military establishment. As I recall there was a perimeter fence with two armed security guards who manned the main gate. Every moment had an aspect of terror about it. One of the guards then asked me to step out of the car. The other guard asked me to put my hands behind my back and to my astonishment he then handcuffed me. Combined with this humiliation I was then blindfolded and forced head first in the back of the car, thereafter the diplomat took over the driving.

As the car rattled and rumbled its way along a lot of disturbing thoughts were going through my mind. There were so many questions I wanted to ask my captors, but still nothing was said or spoken. What the hell is going on I asked myself? Why all the heavy handed stuff. Who are these people? Heaven knows what I've got myself into? I'm a police officer for God's sake, not a common criminal.

We must have driven for about twenty minutes or so when the car coming to an abrupt halt. The car door opened to where I was greeted by more security guards. I then felt a hand taking hold of my arm and thus helping me out of the car, thereafter the handcuffs and blindfold were removed. It began to dawn on me that this was no ordinary place for my observations confirmed it was a research establishment of some considerable size. Suddenly there was movement. Automatic doors slowly opened to reveal an elevator of some considerable size. The diplomat then drove the car inside and in an instant we were dropping down like flies to a bottomless pit. Floor after floor went by till finally we reached ground level some twenty floors below. What confronted me next was the fearful sight of a man dressed in a sort of space-type suit and to my surprise he actually spoke."

"Ok sir, you take a break now," he said. "If you go down to the end of the complex there's a restroom. Help yourself to anything you want."

"It suddenly dawned on me what this place was. Apparently it was made up of a vast honeycomb of laboratories. What they did here didn't bear thinking about. Anyway, my predicament was made more precarious by the numerous passageways and corridors that were scattered about. Thus the fact remained I was a prisoner of persons, hitherto unknown? Feeling tired and weary from my harrowing ordeal I decided to make for the rest room to see what was on offer. In any event I was extremely curious to find some hidden truths about the place. As I twisted and turned down the narrow confines of the complex I had a burning desire to make some sense of my predicament, therefore, I decided to do my own bit of investigating and to hell with it. I had just passed one of the labs when I was almost blinded by a series of bright pulsating lights. Acting on impulse I decided to investigate the matter.

"What happened next almost blew my mind away." Scott continued in a distraught voice. "I allowed myself to stand on the tips of my toes like a ballerina so I could peer over the top of the glass partition. What confronted me next will remain etched on my mind forever. The scene that I was about to witness was like something out of a science fiction horror movie. I was gripped by the growing menace of something sinister that was afoot, when I made a gruesome discovery. In the course of my observations I encountered four scientists that were dressed in white smocks who appeared to be working on a project of some importance. Accompanying the scientists were a number of tiny figures, no bigger than four feet tall. When I got a better look I almost passed out with shock. The tiny figures were no less than an alien species of extraterrestrial beings called the Greys, and to top it all they were working in conjunction with the scientists. The notion of alien creatures here on earth truly horrified me. I was virtually paralysed by fear. It began to dawn on me that this place was solely for the purpose of exchanging technological information with extraterrestrial beings that had probably been captured from a downed ship. In that moment I couldn't move and just froze to the spot. So this is why no one talked or said anything. I ran down to the end of the corridor to where the restroom was situated. I tried to steady myself by pumping several cups of coffee down me. One thing was for sure I wanted to get out of this place, proto. But how? I was a prisoner here. I pondered in deep thought as to how long I would have to stay here? I desperately wanted to contact my wife but there were no phone – just internal ones.

Many hours had passed by when the internal phone rang. A voice at the other end informed me that my party was ready to leave and I was to make my way back to the elevator to where the car was parked. To say I was pleased was an understatement. I'd never been so thankful to get out of the place. In any event when I eventually reached Albuquerque I rang my wife and told her everything I had witnessed, word for word.

"So you guys asked me if I'd ever seen a UFO before," Scott said in a subdued voice. "Well now you know. I'm glad in a way you two guys came along today because I needed to get this business off my chest before I went completely mad. I can assure you no one would ever believe my story, not even my buddies back at the precinct. Mission accomplished, I told my chief that I never wanted to do anything like that again. It must also be remembered however, that not only have I seen a UFO but my wife along with a countless number of other people in the area have also seen strange and weird things, not of this world. You see guys; this is New Mexico, the hot-bed for extraterrestrial activity." Scott reassured us.

When everything was done and dusted we finally paid our respects to Officer Scott and his wife and so left to continue on with our journey. This true and amazing story has since stuck in my mind ever since that fateful day in the year 2000, and not a day goes by when I still think about the incredible experiences we had encountered. In retrospect I felt there was a certain justification in Scott's story that truly fascinated me. It certainly had a solid ring of truth about it, fantastic as that might be. The bottom line is: it seems we are not alone after all and more harrowing is the thought, were the Greys trying to give us a final warning before it's too late?

The Highland Fling

The background to this particular story is as follows. Some time ago I had to attend a meeting of some importance in London. It was one of those, get-rich-quick, pyramid selling schemes. The company proudly proclaimed that in a few short years I could become stinking rich and live the life of a film-star with millionaire status. Their brochure contained lots of photos of flashy cars, luxury yachts, huge mansions, and scantily clad girls. Say no more, I thought, I'll certainly have some of that. Anyway, having earlier exchanged dialogue with the regional sales manager of the company, he invited me to attend a meeting that was being held at a hotel in the Bayswater area of London.

Having arrived at the venue in plenty of good time I got the chance to meet some of the other candidates, who like me, were highly keyed up and raring to go. In all, there were about thirty people in attendance. As I mingled I was introduced to men and women from different backgrounds and cultures. After a while I got the impression that whilst many of them had devoted their entire attention to the acquisition of making money, others however were more interested in scoffing the freebie spread that was laid on. I was then introduced to a rather distinguished looking guy who went by the name of Robert. He was what you might call a true English gentleman – charming, polite, together with impeccable good manners, along with a great personality. However, Robert gave me the impression he was a bit of a scallywag on the quiet. In any event our instant liking for each other proved to be a blessing in disguise. The turning point came when he asked me if I'd be interested in going for a drink with him after the meeting had finished.

And so, over a pint of beer and a packet of crisps the conversation got round to travel, and that he, Robert that is, had got the travel bug, big time. He went on to tell me that he'd been round the world dozens of times as his previous occupation had been a pilot with a well known airline. Now retired and living quite compatibly, he now spends his time writing articles for a travel magazine. Incredibly, there were several places that Robert had not visited before, namely Scotland and the Lake District. Reading between the lines I got the impression that this pyramid selling thing was for neither of us. So therefore, as a result of my chance meeting with him, he asked me if I'd be interested in accompanying him as a friend and travelling companion to visit the places he had mentioned. I nevertheless accepted his offer with both hands. Though I found Robert to be a really smashing bloke there were certain aspects in his character that were slightly puzzling. Admittedly there were a few drawbacks in his make-up, namely his rather eccentric behaviour. This perhaps was a mild statement as you will soon discover.

As I recall, it was some weeks later, after my first initial meeting with my illustrious new friend, when something happened that shook me to the very core. I was going about doing my usual mundane formalities, when from out of the blue I received a phone call. I've got to admit, it was the craziest, most ridiculous phone call I had ever received in my life. The call came from my newly acquired friend called Robert, whereby he began to download his spiel upon me, with words to the effect…………………

"Tabhannaich – Aineach – Uaici – Baidealech – Dachach – Cabhagach – Eaphon – Lala – Maigheach – Nasgadh – Gadheal".

(Plus to go along with this nonsense was a rhyme)

"Up the airy mountain, down the rush glen, we won't be going hunting but cruising round instead".

What in creation is this load of codswallop? I asked myself. Did my eyes deceive me? Am I hearing right? I soon ascertained that a quick translation was needed, but in order to do so I would need the help of a top decoding expert. Holy Moses! Just hold on there a minute. How could I have been so stupid at not being able to understand his amazing vocabulary? Without question it had to be Gaelic dialect, of course. In order to unravel this extraordinary mystery I was then instructed to read the complete works of the

Gaelic language, and once I had mastered the complexities of the situation I would then find the answer to the riddle, which when roughly translated would miraculously turn into pronounceable English grammar.

So imagine my delight when further into the conversation a rather pleasant surprise unfolded, which I am delighted to say came in the form of a one-week's holiday to the Highlands of Scotland. This would take in the wonderful cities of Glasgow, Edinburgh and Perth, before finally finishing up in Inverness, gateway to the Scottish Highlands. Incredibly, the only thing that was required of me was to turn up at Milton Keynes railway station the following Saturday and catch the 09.15 to Glasgow. My train tickets were booked along with the hotels and a bit of cash for spending money, all courtesy of Robert.

The motivation behind this sudden surge of extraordinary behaviour was as follows. Some time ago, Robert had seen a documentary programme on television concerning the Loch Ness Monster mystery. The programme went to great depths as to the whereabouts of the monster, but more importantly, Robert had become a trifle intoxicated with the stunning scenery and the sheer beauty of the place. By his reckoning, if we got ourselves up there, to Loch Ness that is, we could go about and do our very own private investigation, and with a bit of luck, we might even come face to face with the monster himself. Yikes! I trembled in my boots.

All things considered, it was altogether a thoroughly satisfying arrangement and indeed a lovely trip to look forward to. So it came to pass the following week, Saturday, I found myself being magically wafted over to Milton Keynes railway station. But quite unknown to me I was to meet a red Virgin train on platform one. Having mastered the technicalities of boarding, I began the daunting task of trying to locate my friend. But bless my soul, the compartments were brimming with a melee of activity and positively teeming with commuters, packed to the rafters with not a seat to be had. My cunning fiend of a friend had craftily slipped through the net at London's Euston Station and had devilishly sneaked through the gate barriers, past the guards, and somehow had managed to climb on board a red choo-choo train. Robert explained the night before that I was to meet him in the third carriage of the train marked Rear Admiral Horsley, which is of course one of his weird and wonderful jokes. Searching for signs of intelligent life, I unexpectedly stumbled across a rather balding head, glistening in all its glory. It was Robert, sitting there in a first-class seat and beckoning me over to join him.

And so began our long journey as we clicked and clacked, rattled and rolled our way along, sailing past a multitude of industrial towns, then quite dramatically the scenery changed to beautiful rolling landscapes, nestled amid fertile pastures with roaming flocks of livestock. Silhouetted against the greyness of the sky I caught the occasional glint of the sea, darting dandily in and out of the headland. The only minor thing to talk about was the constant hustle and bustle of the vending trolleys, zooming up and down the aisles in search of a customer or two. Our train was passing through the depths of deepest Lancashire when Robert suddenly burst out laughing as his mind drifted away to another world.

"Just imagine the scene," Robert smiled, "if the USS Starship Enterprise was hovering somewhere above the earths' crust and looking down towards Lancashire. I can just visualise the scene. Standing coolly on the bridge of his ship, stood proud the famous Captain James T. Kirk, about to address his crew and orchestrate his authority.

(Captain Kirk) "Spock! I boldly want to go where no man has gone before; therefore, set a course towards Accrington at full speed."

(Spock) "But captain, it is not wise to go down there. I am of the opinion that is not logically possible to go to that part of the universe as there's a strange form of human species known as the Luddites."

(Kirk) "For God's man, it's of vital importance I speak to these people, don't you realise they hold the key to planetary exploration."

"Captain Kirk to Scotty, beam me down to Accrington in lightning speed."

(Scotty) "Not on your life Jim. It's not safe to go down there. These strange people wear funny cloth caps and speak with a strange dialect, not of our world. Please Jim, don't go, you will not be able to understand them."

(Kirk) "Gee, I think you may be right Scotty, and shucks I was so looking forward to meeting these strange beings."

(Kirk) "Bones! Give me a shot of something to steady my nerves, before I go completely mad."

(Bones) "But captain, I've already given you a hypo filled with a mixture of Viagra and rejuvenation fluid."

(Captain) "Thank God for that Bones. I've been a bit on the limp mode for some time now."

"Believe me Jim, after I've finished with you, you'll be stiff as a poker." Bones smiled.

(Captain) "Yippeeeeeeeeeeeeeee!"

"Miss Uhura, set a new course for Pluto, warp factor one."

The journey up from Milton Keynes flew by with remarkable speed and it wasn't long before we found ourselves pulling into Glasgow Central Station. It was now a matter of nipping across town to another station to get a reconnection for Perth. Sometime later, inside Queen's Street station the information monitors were busily flashing up the necessary information to the travelling public. With about twenty minutes to kill, we thought a coffee and a sticky bun would go down rather well. Positioned on the main concourse next to the ticket office was a rather super bar type café. However, taking up our positions inside the place, little did we know what surprises were in store? Our attentions were immediately drawn to a group of men who were lying spread-eagled on the floor, highly intoxicated and in a state of rigor-mortis. Standing over these undesirable heathens was a gathering of the cloth. Three men of the clergy, knocking pints and whiskies back like there was no tomorrow. Were these good men from the forgotten flock of bell-ringers or were they part of the whisky fraternity I asked myself? I knew from past experience that the golden rule for bell-ringers was to keep one's feet firmly on the ground. But little did I know, we are of course in Scotland, where's it's not too uncommon to see people getting seriously drunk on Bell's, their favourite whisky.

Well can you beat that, one of the bevvied boozers was doing his utmost to get up; he went down, but soon managed to claw his way up again. His head swayed from side to side, his hand trying in desperation to grab a drink and his breath by now smelling like a Scottish distillery.

"See you Jimmy!" He spluttered out in a strong Glaswegian accent.

I had the distinct feeling that our short-arsed, pint-sized friend, all of five-foot nothing of him had it in his mind to do a bit of embroidery, thereby to carve his initials with great pride across our faces, thus rendering our features into a grotesque mess of unrecognisable proportions. The well-oiled Jock finally slithered back to the floor again, passionately calling out for a wee dram more. Then in one stint of barbaric madness the place turned to a scene of uproar. Punches and boots went in like sledgehammers. In the middle of this mayhem were our three men of the cloth, who, by the look on their faces were having the time of their lives. The outrageous sight of clergymen, rolling about on the floor, kicking the living daylights out of these poor defenceless people was far too much to take in, and so left to continue on with our journey.

The train journey to Perth did not pass without incident. Some idiot pulled the communication cord. A flasher ran among the passengers, causing the usual chaos associated with flashers, plus an old lady got her handbag pinched by a bogus vicar. Just as things were hotting up our train pulled into Perth, whereupon the vicar did a runner with the finest selection of quality leather handbags.

Thankfully, my travelling companion Robert had conveniently pre-booked us into a hotel for the night called the Rob Roy. But in order to reach the damn thing a taxi was required and, as luck would have it, one was on hand.

"Oh, excuse me driver," Robert enquired. "We'd like to get our heads down for the night, could you take us to the Rob Roy hotel please."

"Heeds did ye say?" The driver asked.

"Yes, that's right, driver, heeds, I mean heads."

"Oh, and driver, before we set off, I'll need a hole-in-the-wall as well, bit short of the old lubricardos, you see." Robert brimmed, pointing towards his empty wallet.

It began to dawn on our Scottish friend, the taxi driver that is, that his two acquired passengers were not of the full shilling, but two raving mad Englishmen, who had nothing else, better to do than flash their wallets about and ask about holes-in-the-wall.

But you see they all think us English lot are stark raving bonkers up here in Scotland. Later, as we climbed the stairs to our rooms Robert complained he felt tired and needed to lie down for a while.

"Look, I'll give you a knock a bit later on, once I've had a chance to recover," he groaned, holding his back his weariness.

Fully rejuvenated, Robert knocked on my door just as the grandfather clock struck its chimes at eight o'clock. Thereafter, he summoned enough energy to pay a visit to a nearby pub, aptly named the Tartan Arms. Apparently, it was the meeting place for up and coming alcoholics. Soon we were mingling it with the rest of the local inhabitants, and like all good Friday night pubs it thronged with noisy vibrancy. Away to our left was a small group of football fanatics who were glued to a giant screen that showed scenes of from a live match with the usual ruckus and foul language associated with football matches.

"Come on, you Ackies, for God's sake score man, shoot you idiot."

"Who and what are the Ackies?" A bewildered Robert inquired.

"Oh, their real name is Hamilton Academicals." I replied back in an informing manner.

"Oh, I see," Robert sighed.

Sitting back enjoying a pint of the local beverage, a surprise came when the door of the snug bar unexpectedly opened. There wedged in the doorway stood this huge framed man, elaborately dressed in a chequered jacket and with it bearing matching trousers and whose accent was that of an American.

"Why, howdy there folks," he began, puffing away on a big cigar. "Could anyone please help me, I'm looking for my long lost cousin by the name of Jamie McDonald. Has anyone seen him? I'll buy anyone a drink with information regarding his whereabouts; just stick your hand up in the air."

Within seconds the entire gathering of the pub had their hands held firmly in the air at the same time pointing towards their beer mugs. The American bought one round, two rounds, three rounds and finally four rounds of beer and just as the bell rang for closing time our American friend was getting mighty anxious as to his cousin's whereabouts.

"Now where the hell's my cousin," he demanded in an angry tone.

A little, red faced, rat-arsed of a Scotsman stood up and declared in a slurred voice.

"Och away man, ye cousin's been dead since 1969."

The American looked dumbfounded. "But all that drink I've pumped into you guys along with the whiskies and cigars I bought for you."

"Aye, ye be a grand man, that's for sure, but can ye come back tomorrow night and I'll tell ye all about the Stuarts?" the deliriously intoxicated Scotsman winked with a feeling of complete satisfaction, so leaving our American friend totally flabbergasted.

The next morning we moved on to Edinburgh. The initial plan was to devote a whole day for sightseeing activities, and then, later on in the day the general plan was to head up to Inverness. My first impressions of Edinburgh was a city of immerse splendour and grandeur. In fact, the history of Edinburgh, I am told, goes back two and a half thousand years to the Iron Age times where the visible legacy starts at Edinburgh Castle which dominates the Edinburgh skyline - and what better way to begin one's journey than in an open-top, double-decker bus. Soon, we were leaving the splendours of George Street and making our way towards a volcanic piece of rock that's set on a high peninsula. Sure enough perched high above the city centre stood the famous Edinburgh Castle. Whereupon our tour guide, aptly named Charlie, gave us an in-depth analysis, together with an account of the castle's chequered past. Charlie explained as we walked along that Edinburgh Castle was built in the twelfth century and was first used as an Abbey, being later transformed in 1639 into the Scottish Parliament buildings. However, the earliest references to the castle go way back to the sixth century, and apparently the oldest surviving building was the Norman Chapel. Along with this mind boggling information, Charlie further informed us that in the eighteenth century Edinburgh Castle was at some point turned into a garrison with a small army of troops which including barracks and a host of military hardware which made Edinburgh Castle, easily defendable.

Fresh from Charlie's amazing history lesson we once again climbed back on board the bus. Close by, cobbled streets led to the oldest part of town. In fact, Lawnmarket is the starting point of the Royal Mile which incorporates such illustrious names as Cannongate, High Street, and Castle Hill. The Royal Mile has best been described as the largest, longest, and one of the finest streets in the world. From my vantage point, I spotted turrets, gables and towering chimneys that could be seen nestled in alongside historical monumental structures. A sudden screech of the brakes brought our bus to a grinding halt somewhere in the Cowgate area, to where the engine fell silent.

Piling out, I found myself standing in a secluded square that was surrounded by the eeriest of old buildings. Tucked away amongst the isolation and quietness were two old churches that were camouflaged with weepy old willow trees. Magdalen Chapel, it became known is sited in Edinburgh's old town near the George IV Bridge. This small, but beautiful sixteenth-century chapel held pride of place for the whole community throughout the centuries. The chapel is of great importance for several reasons. Firstly, it can be said, it had been the cradle of Presbyterianism, holding the first assembly of the new Church of Scotland, dating back to 20th December 1560. Furthermore, it once housed a hospital, looking after the sick and infirm, and then it later passed on to the hands of the Incorporation of Hammermen. From Magdalen Chapel, Charlie escorted us to another secluded square to take in yet another historic building. Hidden behind a cluster of old elm trees was the Kirk of the Greyfriars church, made creepier by the foreboding looking graveyard? Reputedly, it's been a place of worship since the 7th century.

Greyfriars Church, believe it or not, is where the Covenant was signed in 1638, just after the battle of Bothwell Bridge in 1679. For it is said with some reserve that several hundred of the Covenanters were duly imprisoned at Greyfriars. Thus the unfortunate souls were duly executed by one means or another. In addition to these misgivings, this particular part of Edinburgh had seen some of the weirdest goings on. Tales of bodysnatching and ghoulish apparitions were the order of the day. The area became notorious as one of the grizzliest parts of Edinburgh, and it certainly wasn't a place to be hanging around in, especially at night. Charlie explained that over the years strange sightings had accrued on the days that related to the executions. Along with these misgivings, numerous people had encountered the sound of clanking chains and ghostly apparitions. One eye witness actually claimed he saw the headless figure of a man floating through the graveyard. So this is Edinburgh. Yikes! Let's get the hell out of here!

For much of the day we had Edinburgh pretty much to ourselves, but having said that it became acutely aware that our time in Edinburgh was limited so the necessary preparations were made to move on to Inverness. The first time I clapped eyes on Inverness was on a horrible cold windswept night with an easterly gale blowing in from the North Sea. As far as guest houses go the Stornaway was a grand old place that was set high above the town and overlooked the magnificence of the Inverness skyline.

The next morning after a good night's sleep a stroll into town was decided upon. Halfway into our walk we came across a parade of shops that sold a dazzling display of the finest Scottish kilts, bagpipes, tartans and sporrans. Because of Robert's ancestry, the McDoulish clan, the canny cad insisted on buying a tie of that particular persuasion, whose only claim to fame was a bottle over the head incident in the Gorbals area of Glasgow.

Scouring through a tie rack, Robert found the tie in question.

"Here it is the one I want, a McDoulish."

Over came the assistant wearing his full complement of the Campbell Clan but without the bagpipes. The cheeky chappy not only suggested buying a tie but to go with it he urged Robert to go the full hog.

"Oh, but sir, ye cannae just wear a tie," he said. "What ye need to go along with it is a kilt and a sporran," he suggested.

"My dear man," Robert began, looking towards the assistant with some surprise. "If I was to wear a kilt in my local butchers shop, me bits and pieces would be cut off. Plus the fact, if certain people who use dodgy lavatories saw me in that outfit, they'd use my bum as a pincushion, and then stick me privates in a storage jar and use the damn things for the manufacture of the finest red plums."

"Oh but sir, what a lovely way to go," the assistant replied in a campish voice.

For much of the morning we wandered aimlessly around shopping centres and pedestrianised precincts, nosing in and out of shops and doing the usual touristy things. Unfortunately, in the midst of our walkabout we had somehow managed to get caught up with a swarm of Japanese tourists whose sole intention was to bow their heads as if they had just won the lottery, together with their cameras clicking away at anything that resembled an historic building. In our quest for peace and solitude and with our hearts firmly set on jungle-type adventure we took refuge at the local Tourist Information Office. Placed outside was a display board that featured a selection of day trips which read something like this..............

There is something truly wonderful about a coach tour, so why not try one of our very popular day trips which provide the traveller with an ideal opportunity to visit several of Scotland's many renowned beauty spots and historical places of interest. Glide your way in comfort and superb style on board one of our luxury air-conditioned coaches. So for today why not join us on a grand tour of Loch Ness?

Without any further ado, two exclusive tours were duly booked up. Our first trip was an all day excursion to Loch Ness, and for tomorrow we had the resounding pleasure of looking forward to a trip to the Battlefields of Culloden Moor. In no time at all we found ourselves clambering on board a coach bound for Loch Ness with the terrifying prospect of meeting up with our friend Nessie?

For many a person the Highlands are synonymous with Scotland and as our coach made its way through the Scottish countryside, images came before me that resembled a clip from a picture postcard. I witnessed a land of unspoilt beauty, a land of glens, castles and of lochs, magnificently steeped in mountains and heather.

I would like to put one thing straight before I go any further. My understanding of sea serpents is very sketchy, but I do know this: the legend of the Loch Ness monster still persists to this very day and is backed up by the numerous number of near sightings. In short, Loch Ness would be the ideal starting point to begin Robert's investigations. But strange as it may seem, Loch Ness has no need for sea serpents or monsters to worry about, whether they be mythical or not. More worrying is the thought that deep down in that bottomless pit hides the long-necked gorgon called Nessie.

Our tour guide was a chap called Rabbie, who was of the highland persuasion and spoke with a twang that only the cleverest of Orientals could understand. Leaving Inverness to the west, our beast of a coach trundled its way along with gritty determination, twisting and snaking its way through a landscape of wonderful, mountainous terrain. Where lonely roads mingled with lochs and glens all beautifully blended in to form a breath-taking backdrop.

A sign indicated a turn-off point from the main road that fell sharply away, taking us down in zigzag patterns towards the vast sprawl of Loch Ness. Away to our left were the remains and ruins of Urquhart Castle, once used as a major fortress, now a super-duper vantage point to see what our friend Nessie was up to. It was here, from this very spot, when in 1955, a lone photographer claimed he saw a huge head arise from the great depths of the murky waters and quickly took a snapshot of the long-necked fellow – claiming it to be Nessie, the so-called Loch Ness monster.

"Look yonder," a fellow passenger cried out with alarm.

Something sinister stirred from within the blackness of the deep. A mysterious ripple made its way across the dark satanic waters with submarine like appearance that about to submerge. What in creation could it have been? Maybe it was a ripple or indeed a wave or perhaps something far more sinister? The passengers were aghast with horror for with good reason. Because, far from drawing our fears to a close they were only just beginning. Something far more sinister than a ripple or a wave, I shouldn't wonder. More like a sea serpent. In fact if you gaze into the water long enough you may convince yourself that underneath the surface lurks a monster of huge magnitude that darts back and forth and then descends back to the depths.

"Aye" Rabbie sighed, "I do believe that something will stir from the great bowels of the Loch Ness today, a creature so frightening he'll make the likes of Frankenstein look like a Boy Scout. Aye, my beloved Nessie will arise from the deep and his heed will lunge up and gobble up as many of you Sassenachs as he can eat. Aye, Nessie, there'll be a fine dinner for you today, that's for sure."

Rabbie sat there rubbing his beard with a look of glee, simply frightening the lives out of us. However, the punters were not at all too happy as to what Rabbie had said, for there was much worse to come. Rabbie informed us that as part of the package, he'd be taking us out to the middle of the Loch Ness in a paddle boat, where the water is at its deepest and most dangerous. Moments later we were drawing up alongside a jetty. In the water sat this splendid paddle steamer, all nicely tied up and raring to go. Soon, we were being ushered on board. The engines sprang into life and the paddles began to rotate as we slipped gently away from the shore, making headway towards the centre-point of Loch Ness, where we gazed into a deep abyss. It suddenly dawned on me that the colour of the water had mysteriously changed from blue to a menacing black colour.

Rabbie announced that in a few minutes time we would be sitting on the centre point of Loch Ness. Eerily, the engines fell silent as we sat there bobbing about in the water, motionless. Moments later we witnessed a scene of sheer lunacy. For reasons unknown Rabbie decided to lunge himself forward as though he was about to jump off at the deep end for an early morning dip. Had the canny Scot gone mad? For he seemed to be talking to something beneath the water, as he hung half in and half out of the boat.

"Och! Will ye come up Nessie and give us a wee peek at ye, man?" Rabbie pleaded. "We want to see ye in person, please Nessie arise, and don't ye worry, there's plenty of food in the boat for dinner."

"Oh please Rabbie! Let the monster stay down in the depths," a lady passenger cried out in anguish.

Back on dry land again there was further grim news. Rabbie announced it was now on to the monster museum. For heaven's sake, how much more of this onslaught could we Sassenachs take? Actually it turned out rather interesting. The theory goes that Nessie lives out at sea, due to the fact there was absolutely no food in Loch Ness to sustain any form of life, either for fish or monster. This was the scientists' point of view, which I suppose seems quite logical really.

I awoke the next morning covered in a cold sweat, recovering from a series of deeply disturbing nightmares, induced by the sight of naked girls that were removing the scantiest of clothing that dirty old men like me dream about. Furthermore, certain rumours were flying about that our guesthouse had apparently been infiltrated with roaming flocks of whoofters. This was confirmed by the sight of a strange man who was seen wandering in and out of gentlemen's rooms late at night and then craftily reappearing in the morning.

Could I still be dreaming for there was a hand slithering its way under the bedclothes and making its way to a region that only the cheekiest of squirrels know about. Moreover, in view of these rumours I could see the faint outline of a shadowy figure.

"Shush! Don't be frightened," a voice whispered. "It's only me, Santa Claus. Look what Santa's brought you from his grotto," as the dirty old dog unashamedly ripped open his tunic and vigorously shook his raspberry ripple at me. Gulp! They certainly don't make-em like that anymore, I cried. Badly shaken by the experience it did however take me all of three days to get over the incident.

The next morning I found myself strolling across a bleak boggy moorland that was filled with the scent of heather and heath that was deeply entrenched in my nostrils. I was in the heartland of Culloden Moor, and immediately visions of Bonnie Prince Charlie and his brave band of followers were suddenly brought back to life. It was on a murky day in 1746 when Bonnie Prince Charlie deployed his massive army of 5,000 brave Highlanders here on Culloden's bleak moor to challenge the Duke of Cumberland's men. Historically, a huge battle took place on this site pitting Bonnie Prince Charlie's Jacobites against Prince William, Duke of Cumberland and his mighty English army. For it is said with some reserve that the first blood drawn of this great battle came from a Jacobite gun which narrowly missed the Duke of Cumberland's head and, carrying eighteen stone about his person it was surely a prominent target that no one could easily miss. If this is true then the first shot must have been an incredibly lucky one indeed. The Jacobite artillery consisted of some twelve guns that were positioned on the centre and on the flanks. Cumberland's massively rear-aligned artillery under the command of Brevet-Colonel William Belford gave the command to fire and let rip with five-ten-pounders. Such was the damage done on the tightly packed Jacobite ranks; it was one of pure carnage. The battle raged on but in the end the Duke of Cumberland won the day, which to me symbolises a dashing dream for both men to raise their flags in victory.

The following morning we left Inverness and caught the first of a twice daily train service to Fort William, which according to my friend Robert, would be the highlight of our trip - a classic 'steam train' journey. The booking office kindly informed us that as far as 'preserved railways' go, the Fort William to Mallaig line is up there with the grandest and most thrilling train journeys in the world. So impressive is the route that the eighty four mile round trip takes one through a landscape of breathtaking beauty and contrasts.

Sadly, our time in Scotland had all but extinguished so the necessary preparations were made for a hasty return back to dear old blighty. But to hell with it we thought. Where's the old bulldog spirit? However, in the course of our high spirits we had somehow managed to get ourselves lost, ending up in a remote area called Ardnamurchan, and not the sort of place the average tourist would visit. Our 1955 guidebook, picked up at one of Inverness's antique shops, suggested a stay at Dunhoulie Hall, which unfortunately was a decision which would prove most regrettable.

Dunhoulie Hall is one of Scotland's oldest castles and legend has it that no other castle in Scotland could match its nightly goings on. Not just any old castle but a crumbling old, eleventh century relic. For rumour has it Dunhoulie Hall is haunted by all of two ghosts who unfortunately met their deaths in the most grizzliest of ways. For it is said that one poor chap called Sir Archibald carries his severed head under his arm in the hope of meeting the dirty rotten scoundrel who chopped it off. And how could we forget dear old Boris, the ghostliest of ghosts.

As dusk fell we arrived at the castle steps to be greeted by a kindly gentleman called Angus McTavish who acted it would appear, as combined chef, waiter, porter and receptionist - a combination we found somewhat unusual, but I suppose it keeps the wage costs down and wearing a kilt instead of trousers, probably keeps the clothing costs down as well - canny fellows these Jocks.

"Will ye gents be wanting a room for the night?" McTavish enquired.

"Well actually, Jock, we not only require a room, but evening dinner as well."

"Och, let's have a look," Angus sighed, as he cast his eye over the register. "I'll put ye in the East Wing," Angus smiled, rubbing his hands together in glee.

"Oh, and by the way Angus, after dinner we'd like to get our heads down, we're absolutely cream-crackered," Robert injected.

"Heeds did we say, och away, man, ye'll get nae sleep at Dunhoulie Hall, have ye nae heard of the two ghosts that wander the belfries at night?"

"No, certainly not!" Robert declared with a look of surprise.

Angus told us that way back in the fourteenth century several of the occupants had unfortunately met their ends in the most horrific circumstances. Apparently it was the norm in those days. The story goes that the men involved in the reconstruction of the castle had by accident bricked up two gentlemen called Boris and Sir Archibald from within the mighty structures of the castle walls. They were never heard of again so it was assumed the worst that he must have both rotten away from within.

"Well, I suppose it can't be helped, we all make mistakes, but I'm sure the brickies did their best." Robert quipped.

"How many other guests have you got staying at Dunhoulie Hall?" Robert asked.

"Nayn, apart from yourselves, there's only me and Mrs McTavish."

After dinner we got down to the more serious business of a good night's sleep, but would you believe it, I was woken up yet again from a deep sleep, covered in a cold sweat. It was another one of my recurring dreams. This time fresh images came before me of naked men wearing the tiniest of G-strings. More worrying was the thought my passions for the fairer sex were diminishing by the minute. My thoughts were of big burly lorry drivers and hairy all-in wrestlers, roping me down to a bed and giving me one hell of a whipping. Ouch!

I went back to sleep but was woken up yet again this time by the sound of faint footsteps that came from the landing area. Peeking through the crack of the door I could just about make out the faint outline of a shadowy figure that floated majestically through the upper confinements of the castle. To put it in more perspective, I was ruddy-well petrified. To my astonishment I then heard the sound of flushing toilets. But who should step out? You've guessed it; it was none other than Sir Archibald carrying his severed head under his arm. With some urgency the ghostly figure then proceeded to make its way to the pantry cupboard. The next morning, haggard worn and weary I made my way down to the breakfast room only to find Robert, sitting there, looking grumpy and fed-up.

"Robert! I've got some rather disturbing news to tell you. I think I saw one of several ghosts last night. My observations confirmed it was either Sir Archibald or indeed Boris. Whoever it was had the nerve to be carrying his severed head under his arm. Scary as it may seem I definitely saw one of them go through the upper walls of the castle, whereby the ghostly apparition then disappeared into the pantry cupboard."

"Well, blow me! It's funny you should say that because I saw it as well round about three in the morning. Whoever or whatever it was came storming out of pantry cupboard scoffing a load of pork pies and franticly noshing away on a leg of chicken.

"What!!"

"Yes, it's true," Robert insisted.

On hearing my friend's similar story, we immediately dashed down to the pantry to throw some light on the situation. But would you believe it when we got there we found the pantry had been stripped bare with not a morsel of food to be had.

"Now where the hell is Mr and Mrs McTavish to explain all this?" Robert raged. To add to our problems the McTavishes were nowhere to be found. Therefore, having scoured the castle in its entirety we found not a living soul in sight - and in view of the management's failure to provide adequate breakfast facilities it was decided to vacate the establishment and try our luck in the next village.

Sure enough, a couple of miles down the road our journey brought us to a tiny hamlet called Ockle and in no time at all we were tucking into a full Scottish breakfast. The old lady who owned the inn told us she had lived in Ockle all her life and said she knew everyone for miles around.

"I suppose you know the bloody McTavishes." Robert scowled, banging his hand on the table in a rage.

"Ah, yes, but of course, I remember them, but sadly, they died some years ago up in the great castle known as Dunhoulie Hall."

"Impossible! We were only talking to them last night, in fact we stayed there."

(The old lady laughed) "But ye cannae be serious, sir, for the castle burnt down to the ground some fifty years ago, taking Mr and Mrs McTavish along with it, all ye'll find up there is a load of crumbling ruins."

"Hey Robert! She must think we're stark raving bonkers, for you and I know we stayed there last night and now she tells us it's just a ruin."

Settling up terms with the lady, we immediately drove back to the place from wench we came and to the exact spot where Dunhoulie Hall had stood, but to our utter amazement, there was nothing. It began to dawn on us that perhaps Dunhoulie Hall didn't exist after all, for as we gazed across a bleak foggy moorland, the only thing we found were a few crumbling ruins, filled with empty fields and roaming herds of cattle. Dunhoulie Hall had completely vanished just like the old lady had said.

The Lime Coloured Suit

Joe Valucci was born on Sunday 28th April 1939 in the Bronx district of New York City, and surprisingly he came in weighing a hefty 10lb, and inevitably, such a weight would later take him on to become the future heavyweight boxing champion of the world. As far as immigrants go the first band of brave souls had arrived in America by the turn of the century. They had come to the land of opportunity on ships packed in like sardines in search for a better life. On most days the harbour area was filled with a long line of immigrants who had come from every corner of the globe. By the time most Italians had managed to sort themselves out and found a place to live, it didn't take long for them to become totally disillusioned with the place. The Valucci family were no different, so off they went off in search of a little piece of homeland which surprisingly turned out to be a little piece of Italy, neatly packed into a square mile of land.

As time passed by the Valucci family were at last beginning to get reasonably acquainted with life in the United States, but all was not well however. The truth of the matter, alas, was one of squalor, hardship and poverty that the family had to put up with. Joe Valucci grew up in conditions not unlike many a family before him. Nevertheless, it was impossible to overstate the desperate situation they were in. However, Joe grew up with the knowledge that something much more favourable lay ahead of him.

Like most areas in New York the place was riddled with crime and corruption. From an early age Joe seemed to attract trouble wherever he went and it didn't take long for him to fall into petty crime. It was quite customary for gangs and hoodlums to settle their differences with fists, boots and flick-knives. Let us not forget that these were the toughest kids in town. Joe soon found out that the streets of New York were not paved with gold as otherwise told by people back in Italy. At school he was a complete failure at just about everything, except sport, where he excelled as a fine young athlete.

By the time he had left school and without any meaningful qualifications he quickly landed up in trouble.

Joe's fortunes began however when his father presented him with a pair of boxing gloves for his fortieth birthday, and that started off the whole crazy thing off. Initially, Joe wanted to follow in his father's footsteps as a steeplejack, but hence began his working life at a local gym, doing a variety of menial jobs, like sweeping up and making the coffee, more or less a dog's body, but with youth on his side he would later develop into a world champ and, like many a boxer before him he found that boxing was a passport to a relatively easy lifestyle.

The following years were taken up at amateur level; gradually working his way through the ranks and up to heavyweight class and in no time at all he was ranked as a phenomenally talented boxer who perfected his boxing skills in deadly-like fashion. He first came to prominence when he won the middleweight title in1959. As Joe continued to develop he showed a remarkable aptitude of graceful agility, amazing speed and sheer strength. He was the epitome of toughness in the ring and in no time at all he was ranked heavyweight. After a series professional fights he now faced the legendary Max Muller for a crack at the world heavyweight title.

The showdown was to be held on the 26th of June 1962 at Caesars Palace in Las Vegas. The fight was billed by the media as the fight of the century. Valucci and his entourage took up residence at the Sands Inn Motel while Muller and his party preferred to stay at the Golden Nugget. As predicted it would turn out to be one of the most controversial fights of all time. The night before the fight the two boxers gave a press conference which had produced the usual banter and playmanship, having earlier been involved in a much heated debate by the two different camps, calling each other names of the most ludicrous and farcical nature. But surely Joe had come to Las Vegas fancying his chances against Muller. On the contrary it was Valucci who had struggled in his last fight against the Argentine Emanuel Elburo, winning marginally on points in the tenth round. Muller on the other hand had this impressive twelve match unbeaten run, winning all of his previous fights by clear knock-outs. Clearly, Muller had the unparalleled advantage over his opponent by his sheer size, height and reach. In comparison to Valucci, Muller was a giant of a man and it proved once again that he was the best heavyweight boxer in the business. Let's face it there weren't many boxers who fancied their chances against the German. On the other hand, Valucci was up against a man whose troubled past made him a dour old affair. In contrast Valucci was considered a legend in his own right, losing only one of his last eight fights. At the time he was ranked heavyweight outside contender and in line for the crown. He had this deadly combination of hard-hitting left jabs and fierce undercuts that would knock a donkey off its hind legs. As predicted the fight would turn out to be one of the most awesome displays of fighting power, which according to the ratings, Muller would win in relatively easy fashion. Muller was a hard act to follow and Valucci would have to be at his best if was to beat the German.

('Twas the night of the big fight)

Amid the furnace like heat of the night a thick blanket of tobacco smoke had filled the air in the vast auditorium as the two boxers made their way into the ring. You could almost smell the tension created by the pungent sweat-filled air. All eyes were focused on the compare as he took hold of the microphone and went about doing the introductions.

"Ladies and gentlemen it gives me the greatest pleasure to introduce to you, in the red corner from Hamburg, Germany, weighing in at 182lbs, please welcome the one and only Hans Muller. And in the blue corner ladies and gentlemen, from the Bronx, New York City, weighing in at 176lbs, I give you Joe Valucci. Centre ringed, the referee, Tommy Boyd summoned the two boxers together to start with proceedings. Once the instructions had been given the two men glared at each other with intense hatred. But it was Muller who gave the meanest look imaginable. He even had the cheek to grin at Valucci through his gum shields at the same time flapping his arms about trying to fluster his man. When at last both men touched gloves and nodded their heads in approval for the fight to begin.

The bell rang for round one to begin and both men came out from their corners ready to fight. Typically, it was Muller who came out in true Muller fashion, applying the pressure on Valucci from the start. About a minute into the fight saw an unusually aggressive Muller laying into his opponent with short left hand jabs to the head. Vallucci returned the compliment with a series of punches to the stomach, but it seemed to have little effect on the German.

(Round 2) The second round picked up where the first round left off and it was pretty much even Stevens. However, it was Valucci who looked the more composed as he glided his way in and out of trouble. It was considered a good safe sensible round for both boxers and the panel of judges awarded even scores.

(Round 3) Round three saw Valucci in a much more determined frame of mind as he went at Muller like hammer and tongs. Valucci moved gracefully around the ring like a floating ballerina. The German came back like a man possessed; his eyes were filled with fire and hatred. Muller threw a real blockbuster of a punch that landed on Valucci's chin, dropping him to the floor like a ton of bricks. Dazed, he staggered up and on the count of three returned the compliment by sending in a thunderous right hook which forced the German back on the ropes. Both men gave as good as they got.

(Round 4) The contest by now had turned into a bruising encounter whereby both men were showing signs of tiredness. The audience was baying for Muller's blood. In contrast, the fans believed they had a man in Valucci who could whip the ass off the German and go on to win the fight. Muller threw a dangerous left hook which grazed Valucci's eye which produced a slight trickle of blood. Another bone-crushing left hook went in, forcing his opponent back on the ropes. In a tight clinch the referee separated them. Valucci ducked and dived as he tried in desperation to avoid the ferocious onslaught. The round went to Muller.

(Round 5) The bell went for round five and both men came out of their corners determined to win the fight. It would turn out to be a bruising encounter of pure savagery. Muller started off by throwing a combination of fast and furious left-hand jabs to Valucci's head. One got through and grazed his opponents head. For a moment Valucci was almost blinded by the punch which sent him crashing against the ropes, before finally sinking him to the floor. To the count of six he staggered back to his feet. But it was Valucci who showed remarkable powers of recovery and in a situation like this it was imperative that he tried to finish off the fight as quickly as possible. Then, in one moment of sheer brilliance Valucci produced a devastating display of punching power that worked to perfection that had the audience on their feet. Joe sent in a blistering right uppercut to Muller's head which sent the German flying across the ring, saved only by the ropes. Absorbed by a further onslaught of punches to the head and stomach, Valucci pursued his man and went in for the kill, throwing an almighty left hook that connected up to Muller's right eye, leaving in its wake an avalanche of blood. The German wobbled and it resembled a man who had lost both his legs. Obviously dazed and hurt by the ferocity of the punch it was only a matter of time before the gash would turn into a raging torrent of blood. Surely, one more clear punch to Muller's head would win the fight for Vallucci. Muller could not possibly go on and it was only a matter of time before the referee, Tommy Boyd had little choice but to stop the fight in fifth round. Joe Valucci walked gingerly across the ring with both arms raised in triumph. The fight was won and Joe Vallucci was now heavyweight champion of the world.

It was inevitable however that Joe would go on to box for just a few more short months before his life would take on a disastrous turn for the worse. After winning the fight he collected a staggering fortune which in one sense would turn out to be his downfall. His vast empire of wealth seemed to disappear overnight as a result of acquiring gambling addictions and a partiality to drink, drugs and loose women, whose only interest in Joe was to part him from his money. These events coming so close together had a profoundly unsettling effect on poor old Joe. So consequently, over a period of time Joe had drifted into a life of a vagrant and misfit, and by now a lonely man who spends his time drifting from one town to another, sleeping rough and more or not thumbing a lift or taking a ride in a boxcar, travelling distances that were staggering and yet going anywhere but nowhere. It was on such a journey that something incredible was about to happen which would change Joe's life forever.

By now, his discarded clothes hung distastefully from his body, accompanied by the stench of stale sweat and urine. Let us not forget that this was one of the greatest boxers in living memory. Maybe the next town would bring our beleaguered boxer, fresh fortunes? For indeed, it would be in such a town called Santa Fe that Joe's life would take on a whole new meaning. Earlier on in the day Joe had heard a group of men taking in town that a freight train was leaving for around nine o'clock that evening - bound for Santa Fe. As darkness fell Joe made his way to the freight yard on the west side of town and there he hid behind some loco sheds. From his position Joe peered feverishly towards the railway sidings upon which a huge freight train was waiting patiently to embark on its journey. Joe sits and waits for an opportunity to climb on board a suitable boxcar. Several minutes had passed by and Joe could wait no longer. Suddenly, he hears the sound of a loco, huffing and puffing, and getting itself nicely warmed up. With some urgency Joe makes his way along the railway track, being particularly careful to avoid anyone in authority. One by one he tries to prize open a boxcar, but to his frustration they were shut tight - when at last he finds one open. Sliding the door back Joe is greeted by the sight of straw bales of hay that were lying sparingly on the floor. This was perfect he thinks and will make a perfect environment for him. It was just like having central heating but without the hot water. In that instance Joe hears the sound of a whistle and the vibration of the train taking up its slack. Slowly but surely the train begins to move off from its urban sprawl to begin its long journey mid-west. Snug as a bug Joe settles down for the night and gracefully dozes off to another world. His sleep takes him back to one of his big fights. The scene is Madison Square Garden's in New York. He's in the middle of round three. His contestant is the Mexico, Amondo Calibra. Punches rain in thick and fast as the Mexican throws a humdinger of a punch to Joe's chin. He wobbles, but immediately comes back with an almighty blockbuster of a punch that sends the Mexican to his knees.

Just as the bell goes for round four Joe is woken up by the thunderous sound of a passing train. The endless line of freight wagons sound almost musical as they rattle and rumble their way along, getting louder and louder and turning poor old Joe to the point of deafness. The train passes through the obscurity of open prairie country before finally descending upon the great plains of the mid-west. As the hours drift by something incredible happens that startles Joe. As it happened Joe is drawn to the far corner of the box-car. Surprise comes when he hears the rustle of straw which brings forth the appearance of a human hand, followed by a head. What in creation? Joe's truly startled because he thought he was completely alone. The uninvited guest brushes away the straw from his person and reveals himself. To Joe's amazement it was another hobo who had probably sneaked on board the train without his knowledge. Hey, wait a minute Joe thinks, that face looks familiar - but surely not?

The hobo was the double of a man he once knew called Tony Ferigo who had formally been his trainer. Joe suspicions were truly justified for without question it was his old friend and mentor, Tony Ferigo. But how on earth did his old buddy get himself into a situation like this. The last time he saw Tony was after his big fight in Las Vegas. At that particular time he was doing really well. Having exchanged the mandatory handshakes and pleasantries the conversation continued on the subject of their past lives and almost at once a feeling of overwhelming admiration came from both men. Tony suggested to his old buddy that he should try and pull himself together and get his life sorted out; after all he was the greatest boxer in living memory. His ex-trainer takes great pity on Joe and suggests to him once they had reached Santa Fe there was an organisation in town that could possibly help them.

So it came to pass on a glorious spring-like morning, the two friends had finally arrived in Santa Fe having endured their epic journey across America. Without any further ado they immediately homed in on the organisation that helped homeless people. Having put pen to paper and gone through a series of forms and interviews both men were given the opportunity to acquire suitable accommodation within the Santa Fe area.

In the course of the day Joe found himself walking up the steps of a house on the east side of town, thereafter; he had the resounding pleasure of meeting his new landlady called Elizabeth. She proves to be a very kind and sympathetic person who takes great pity on Joe - knowing of his past, and, as a result, Joe's whole attitude and lifestyle was miraculously transformed in just a few short weeks. Over a period of time Joe had developed into a completely changed man. He was now well fed, tidily dressed, sober, and moreover, off the drink and is much happier all round as a person.

One memorable day Joe was returning back from a work-out at his local gym, and there to greet him was Elizabeth with some important news, and so the conversation moved on to Joe's wellbeing.

"Look Joe," Elizabeth began. "For some time now I've been thinking of clearing out the room on the top floor of the house, previously used by another lodger. So how do you feel about helping me with the work," she asks Joe, whose disinclination to any form of work had almost disappeared. In response, he tells Elizabeth he would be only too happy to assist her in any way possible in gratitude for all her help and kindness she has shown him.

Joe was led up a flight of stairs that led to the upper part of the house to where the said room was situated. Upon opening the door they were greeted by a worthless pile of junk that was scattered about, none of it appearing to be any use to mankind. Joe had been given the melancholy task of shifting everything downstairs to leave for the trash men to take away. Once the worse was over Joe began on getting the place cleaned up. It proves a big task and it takes all of two weeks of hard work to complete the work properly. The only notable thing of interest in the room was an old Victorian wardrobe that was tucked away in the far corner which Joe thinks it might have some antique value. There was a momentous look of trepidation as the wardrobe was duly opened. Its contents revealed a beautiful selection of the finest gentlemen's clothing.

"Upon my word," Joe smiled, as he cast his eyes on one particular garment

Low and behold it was the 'Lime-Coloured Suit'.

Elizabeth states with some sadness that she bought the suit for her husband (now deceased) just before they got married. "Sadly he only wore it the once," Elizabeth said in a subdued voice.

As a reward for his commitment and effort Elizabeth gladly gives the suit to Joe in recognition for the hard work and endeavour that he has put in. In addition, she therefore invites Joe to move into the room, forthwith, suggesting it would be an ideal setting and much more comfortable for him. Once the room had been thoroughly cleaned and painted along with new carpets laid, Joe though it would be just perfect for him. It seemed a far cry from the misery of living on the streets. It was nonetheless a most wonderful offer on Elizabeth's part. Several weeks later Joe moved in to his new surroundings with the enthusiasm of a schoolboy with a new mechanical toy. And so began a new chapter in Joe's life which in one sense would turn out to be the happiness he had ever experienced.

Now firmly established in his new surroundings Joe thought it was about time he paid a visit to his local cinema, the Roxy. Therefore, feeling a little flush he decided to venture into town and take in the afternoon's matinee. Acting on impulse Joe decided to try on his new suit, the one Elizabeth gave him - the Lime-Coloured suit. On admiring himself in the mirror Joe believed the suit had given him a certain charismatic and benevolent appearance. Without any further ado he sets off into town with a swagger and a smile that had previously deserted him. As he approached the cinema Joe noted with a certain amount of displeasure that a big queue had formed outside. On the face of it he thought it rather strange that the entire row of patrons was made up, entirely of males. Then without warning a big bruiser of a man appears and annoyingly starts to jostle everyone.

"Come on you guys hurry up we haven't got all day!" the man yells.

Joe wonders what the hell is going on. At first he thought it must be the security staff, but no. The next thing he knew was being marshalled inside the cinemas complex where he found himself standing on a stage along with fifty or so other guys. From that moment a man's voice could be heard bellowing out instructions on a megaphone. It began to dawn on the ex-champ that he'd got himself into a right old pickle.

"All I want you guys to do is walk slowly across the stage one by one, and then turn and face me, that's all you've got to do." The voice said in a forceful manner.

The moment of truth came when Joe discovers he's mistakenly landed up for an audition with a big movie company that were in town. Apparently, they were looking for a budding new actor to take part in their new film. Joe decides to go along with the whole thing and do what is expected of him, and thought it could turn out to be quite interesting. With some reluctance, Joe regained both his breath and composure before finally plucking up the courage to do as instructed of him. His every step was being closely monitored by two brightly lit spotlights that followed his every move. Joe takes his turn to walk across the stage as suavely as can be, and then turns to face his receivers at the same time trying to appear charismatic as possible in his wonderful new suit and wondered what the effect will be.

The guy with the megaphone turned to his casting crew and said: "hey the guy in the Lime-Colour Suit. If he can talk as good as his looks then that's our man, make no mistake, that's our man."

Once the auditions were over, everyone was sent home, except Joe. He was immediately given a voice test which instantly makes a lasting impression with the director and co-producer.

Having emerged from his harrowing ordeal Joe was rewarded with a screen test and as a result he'd been cast to play a professional boxer, which indeed was music to his ears. The ex-champ was back in business once more - Hollywood here I come. Nonetheless, Joe felt an extraordinary feeling of immense achievement at having pulled off this amazing feat. Over a period of time Joe had successfully starred in a number of lucrative films. This time he is a role model in life. No more gambling, drink or drugs. Practically overnight he had become a man of immense wealth, but the funny thing is he still lives at the same address with Elizabeth to keep him in check.

One afternoon Joe was returning back from a shopping trip armed to the teeth with a variety of goodies and there to greet him was Elizabeth. The discussion that followed moved on to the Lime-Coloured suit.

Elizabeth explains to Joe that for some time now she's been thinking of getting rid of the Lime Coloured suit now that it has served its purpose and brought Joe incredible good fortune. She therefore intends to drop the suit off at a local charity shop the very next day. And there the suit remained till finally a man walked in a week later and puts his case to staff. He states he is in desperate need of a suit to wear as he has a very important interview the next day and needs something that will stand out from the crowd. So, having flicked through the endless rows of gentlemen's clothing he comes across a suit to his liking. Low and behold it was the 'Lime Coloured Suit'. A few days later the man returned to the charity shop armed with a suit in his hand together with a huge smile on his face.

"Hey would you believe it," the man smiles. "That suit I purchased from you, the Lime Coloured suit. Well, it seems to have brought me mighty good luck. My interview went well, and, as a result, I was offered a sales position with a car dealership. I would like to return the suit and perhaps it will bring someone else good fortune."

Two days later another man walks into the charity shop of ill-repute. It was a hobo in desperate need of clothing. Almost at once he comes across the Lime-Coloured Suit and tries it on. "I'll take it ma'am." The hobo beams with a huge smile.

Just as the hobo was about to leave the lady assistant takes from her purse a five dollar bill and gives it to the hobo.

"Hey, go buy yourself some food, and whilst you're about it, stick a couple of bucks on a lottery ticket." She says jokingly.

"Why gee thanks ma'am. If my ticket comes up trumps then I'll be back with the winnings."

Three days later the hobo returned to the charity shop the day after the lottery had been drawn. This time he is immaculately dressed in a pin-striped suit, accompanied by a trilby and the shiniest of black shoes. He takes from a carrier bag the Lime-Coloured Suit. "Ma'am, I want to thank you from the bottom of my heart. You see that money you gave me, the five dollars. Well, I struck two bucks on a lottery ticket and would you believe it my ticket came up trumps. I won a million dollars. So ma'am, I am returning the suit plus leaving you a mighty generous donation."

The conclusion to this story is that the Lime-Coloured Suit has the ability to bring incredible good fortune to whoever wears it.

Escape to the East

Senior Aircraft-man John Jackson had been lying fast asleep in his bed for almost two hours that evening in barrack room 4C at RAF Station Kuhlendorf in West Germany. Positioned next to him was fellow 'D' Watch Electronics Operator, SAC David Atkinson, who was admiring the razor sharp crease he had worked so hard to get after spending hours of effortless work with the steam iron. Atkinson liked showing people up like John Jackson whose turnout always seemed to look poor in comparison to his pristine immaculateness. On another bed to John's right was SAC Bob Gregory who was shining up his cap badge after having wiped it with metal polish he had most diligently applied. Bob Gregory noticed it was 22.38 hours and remembered that John Jackson wanted to be awakened ten minutes before the Watch bus was due to take his unit to a top-secret communications compound at 302 Signals Unit. Bob stood up and walked over the highly polished lino between the two beds. It took several light taps on John Jackson's right cheek of increasing force before he saw his eyes slowly open to reveal an overwhelming desire to go back to sleep. Rather reluctantly, John's sleepy eyes unenthusiastically focused on Bob's.

"Hey oop John!" said Bob. "Fraid it's time to get your rear end into gear. Bus will be here in ten minutes. Just think of it, after tonight, we've got just one more night shift to do before we go back on days again, so the news is not all grim."

Bob noticed a total disinclination on John's part to make any effort to stir himself from his deep slumber, so he added. "Look, its best if you bounce out of it my old mucker. You realise there's this big purge going on at the moment regarding lads not properly turned out. We don't want to get lumbered with twerps like Wilson as our Officer, so I reckon you'll need to spend the next ten minutes sticking your head under the cold tap."

John at this point was calculating all the odds that were stacked against him, who, unlike his colleagues, avoided anything that was associated with discipline. John's worse misdemeanour was repeatedly being put on endless charges called 'Fizzers' as they were referred to in the RAF.

Bob decided to give his lazy friend another good shake to wake him up. If John dropped off to sleep again it was curtains for him. He therefore decided that he could at least lay there for a few more minutes before all hell broke loose.

In truth, John Jackson's feelings about the RAF were pretty much at rock bottom. The motivation behind his thinking was one of bitterness and frustration. Up to this point in his life he was feeling thoroughly depressed with anything that was associated with military life, especially with all the endless bull-shit that he had to endure. This apparent depression had mainly been brought about when earlier in the day in the village of Neustadt he had been thrown out of his fiancé's flat, with words to the effect. "I never want to see you again, you Englander pig." John was very much in love with Fraulein Gertrude Muller. He had the great fortune of meeting her shortly after arriving in Germany. It was his first operational posting just after he had completed his specialist trade training in Lincolnshire. John had spent many wonderful moments with Gertrude but it seemed the romance was all but over. The whole stupid thing started when he had failed to turn up at Furst Biergarten railway station. John tried to explain to Gertrude that he had been put on three days Jankers for a 'slovenly bed pack' and had also failed to scrub the ablutions of barrack room 4 C to the required standard to the Co's inspection, but Gertrude didn't believe a word of it. She told him she had been thoroughly humiliated by his not turning up, as it was not the first time he had let her down.

The ending of his love affair with his beautiful Gertrude made him feel he'd had enough of RAF life. It was only her love and intellectual conversation that provided him with some sense of normality from the endless shifts and parades that he had to endure.

It was this 'RAF mentality' he had grown so much to hate. What really irked him, he knew as a Radio Operator he was better than most and had tried to put in tremendous effort and reliability into his work, but it was clear that 'idiot' Officers and NCOs didn't give a damn about him or his work. All they seemed to care about was the way blokes made their bed-packs, or how high they could raise their arms when marching, or whether they saluted officers in a smartly and correctly fashion, or whether brasses were dazzling to almost blind them. His fellow officers seemed similarly obsessed with this theology. John, therefore, desperately needed Gertrude's love to keep him sane. In fact his reaction to Gertrude's news was met with a feeling of deep depression and bitter disappointment.

John's sleepy thoughts were interrupted by the raucous voice of SAC Pat O'Hara.

"The bus is here lads, time for our ride to a jolly night of giggles at the compound."

The other men in the barrack room duly filed out as Bob Gregory gave John a final shove as he passed his bed. John suddenly realised that unless he moved himself with some urgency he was going to be late for his Watch and miss the bus. At last with some reluctance he bounced off his bed, pulled his shirt over his underclothes that he had been sleeping in, pulled his blue working trousers up and his blue top and stuffed his collar, tie and socks into his pocket before rushing out with his laces not tied and just managing to jump on the bus before it pulled away, much to the amusement of his fellow officers.

During the six-minute journey, John had managed to get his socks on and shoe laces tied together with his collar on and tie properly knotted. He pulled out his handkerchief and tried to scrap the mud off his shoes, but as usual, he had only been partly been successful when the bus dumped them at the gate of 302 Signals Unit compound for what the RAF terminology is called, 'e-bussing procedure.'

Finally, they all filed through to have their identity cards checked and their high security badges issued for the appropriate grade by the RAF police. As the queue moved forward John noticed that the new Watch Officer, Flying Officer Wilson, was standing in the police room behind the corporal as they began to scrutinise the men as they passed through. Flying Officer Wilson had been posted in from a 'square bashing' camp in England and had already acquired a reputation for making it known about the high levels of discipline he expected from his men at 302 SU which he gathered it was not up to his standards. Wilson came to the conclusion that things in the personnel department were extremely slack and needed to be tightened up.

As John came up to the window to be security checked. Flying Officer Wilson eyed him up and down disdainfully.

"SAC Jackson!" he said in his irritating public school voice. "Your appearance is an absolute disgrace. Your collar is filthy, your tie is not tied correctly, your cap badge is in a disgraceful state of neglect, and by the look of it you haven't washed or shaved for the last two weeks! As for your shoes it looks as though they'd been dragged through a hedge backwards. I will not tolerate such slackness among men on my Watch. You are a disgrace Jackson!"

"CORPORAL, PUT THIS MAN ON A CHARGE!" Flying Officer Wilson shouted with great enthusiasm.

John is duly ordered to report to Flying Officer Wilson immediately after his Watch had finished and there to be charged. As John made his way through the complex of the building he was feeling thoroughly fed up, in fact his temper nearly erupted when he heard ex-boy entrant SAC Atkinson, walking behind him with his bulled up shoes and gleaming like mad, as ever.

"It's entirely your fault, Jackson." Atkinson grumbled. "We warned you about your laziness. Look at your filthy shoes compared to mine. As you've had previous form your Conduct Sheet I should think will land fourteen days Jankers. Maybe it will teach you a lesson not to be so bloody idle and disgrace our Watch by your scruffiness."

Somehow John had managed to hold back from planting one on

SAC Atkinson's chin, and pretending not to hear him. John had just turned left into 'Blue Unit' communications room to relieve his 'B' Watch counterpart, SAC Macpherson, on position eighteen which covered the Soviet Air Defence network in the West Ukraine.

"Welcome to heaven." Macpherson said as he greeted John in his raw Glaswegian brogue, who was extremely delighted to see his relief take over. "God, it's been a ruddy long stint tonight, I thought it would never end. It seems the Ruskies transmitters have all but gone off the air or else the buggers got plastered on the Vodka. In truth I wanted to fall asleep but bloody Corporal Skinner kept coming round and telling me to 'do some work', and calling me a 'LAZY Git'. How can I do work if there's no bloody work to do! Your turn to be downright bored stiff for hours on end, I'm off to my pit."

After signing-on and taking up his position John Jackson soon settled into his night's work. The first thing he noticed was a mistake that SAC Macpherson had made. For some unknown reason he had mistakenly tuned the receivers in to an unknown band of frequency which was presently locked on to an idle band which had caused both outstation receivers to be mistuned. One band to his amazement was receiving Radio Luxembourg while listening to music instead of the Soviet Group's correct frequency of 3,896 kHz. John retuned each receiver in which he whipped into shape and brought the correct band into focus whereby the remaining band on outstation 12 KHz high from where McPherson had the Racal receivers tuned in.

John never liked dropping other men in it so he therefore decided to cover up his fellow colleagues mistake by making the correct entry in the log - stating that the stations had been working perfectly and correctly tuned in after being somewhat idle, if only for a few minutes. But soon the undulators were busily clicking away like mad and printing out the Cyrillic's in Latin type font. As the night wore on, John worked tirelessly on, but his thoughts were dominated by his deep depression at losing his beloved Gertrude. Coupled with this thought he still had the unwelcoming vision of doing his fourteen days on Jankers. John ascertained that his feelings about the RAF were thoroughly demoralising. It seemed that SAC Atkinson's taunt about his laziness and scruffiness was likely to prove correct. Apart from last week's charge over his slovenly bed pack and unsatisfactory scrubbing of the barrack room ablutions which he had previously been charged with, he felt he had also been admonished for Blanco on his webbing brass and Duraglit residue on his webbing belt and Kit Inspection. For that crime he had been 'admonished'.

The damming verdict would soon come around for the unsatisfactorily presentation of his un-pressed trousers and of course his tie not correctly positioned. For this it was Jankers for him. All these failings and warnings were recorded on his Conduct Sheet so when Corporal Moss's charge finally went through and the said Officer inspected his charge sheet he was certain they would decide to give him a heavy punishment of fourteen days which seemed quite likely. John dreaded the thought of doing fourteen days Jankers and spending countless days doing such harsh fatigues set out by the RAF. The sheer thought of getting up at 0500 hours and doing square bashing till his shoes were practically worn out was punishment enough. But the thought of doing Jankers made him more depressed than ever. He continued working through the night and taking tapes of the Russian network. The toughest part of being put on a charge was not being able to get out of the camp during for his off-duty hours. Even more humiliating would be the continuous taunts from the likes of SAC Atkinson. The sheer lunacy of it all truly horrified poor old John.

By hook or crook, he therefore decided to escape from his RAF hell and spend the rest of his days in the Eastern Bloc. There he could become a free man and do whatever he liked. His RAF job was okay in itself but the discipline was far just too harsh, and without Gertrude in his life it wasn't worth living. At first he thought of returning back to the UK. But he knew this was totally out of the question as the RAF police was sure to find him and have him instantly arrested and brought back to camp. He didn't really want to go back to England. He hated his father and had unhappy memories of his childhood in England. But unlike most 'Brit' servicemen, he very much liked Germany and the German way of life. People were certainly much more pleasant, and far more intellectual. However, the truth of the matter was that the RAF hierarchy together with the military police worked very closely with the West German authorities, so wherever he went or tried to hide, they would soon find him and bring him back to his defaulters for punishment. And then a possible solution came into being. The thought had accrued to him that he could cross over the border into East Germany and thereby ask for political asylum. Needless to say, there was some scepticism on John's part, but in truth he was adamant about escaping. With the knowledge he had of 302 Signals Unit he thought he would be of great value to the Russians. And then another thought had crossed his mind. What would make his escape more desirable if he could get his hands on a number of top secret documents that the Communists would find invaluable? This in itself would surely guarantee his future. John was fully aware of the difficulties that confronted him, but he was adamant about escaping. As the night wore on he continued working on the undulators that were busily clicking away with far more traffic than usual.

It then transpired that the time had reached 0710 and John noted that there was just fifty minutes to go before 'C' Watch came in to relieve him. And so, after much thought and deliberation and having gone through every conceivable aspect of his intentions, he therefore decided the only way out of his predicament was to escape to East Germany by way of a train journey from the British Sector in West Berlin to the Eastern Frontier. But what would make his escape more exciting, if he pretended to be a tourist from somewhere like Sweden or Denmark. Then a brainwave of an idea had suddenly shot through his head. His escape plan would surely be made more desirable if he could get his hands on a number of 'Top Secret' documents? This in itself would surely be his bargaining point. Once he had crossed over the border he would then present the documents to the Russian authorities and thereby ask for 'political asylum'.

Noting that Corporal Dickson was out of the room John decided to walk along the passageway to J2 Traffic Control room, which was a grade 'A' security area. He knew full well that the room contained highly classified material. As he didn't have the means of entry, he thought it might be a bit tricky. However, all that was needed was a few moments of undisturbed peace without being detected. This act of skulduggery would surely be the key to his future. But just as he passed the room in question he discovered it was locked. To open it would be far too dangerous as he was a mere radio operator and not allowed into a 'Red Badge' security area without special clearance.

Quite by chance the door in question suddenly opened and from it emerged; Flying Officer Wilson who carelessly left the door ajar. Wilson then went into the Yellow communications room while glancing at John and had assumed he was on his way to the compound abductions. As there was nobody else around, unseen, John craftily slipped into the room and there went about doing his dirty deed. By an incredible stroke of luck he noticed a pile of documents lying on top of the table, labelled 'Eastern Bloc Decoding Formula' and marked most 'Most Secret'. John couldn't resist the temptation. He at once picked them up and quickly stuffed them under his working blue uniform. Speed was of the utmost importance. He casually walked out of the room and made his way to gent's toilet.

John couldn't believe his luck and felt an enormous sense of triumph, realising the decoding books were bound to be of great value to the communists and knowing full well to the extent of which Western Intelligence had cracked their communications codes. This he thought would be his ticket to freedom and would give him the means to start a new life in the East. More to the point, he felt the RAF would pay for the pitiful way they had treated him over the years. The only thing on his mind at this moment in time was to get the documents out of the compound and out of RAF Station Kuhlendorf and especially without it being detected. But just then Sergeant Scott of D Watch appeared. He was the NCO in charge of J2 section, but rather annoyingly he was standing in the passageway and had apparently seen John coming out of Traffic Control J2 which he knew perfectly well was out of bounds to him. To John's horror the decoding book seemed to bulge out of his uniform. If Sergeant Scott spotted anything suspicious he would be in really serious trouble. His whole plan to escape would be wrecked before it got started. It would be inconceivable if his plans were to falter at this stage. Undoughtedly, his actions and movements would be scrutinised if he wasn't careful. At all costs he must try and avoid suspicion, but how could he explain his actions to Sergeant Scott?

"Jackson! What the hell are you doing in that room?" Sergeant Scott shouted. John had no time to think. His heart was beating like a raging inferno. He said the first thing that came into his head, trying to concoct an excuse. His excuse was neither concise nor easy to believe. Therefore he invented a tactile one.

"Oh, I'm sorry, Sarge, I thought you were in there. I went into the room because Flying Officer Wilson left the door ajar so I went in to see if there was anybody else left in there. Also Sarge, I want to draw your attention to my control, there was a signal coming up at 5959 and I thought it may be of some importance. Could you take a look at it sir before 'C' Watch come on duty and get all the credit."

John knew perfectly well that 5959 was a very routine signal which was sent out on numerous occasions. He knew his Group well, but he hoped Sergeant Scott did not. He just might be taken in by it and buy him a few minutes of breathing space as well as being a feeble excuse for being in an area that was out of bounds to him.

"Okay, but that is no reason to break security procedures. You know you are supposed to knock and wait outside if you want to see somebody in a Grade 'A' area. Just because that stupid pillock Wilson breaks procedures there is no bloody reason for you to do so! Now, let's go and have a look at this signal."

Sergeant Scott followed John to his operating position and checked through the print-out.

"My word, you're right Jackson, it was sent 5959, and this

Russian text looks interesting? Hmm. This could be very important, very important indeed! It was right of you to bring it to my attention. We can't have those idiots on 'C' Watch getting all the credit for our work, can we? I'll take it through."

Sergeant Scott then left the room taking with him the print-out. John looked at his watch, there was just 38 minutes to go before 'C' Watch came on duty. Would he able get away with his bluff and avoid a complete disaster? Undoubtedly, his main objective at this moment was to press on regardless. It would inconceivable if someone was to discover that the documents were missing? The minutes seemed to tick by at a snail's pace, after what seemed like an eternity, but to his delight Sergeant Scott had not returned. John then saw the airmen from 'C' Watch coming into the room, including his own relief SAC Stuart Webb. John was desperate to get out of the compound and as far away from camp as possible with his precious documents.

"Hello Jackson," Webb said, "you still on this one, good."

"To be honest it's been pretty quiet. However, Krivoy Rog just sent a print-out with a coded message of 5959. Our intelligence expert, Sergeant Scott reckons it's significant." John knew only too well that SAC Webb was fully aware that 5959 was just a routine signal which was often sent out, so he didn't argue the matter.

"They are paid to think, not us! Ours is not to reason why, eh?"
John knew that sending 'The Brains' on a wild-goose chase was never liked.

SAC Webb grinned at him. "I'll probably get a rollicking for your mistake later on, you fool" he said laughingly. "Go on, get out and enjoy your time in your nice warm bed."

John was a bit surprised that Sergeant Scott had not returned to 'rollick' him for sending him on a 'wild goose chase'. But right now John had more important matters to attend to. What he really needed was to set up a false trial so as to cover his tracks so to speak.

"Cheerio chaps, see you in the morning," John smiled, knowing full well he would never see SAC Webb or any of them again. He proceeded to make his way towards the exit point to be checked out at the same time he was feeling somewhat apprehensive that the decoding documents would be found, but just as he got to the main gate to be security checked a long queue had formed outside. Apparently, the RAF police were having one of their rigorous searches and was asking everyone to turn out their pockets.

"Don't tell me they've discovered the documents were missing or is it just a routine check?" he thought. What John feared most was that one of the officers would discover his deception. His whole plan to escape would be in jeopardy before it got started. Therefore an atmosphere of suspicion and fear had suddenly crept into the equation. To leave the queue now, for whatever reason, would merely give the game away. He prayed they would let him through without finding anything on him. If not, his master plan to escape looked like collapsing.

While the search continued to move forward each airman was made to turn out his pockets, as well as their rucksacks. This apparently was not one of those random security checks with just one or two men being picked out; every man was being done scrupulously. Someone must have noticed the documents were missing, John thought. That could be the only reason why they were checking on everybody. Just as he was about to step forward, John foolishly gave them a piece of his mind. "What the hell are you looking for?" He said distastefully and wondered if it would deem it a more serious offence, other than making bed packs which seemed to be the regular RAF mentality.

John made his way forward in the cheque and was adjacent to the door which incorporated the RAF police room. In front of him was LAC White, and after that it would be John's turn to be searched. Inside the police room Corporal Moss who was busily writing out a report and would not be involved in the security check. However, John had come up with a brainwave of an idea which could possibly get him off the hook. He suddenly remembered that he had been ordered by Corporal Moss to report to him at 0800. The time was now 07:58. Could this possibly confuse things by the RAF Police for letting him through without being searched? Worth a try, John thought.

"Excuse me, Corporal," John said. "You wanted me to report to you at 0800, do you want me to see you after the security check?"

Corporal Moss paused from writing up in his logbook and a smile that adorned his face.

"Ah yes, that's right SAC Jackson. You and I have to a little matter of a Fizzer to attend to. Please step inside and we'll get this matter sorted out."

John rapidly left the queue just as LAC White was due to be searched by Corporal Jones and instead went into the police room where Corporal Moss was working. Corporal Moss then asked his counterpart to have a brief word with Corporal Jones.

"I'll look after this blockhead Corporal Moss," Jones said with a cynical grin.

"About time you took on a bit of the work, you're welcome to him." Corporal Jones said, and immediately made his way outside to carry on checking the others in the queue.

Meanwhile Corporal Moss demanded to see John's ID card which he immediately pulled out from his top pocket. Corporal Moss then pulled out an unused RAF form 252 from his desk drawer, the most dreaded of all RAF forms, especially among airmen, because everybody knew that once your name went down on one your destiny of forthcoming unhappiness was 'in the pipeline'.

Corporal Moss took his time copying John's RAF number, rank and name on to the form 252 in his big, neat capitals. John realised a few more successful charges under his belt would look good on his record and enhance the prospects of him getting that third tape he so badly wanted. Corporal Moss signed the 252 form with a huge grin on his face and informed John that he was being charged, noting he made 'no response' to be quoted in his statement. John was well aware that any recorded comment would land him in further trouble when his C badge went through, but of course he wouldn't be there to collect his unwelcomed punishment.

Meanwhile, all the others on 'D' Watch were on board the compound bus. Corporal Moss had noted this and shouted to the MT driver who was looking rather impatient. "Hang on a mo driver, one more in here to come on board." Corporal Moss then turned to John with a foreboding smile, and said. "Better get your rear-end into gear and jump on the bus, fast. We don't want you to be late for bed, do we? I want you to be nice and fresh to start your Jankers."

John responded as ordered and in lightning speed he rushed outside to the waiting bus. He of all people had not been searched which was met with a great sense of relief. As he sat there on the bus a thought had suddenly crossed his mind. Once he was safely across the Eastern Frontier it would then transpire that Corporal Moss would be the likely culprit for stealing the missing documents. Perhaps Flying Officer Wilson would also be severely reprimanded for leaving the J2 door open. The whole lot of them would get their just desserts. For the first time in months John felt an overwhelming sense of immense triumph. However, he knew full well he could not divulge his thoughts to any of his colleagues back at the base. Therefore, he must refrain at all costs from sharing his thoughts to anyone.

During the short bus ride back to the main camp John continued on with his escape plan. On his arrival at barrack block 4, he waited for the others to leave for the Airmen's Mess where they always had their breakfast before going to their various pits. John however always climbed straight into bed as he hated breakfast. As soon as the room was empty he transferred the top secret documents into his RAF rucksack and then went to his locker and got out his United Kingdom Passport, his wallet, along with his Spiesenbank pass-book, which he knew he had over Five-Hundred Marks to provide funds for his journey.

After a quick wash and brush up in the same ablutions that he had previously failed to clean, and, with a heavy heart and a feeling of great sadness he looked around for the very last time at his RAF surroundings. Just think of it, he thought: no more making bed-packs and no more Jankers. John had always been hopeless at making his bed-pack ever since his square bashing days. He was just about to walk out when he heard SACs O'Hara, Atkinson and Sergeant Thompson coming back from the Airmen's Mess, carrying their beer mugs and commenting on what a 'load of rubbish' their night had turned out. John knew all too well that whenever that lot came back from the Airman's Mess, they were always well and truly plastered. SAC O'Hara, on seeing John in civvies, said, "What, not in your pit? Haven't you had enough of this bloody place?"

"I'm tired all right," John replied. "But as you know I've been put on a fizzer and it seems to be my last day of freedom before my charge comes up. I've been informed by the powers that be it could come up on Thursday or even tomorrow. I'm not spending my LAST DAY OF FREEDOM in a raff pit."

"Aye up, John," interjected Bob Gregory. "I recon you're going to see that Kraut bird of yours again, you lucky bugger?"

John reasoned that when the RAF police was informed of his desertion it will hopefully send them off on a false trail and he replied. "You bet I am! Can you think of a better way for a bloke to spend his last day of freedom?"

At this point Dave Atkinson began his usual taunting. "You would not be on your last day of freedom if you weren't such an idle lazy git, thick a pigs shit and a disgrace to your uniform, you manky bugger!"

SAC O'Hara tried to shut Atkinson up. John decided he would not respond to the foul mouthed moron. Anyway, he would not be seeing any of them again, so 'good riddance!' to the lot of them, he thought.

John left 4C room while the others were preparing to climb into their various pits.
Diligently, he slowly but surely made his way towards the main gate where he realised he would have to show his ID card, but unless he was on the Jankers list, which he wasn't at the moment, he would not be stopped from going out. Cool as a cucumber he casually walked out of the main gate and caught the 08.35 bus to Neustadt, one of four buses that left the camp each day. On arrival at the town of Neustadt he then picked up the city Auto bus which would take him to the centre of Luneburg.

Over a period of time John had carefully worked out a strategic plan of action. He therefore decided he would not attempt to cross the eastern frontier at Helstadt but instead to the south. That he reasoned was far too risky as it was frequently used by military convoys. He knew from what Gertrude had told him that most Germans could pick out a British serviceman a mile off from their features, such as the standard RAF haircut. So to avoid being stopped at the western side of the frontier he decided to change that. He knew of a theatrical costume shop in town and a visit there enabled him to pick out a disguise that would effectively cover his short back and sides, which hopefully, would make him, look like a student tourist. After purchasing the said items, the disguises looked so realistic John thought it impossible for anyone to assume he was no other than a true German.

John had earlier told staff at the costume shop that he had the great honour of performing in a stage play, Mozart's Die Zauberflote and needed to match the part in the appropriate costume. To go along with his acting skills John had also managed to purchase a pair of false spectacles along with a full length beard. These disguises, if anything, actually made him look slightly more suspicious than the photo on his passport. But of course when you're in the RAF everybody had to have their hair cut down to size like a hooligan 'Skinhead', otherwise you got put on 'a charge' for looking like a normal human being.

Having arrived at Hauptbanhoff railway station he changed from his RAF uniform to one of civvies in an old toilet block at the station. John at this point of his journey was feeling pretty confident that nobody would suspect him as being in the RAF and remembered what Gertrude had once told him that most German people could pick out anybody who talked German as English, although, thanks to his association with her, he decided to speak in a different dialect and to convey the impression he was Swedish. This in itself would hopefully conceal his true country of origin, just so long as he did not bump into a real Swede. Sometime later John made his way to the station ticket office to purchase his ticket. He thereby went through a procedure of putting his fingers, plus of course his money through a tiny glass slit, whereby a lady who sat behind a glass screen, pressed a couple of buttons on her old fashioned ticket machine, and then, hey presto, a ticket shot out.

Regaining his composure John began to make inquiries about his train journey.

"Oh excuse Madame, can you tell me when the next train leaves for Berlin?" John inquired in his new style Swedish accent. "You see Madame; I am over here in Germany for a few days' vacation from Gothenburg University and have been told Berlin is well worth a visit before I return back to Sweden."

The lady was most pleased to help. "But of course sir. West Berlin is certainly worth a visit. Oh by the way, the next train to leave is from platform eight at 13.42 and arrives in West Berlin at 17.20 - or if you like you can travel across via the wall into East Berlin to Friedrichstrasse," she politely replied. She also pointed out there was no problem crossing the border. Further to this information, she went on to say that he could purchase a Transit Visa from the East German officials once he had boarded the train. After thanking the ticket lady in his attempted Swedish dialect he duly moved over to the Fahrkartenschalter where he hoped and prayed they would not check his passport. But just in case, John thought it wise to speak in his normal English accent, and stated that he wanted to go to West Berlin.

"Single or return sir," asked the booking clerk curtly in English.

John thought there was no way he wanted a return. So as not to create suspicion, he replied. "Oh, I will be flying back so I only want a Single, please." He thus handed over twenty Deutschmarks and was immediately was issued with an international Deutsche Reichsbahn coupon which would take him through to Berlin Stadtbahn. John noted with a feeling of tremendous excitement that it indicated via Schwanheide. Schwanheide to John's delight was in the Soviet zone and is where he intended to seek political asylum. Once he was safely across the border he would immediately inform the Soviets that he had top secret documents on him. Then at last his worries would all be over and completely free from his RAF hell. Just think of it, John thought, no more making bed packs and no more Jankers. Could his luck hold out or would something go terribly wrong at the last moment? Up to this point of his journey John was feeling extremely tired as he hadn't sleep for some time now, but he didn't care? With the usual hiccups associated with rail travel, John eventually arrived at Schwanheide with five or so minutes to spare. Making the necessary inquiries that was connected with his journey a very helpful porter informed him that his train was waiting on platform two. Finding an empty non-smoking carriage he quickly boarded and made himself comfortable. But just as he was getting ready for the big off, the door of the compartment unexpectedly opened. It revealed a man and a woman who were exquisitely dressed in bright brash clothes.

"Oh excuse me honey," the lady smiled. "Do you mind if we join you?"

John withdrew his cigarette and began to scrutinise his unwelcome guests with some scepticism. He at once recognised their originality by their loud drawl. It appeared they were Americans. John was just about to tell them to bugger off and go find another compartment, but had second thoughts. Nevertheless, he would have to be careful if he was to continue to play the part of being a tourist. It may come about that he would have to admit as being British as he might have to show his passport. He certainly didn't want to appear suspicious in any way, so he would stick to his story of being Swedish. These intruders were really beginning to spoil his plans, therefore, he would have to be polite and not rock the boat.

"Yes, I'd be delighted for you to join me." John replied.

"Oh, you must be British," the lady smiled. "Oh I do love your British accent. You see, me and hubby here are over here on vacation from Houston Texas. We had such a nice time in England and just love your Queen and Royal Family."

John thought it polite to make meaningful conversation with the Americans and knowing of the special relationship there was between the two countries. However, he was feeling far from easy with their presence. The last thing he needed right now was the existence of two ultra-patriotic Americans in his compartment.

To confuse the Americans he could easily say he wanted to go to the toilet once the train had crossed over to the eastern frontier and there go about finding an East German border guard and so releasing the secret documents he had about his person. But he was a bit concerned as to whether the West German authorities would check his passport on the Buchan side. He thought it highly probable that the decoding books which had come into his possession would have been noted by now, back at RAF Kuhlendorf. It might also come about that the German police could be tipped off as to John Jackson being the likely suspect. Therefore, he came to the conclusion that the authorities would not bother to check his passport as the train was going straight through to West Berlin. On the dot of 13.42 hours the train pulled out of Hamburg Hauptbanhoff and set about its journey.

Meanwhile his two American friends clearly wanted to make some meaningful conversation with the RAF escapee, but John was certainly not in the mood for chatting or otherwise. Instead, he had the Gaul to tell them he was taking a degree at Oxford University in electronics and sincerely hoped the Americans were not experts on such matters, although with his RAF training at both Compton Basset and Digby, he felt certain he knew a thing or two about electronics. He therefore decided to test them out and begin to ask a few inquiring questions. But it turned out the American's been in oil and knew nothing about electronics.

Just as well, he thought.

His newly acquired companions decided to enlighten John with their travel plans. It then transpired the Americans were going to West Berlin on a business trip and were absolutely thrilled to be going there, especially at the thought of going behind the Iron Curtain. But instead of flying they decided to go by train, rather than fly. John hoped they would not be able to notice anything unusual about his appearance as he was getting a little jittery about his false disguise. He endeavoured with some reluctance to conceal his long beard, wig and fake spectacles; but to his joy they did not seem to notice.

He knew from what the Fraulein told him at the ticket office that it took just fifty minutes after leaving the station before the train reached the Soviet zone. He also realised that German trains always run on time, unlike those in the UK. He kept looking at his watch, counting the minutes as the train passed through the magnificence of the German countryside. Then his worse fears were confirmed. A West German official entered his compartment and demanded to see his, 'Ihre Reisepass bitte', which John knew all too well they wanted to see everyone's passports. But was this normal practice John thought to check on peoples passports while the train was under way? He doubted it. It was probably just a routine check?

Up to this point of his journey it looked as though he would be caught red-handed. However, it was with a sense of anticipation together with the knowledge that something almost certainly would go frightfully wrong, when he was so near to fulfilling his dream. There was only one possible solution to his thinking. Sergeant Scott must have given John's name to the RAF police, who had then passed it on to the West German authorities. That could be the only explanation? John had noted with a look of surprise that the two officials on the train had examined the Americans passports and now wanted his. With a certain amount of trepidation he opened his top pocket and handed it over his passport over to the Police. Once they saw his name, 'John Jackson,' he was sure they would inform him he was under arrest and his bid for freedom would be thwarted, just when he seemed to have made it.

John's inner thoughts came to bear a sense of guilt. "Why on earth did I steal those documents? I could have easily asked for political asylum. It would have been my own stupidity if I had got myself caught, but to his amazement the West German policeman politely handed him back his passport and said. "Have a nice stay in West Berlin, Mr Jackson!"

To his immense relief they were letting him stay on the train. The fact remained he was not going to be arrested after all and it seemed his name meant nothing to the officials other than that of a presumed English tourist. In any event he could not believe his luck. Having arrived at Buchen station John felt conscientiously secure that he would not be discovered. Could there be another passport check, he wondered? Indeed, there was one aspect to his thoughts which with all his dexterity of disguise, could not conceal, or daren't. Perhaps somebody at Buchen would recognise him as being a British Serviceman? He alighted at Buchen railway station along with the two American passengers, where they waited for a reconnection to East Berlin. Twenty minutes later he was on his way to freedom. Or so he thought? The east bound train treaded its way through the openness of the German countryside and continued to head for the checkpoint border crossing. But what greeted John and his fellow passengers next was met with a feeling of total numbness. While a riveting conversation was going on with his two American friends the sudden and unexpected sound of rapid machine gun fire could be heard. For a split second there was a sense of panic. John decided to investigate the matter along with the other passengers. The sound was apparently coming from two watch towers that were positioned on either side of the track. The train had no option but to slow down and stop. The scene they were about to be witness was one of pure horror. There by the side of the railway track was the body of a man. It was the disfigured remains of a young man who had clearly been shot. The dead man was lying by the side of the track, face upwards, and apparently riddled with bullets.

"My God, they've just shot a man trying to escape over the wire." The American lady said disapprovingly. "It seems the poor guy was trying to escape to his freedom."

"It really comes home to you when something like this happens, and aren't we lucky to be living in the West," her husband confirmed.

John's face took on an expression of deep shock. He couldn't believe his eyes to what he had just witnessed. There was a stunned silence as his fellow passengers continued to gaze at the dead body. The American lady tried to say a few words of comfort.

Turning to John, she said. "Doesn't it make you feel how lucky you are to be British? All that poor guy wanted was his freedom but of course over here they shoot you rather than let you escape."

After a long delay the train finally continued on with its journey, leaving behind such dreadful scenes of devastation. John concluded that could have been him lying there in the freezing cold, riddled with bullets. "In fact the young man looked very similar to me, "but now he is 'DEAD'. John began to wonder, if perhaps, he was making a big mistake by becoming an East German citizen? Jankers was surely a lot better prospect than the harsh punishments this lot were handing out. When he first signed on in the RAF he thought it was wonderful, his ideal future. John summarised that perhaps he was making a big 'mistake' by defecting to the 'East'. Could there yet be time to prevent him from making another big mistake before it was too late? He considered for a moment the disastrous implications he had just witnessed and endeavoured to come to terms with the situation.

The train pulled into Schwanheide station. Schwanheide to John's delight was the said place he intended to make his bid for freedom. He had some serious thinking to do. He looked at the unwelcoming officials on the platform and the cold and grey looking foreboding buildings. Somehow he did not feel like attempting to go over to the other side? The sound of machine gun fire was still echoing in his ears. The next time it could be me they were shooting at.

Surprisingly, no other officials came into the compartment and soon the train eased its way out of the station. Should he, or should he not, give himself up? He suddenly remembered Gertrude. What if he ever wanted to return to West Germany to see her? Would he then be shot? He was beginning to feel that he would rather be doing his dreaded Jankers, where at least, after serving his time he could at least see Gertrude again. If he stayed in East Germany there was no such hope of seeing Gertrude or indeed England again. He suddenly had a craving to see the Old Market in Bristol again. He thought of the Clifton Suspension Bridge and the Mendip Hills where he used to go walking. Or was it just a pipe dream. In truth, he wouldn't be able to see those lovely hills again? He remembered his trips as a child to the beach at Weston Super Mare. John gazed out of the window at the uninviting flat landscape with the rain now beating down. Somehow East Germany did not seem a better alternative to one in the RAF.

It was at this point when an East German Immigration official came into his compartment. He asked the American couple whether they were going to East or West Berlin. "West Berlin" they both replied and were immediately issued with a Transitvisum. The official then turned to John and asked whether he was going to East or West Berlin? This was his big chance. Should he say he was seeking political asylum in the East and had about him a number of secret documents that would be of vital importance to their country?

The American couple looked at John with intense interest as they waited for his reply. "I'm going to West Berlin too." John replied. He at once realised this was not what he was supposed to say, but it was too late. The sour looking official handed him his DDR 'Transitvisum' and stamped his passport with 'DDR' and left the compartment. John had reached his decision and there was no going back. He would unreservedly go through to West Berlin and go back to the RAF and do his fourteen days Jankers, and thereby go back to making bed packs again. Maybe he would get a bigger punishment as a result of his little trip but it was still a lot better than being stuck in East Germany and certainly much better than being shot.

The train continued on with its journey through the same sort of flat unattractive countryside as it passed through the poverty stricken looking towns of Ludwigslust and Wittenberger. It began to dawn on John that he must have been out of his tiny mind to even consider living in such a miserable looking place where there was so much evidence of deprivation.

As the train neared the fringes of East Berlin a terrifying though had crossed his mind. The East German official who had issued his transit visa might have recognised him as being a serviceman from his passport. Perhaps they were planning to have him arrested and taken off the train to an interrogation centre by the Secret Police before the train crossed over to West Berlin. He noted that once or twice an East German official had passed by his compartment and peered in, as if to make sure the 'English espionage agent' was still there, ready to be arrested by the KGB.

While the train continued on with its journey John saw the same sort of watch towers that he had witnessed at Schwanheide where the unhappy East German lad had been machine gunned to death. The thought of these events continued to fill John's inner feelings with a sense of inner hysteria. In all probability he had been so close to sentencing himself to a living hell that would make Jankers seem like paradise.

Things came to a sudden climax when the train chugged its way through the confinements of a sprawling city. But what greeted him and his fellow passengers next was the unexpected sight of happy smiling faces. To his joy and relief he was back in Berlin once more and had arrived at Spandau.

It gradually began to dawn on him that his nightmarish hell could finally be over. He had escaped from East Germany and had reached 'freedom,' at last. The train finally pulled into Bahnhof Zoological Garten station, just a few minutes late, at 5.24pm. He said goodbye to his American friends and wished them a happy and safe trip. But little did they know however, how their simple remarks had persuaded him against making the biggest mistake of his life?

Having gone through every conceivable aspect of his intentions John made a conscious decision to get himself back to RAF Kuhlendorf as fast as possible. Therefore, the motivation behind his rationale thinking was one of extreme urgency. John ascertained that his immediate priority at this moment in time was to catch the next available train to the town of Tegel where he intended to alight and then another train to the town of Luneburg. Then from there it was a matter of picking up the Autobus which would finally take him back to the British Sector in West Berlin. It was a whisker away from 22.00 hours when John duly arrived back at base camp at RAF Kuhlendorf. He had exactly thirty minutes to change into his RAF uniform and report for duty to communications room 4c to start his night-shift. He couldn't have cut it finer.

On entering the very same barrack room which he had previously left, he saw his RAF 'pit' together with his locker and his RAF uniform and kit still undisturbed. This time he was determined to pull out all the stops and make damn sure he looked immaculate as his fellow officer, SAC Atkinson. But who should walk in at that very moment. It was Bob Gregory.

"Hey up, John! I thought you said you were going to spend the day with that lovely German bird of yours?" Bob inquired. "Gertrude Muller wasn't it?" John thought it rather strange as to how Bob Gregory knew her name as he had never mentioned it before.

"I intended to go and see her," John said, "but I changed my mind and went down to Luneburg instead, why do you ask?"

"Hey up John, it's just that she's been through to the NAAFI on the phone three times today. Apparently, she was desperate to speak with you. We couldn't find you anywhere so I talked to her on the phone for a while and said I would pass the message on to you. In fact her exact words were: please come back to me John, I love you very much and can't bear to lose you. I explained to her that you'd been put on Jankers for the umpteenth time and you found it impossible to get out of camp without getting into more serious trouble. She said she is very sorry that she was so unreasonable with you last week and now realises it wasn't your fault. My God Jackson! You're a lucky bugger to have such a fabulous bird as Gertrude. How I wish I had someone like her."

It suddenly dawned on John that perhaps being in the RAF for another eight years was not such a bad idea, after all. All he wanted more than ever was to get back with Gertrude once more, but now he would have to wait another fourteen days to see her until he had finished his new lot of Jankers. He decided that first thing in the morning he would nip over and see Gertrude before he went on duty.

As he boarded the compound bus he made a firm pledge to himself. This time he intended to pull out all the stops. Therefore, he made a firm decision to polish up his cap badge along with his shoes, press his uniform and then go about putting a clean collar on together with a regimental tie. He suddenly remembered he still had those wretched decoding documents on him and wanted more than ever to get rid of them before he started his Watch. If not, he would be in really serious trouble if they were found. It was imperative that the documents were not left in the barrack room overnight. They never search you going into the compound, but always going out. He therefore decided the safest thing to do was to smuggle them back inside the compound and then plant them back in the J2 room again.

Amazingly, John arrived at his Watch with a few minutes to spare and made sure there were no mishaps on the way in, and thereby duly relieved SAC Macpherson. This time he actually had both two undulators copying traffic, before John took over and Macpherson never swore once. About thirty minutes into his work John noticed Corporal Dickson had gone out of the room. This was his big chance to slip the decoding books back into the J2 room without anybody seeing him and out of sight of other personal in the vicinity, and hoped nobody would query him about his movements. They would otherwise think he was getting a replenishment of undulation tape. With nerves of steel he craftily slipped over to the J2 room, got the decoding books out and made sure nobody was looking. He then carefully slipped them under a pile of other documents and then went back to take up his position while taking with him a new roll of tape together with a logbook.

As he carried on working Sergeant Scott came in and sat at the supervisor's desk next to Corporal Dickson. John heard Sergeant Scott open a drawer on his desk. He was dying to have look round but thought otherwise. He carried on working and pretended to be concentrating on his work. John then heard Sergeant Scott speak to Corporal Dickson.

"What the hell are those bloody Eastern Bloc Decoding Documents doing in here? I thought the confounded things had been chucked out ages ago? Damn things are totally out of date and ruddy-well useless." In disgust, Sergeant Scott threw the said items into the administration waste paper basket.

As Sergeant Scott walked past John's position he at once recognised him. But what made John's return more remarkable was the fact that Sergeant Scott gave him the thumbs up together with the most incredible smile. All of a sudden Sergeant Scott was showing all the signs of being his best mate but it seemed he didn't have time to stop and chat. This was another pleasant surprise that John had not anticipated. However, he was slightly worried about getting a damn good rollicking when Sergeant Scott realised he'd been given a 'bum steer' on the previous night.

Once John had finished his stint on night shift he returned to his barrack room to get some sleep. He was absolutely exhausted and dog tired and was desperate to get to bed but at the same time he was determined to get out of camp first thing in the morning to see his beloved Gertrude that was of course if his charge hadn't gone through. He was just about to put his pyjamas on when LAC Smith from Station Headquarters came into the billet.

"Which one of you's SAC Jackson?" he inquired. John immediately identified himself as that person and was ordered down at the 'Disciple Office' IMMEDIATELY. His Charge Sheet had gone though. John immediately realised the moment of truth had finally arrived. This time he decided to pull out all the stops. Thereby, he put on his best blue uniform, and polished up his shoes in addition to his cap badge and then set off to the 'Disciplinary Office'. Once again the same trembling feeling came over him that he had experienced when he attempted to cross over to Eastern Frontier. It had come to John's attention that the Unit C.O. Squadron Leader Evans was to take the Charge, not Flight Lieutenant Carter.

Corporal Moss came in beaming from the officers married quarters where he awaited the dreaded moment of his being frog-marched-in to face the music. John at this point was understandably at his lowest ebb. Squadron Leader Evans was be bound to ask to see John's Conduct Sheet and the three previous entries and warnings he had been issued with. What made John utterly pig-sick was that the charge had come up so quickly. This would mean he would lose all his privileges which in theory would be in force with immediate effect. In the meantime he was confined to camp. It suddenly dawned on him that he would not be able to get out of camp to see his lovely Gertrude again, not until he finished his period on Jankers.

John pondered for a moment. If he didn't get out of camp Gertrude would regard this as deliberate attempt to snub her and thereby finish their love affair for good. He loved her very much and hoped and prayed that Squadron Leader Evan's might be lenient and just give him seven days or perhaps three or even four days, but he feared there was not a cat in hell's chance of that?

The Station Warrant Officer then marched John into the office behind the escort. "Left, right, left, right, left ... pick your knees up ... left, right, left right. HALT! Escort and accused, LEFT TURN." John stood there with his hat off before Squadron Leader Evan's who looked particularly stern and forthright. Details of the charge were read off, whereby Corporal Moss was marched in to give his evidence. He did so very professionally as he was so used to doing after the many 252s he had submitted for so many others, going through each of SAC Jackson's faults as commented on by Flying Officer Wilson with great emphasis and ending with these words: "In view of the untidy state of SAC Jackson's appearance and the very appropriate comments made by Flying Officer Wilson that he had disgraced 302 Signals Unit and D Watch. I therefore charge SAC Jackson with failing to comply with Unit Standing Order, number 3C, and Station Routine Order, number 516, paragraph one; both signed by yourself, SIR!"

Corporal Moss was marched out, and John noted a huge grin on his face as he left, obviously overjoyed at seeing him in trouble. John had come to the conclusion that Corporal Moss was an utter swine.

"Well, what have you to say for yourself, Jackson?" Squadron Leader Evans asked in a foreboding voice.

"Well sir, I'm very sorry. You see I overslept before my Watch started. I didn't have time to properly prepare my turn out. It won't happen again. I promise you in the future I will always be smartly turned out. I am very sorry to have disgraced the Unit, Sir." John knew it was hopeless? Or was it?

"Thank you, Jackson".... replied Squadron Leader Evans. "I accept your assurances and I do think Flying Officer Wilson was a little over zealous for an operational unit, particularly on a night shift, and I shall be speaking to him. "No, I do not think you have disgraced the Unit. Far from it Jackson, you have been anything but a disgrace to D Watch. It so happens that yesterday afternoon you were the cause of tremendous pride to all of us when I had talks with the C.O. and the Director of Operations. He went on to tell me"..................

"After you left the compound yesterday morning we copied the full traffic report and as a result we were able to break the Soviet cypher of the day. So what we got in fact was an early warning of an attempt to shoot down an American U2 intelligence flight and thereby took evasive action. Sergeant Scott tells me that it was 'YOU' who personally directed his attention at the very start of the operation which he could never have detected without your timely and knowledgeable advice. So Our Unit was way ahead of everybody else including all the American Signet Units. I've just received a highly commendable communiqué from the Home Office and the bottom line is: it was you and Sergeant Scott who has brought tremendous credit to us all. There is no question of my punishing you for such an unnecessary charge. Indeed, Jackson, it is my recommendation you are now very much in line for promotion. So, please don't appear before me again on any silly charges. "CASE DISMISSED. March Mr Jackson out, Mr Foster."

He didn't even ask to see John's Conduct Sheet!

John was frogmarched out of Squadron Evan's office, "LEFT-RIGHT-LEFT-RIGHT-LEFT" by the Station Warrant Officer. As John made his way back to his billet it suddenly dawned on him that he was sometimes wrong with his predictions in life. Well almost, he thought. Everything that had transpired over the last few days would remain his private secret. It was clearly evident that nobody should know about his trip to the Eastern Frontier? Furthermore, it was also imperative that no one should ever find out about his little escapade.

For a start his Passport along with the East German transit stamps would be thoroughly shredded, whereby, he immediately intended to apply for a new passport as soon as possible. However, instead of spending the next fortnight on defaulters or in East Germany, he would be spending every single minute in the arms of his beloved Gertrude. To make his comeback truly memorable John was married to Gertrude four weeks later. The announcement of his promotion to Corporal which meant no more making bed packs and his upgrading to the highest level of security clearance came through two weeks later. His very first duty in his new role as Corporal would be to provide a Charge Form 252 which would have the name, rank and serial number of 'SAC Atkinson' on the 'Charge against Form' for his 'laziness in his work performance. John was looking forward to seeing how 'that twerp' enjoyed being put on the same punishment as he had been subject to. Or maybe he will decide to cross over to the Eastern Frontier. That is of course if he's stupid enough!

Good Morning Vicar

Let me first introduce myself, my name is Cyril Stanley Saunders but just call me Cyril for now. I came into this world in the winter of 1939 and my place of abode at the time was situated in the plush borough of Bermondsey in London. I hence came from a big family that consisted of five brothers and three sisters. As I matured my main objective in life was to follow in my father's footsteps as a well-respected burglar, doing mostly houses and the occasional warehouse, but funnily enough the old codger collected stamps would you believe. (Can't be a bad bloke) My mother Aida, God bless her, took great pride in bringing us up and especially as we turned out a right load of thieves and scallywags, along with anything else that was associated with crime. I personally yearned for job satisfaction and independence. Yet for some mysterious reason I landed up getting nicked just before my fourteenth birthday - but anyway on with my story. Whether for this reason or another I got into more serious trouble just after leaving school, just when as I was beginning to the hang of things. Once I had reached my late teens I began to do even bigger jobs and getting more daring with it.

My big break came when I was approached by two talent scouts - villains that is. I was thereby invited to join a London mob called the 'Big D' outfit that was situated in the East End of London, and boy, I was on my way. They had the lot working for them, safe crackers, dynamite experts, forgers, and top-notch getaway drivers. The operation was run by a man called 'The Major', ex-army type who had previously been engaged in military type operations, here and overseas. It must have been around 1959 when The Major boasted he was going to pull off one of the biggest jobs in history. I was thereby summoned to a meeting at one of his many warehouses, whereby, all interested parties were to be given an in-depth briefing session. Standing on top of an old tea-chest stood proud our beloved leader. Little by little he began to give us the low-down on the job. The lights were dimmed and so began a short film session which unveiled the general layout of the robbery. The job as it turned out was going to be an armed robbery of a security van that belonged to a firm called Sutton and Cartwright, the very same people who specialised in the transportation of gold bullion and whose headquarters was situated in Church Grace Street, London. In the course of his briefing The Major outlined a combination of cleverly worked out strategy plans which went something like this. At the said hour a security van would thus depart from the bank loaded up with a shipment of gold bullion and cash to the tune of one million pounds or more. The priceless cargo would then leave the bank and tread its way through the city of London with military like precision. Lying in wait would be our firm, gathered together in two separate vehicles, ready and waiting to pounce. At a precise moment two things would happen. Firstly, smoke bombs would be used to knock out the guards and anyone in the vicinity. This was accompanied by the use of tear gas which would enable our gang to move in and immobilise the vehicle. The security van would then be winched on to a low-loader truck and hence taken back to our warehouse where we'd go to work on it with the acetylene equipment, thereby, cutting a hole through the rear doors and enter, thereafter. In short once the job had been successfully completed the gold bullion and cash would then be distributed amongst ourselves and hence going our separate ways, moreover, becoming stinking rich overnight. The Major in all his wisdom, described the job as the most audacious crime of the century. By now, the poor old chap had worked himself into a state uncontrollable frenzy at the very thought of getting his hands on all that lovely loot. So the scene was set for one of the most daring robberies to come out of London.

In any event the job went off like clockwork. However, in the ensuing days that followed the police and media people were quick to speculate it was an inside job. Little did they know however, it was the brain-child of our beloved leader? As I say the job went off like clockwork apart from one little mishap. Let's face it even the best-laid plans can sometimes go wrong. During the execution of the robbery my wristwatch had regrettably gone missing. The worrying thing was it had my name stamped on the reverse side of the damn thing. It didn't take long for the police to put two and two together which later led to my downfall. In fact a week later there was a knock on my door. The bogies picked me up and took me back to the local nick and later charged with armed robbery, along with the rest of our crew. So consequently as a result of my stupidity, in September 1959, I appeared before Bow Street Magistrate's court for sentencing. The Judge, a well-respected man by the name Lord Chief Justice Chaffney Brown, gave his rather disturbing verdict. Whilst standing there in dock he had the audacity to announce...

"Let the scrum bags rot in hell!"

In his final summing up, he said: "Cyril Stanley Saunders, you have been a thorn in the side to every police officer in the land and, as you've had previous form, I thereby sentence you to a term of twenty five years in prison."

To say I was devastated by his harsh sentence was an understatement. But little did they know I had the intelligence and wit to starch my share of the booty away. Only I and I alone knew of its whereabouts. What I had done in fact was to bury my share of the loot in the grounds of an old church called St Ethelbert's, just off the Wandsworth High Street. So with this in mind I had the great satisfaction of a vast fortune waiting at my disposal once I had done my porridge. Undoubtedly, all I had to do was dig the darned thing up as and when the moment was right. With twenty five years in the nick to look forward to all I could do was to sit back and bide my time. The first ten years was the worse really. However, whilst serving out my sentence I'd managed to strike up a remarkable bond with several of the inmates. Let me see now, there was Snowy, the picket pocket along with Charlie the get-away driver, Sid the forger, but not forgetting Gelignite George, safe blower and dynamite expert- all-in-all a right bunch of villains.

As time drifted wearily by incarcerated in the solitude of prison life, I made a firm pledge to myself. I therefore decided that I never wanted to go back to prison life, ever again. The years had taken their toll on me and had changed my whole way of thinking. I wanted more than ever to become a man of respectability - a man that people could look up to. Let's face it, having been banged up for the best part of my life I had plenty of time to do some serious thinking. In the end my plan was to buy me a slice of respectability.

Fifteen years had passed by when I summoned before the board of governors of to attend a review for parole. Mercifully, they granted me my wish. For being a model prisoner and for good behaviour they granted me my freedom. So as a result of my good fortune I was set to leave Wandsworth Prison, forthwith. The saddest part of it all was leaving my fellow inmates behind. I made them a parting promise to them. Once they had got their paroles sorted out my intention was to meet up with them in London for an old lags reunion and get ruddy-well plastered.

The following week I walked out of Wandsworth Prison a free man, armed with a rail ticket plus a few bob in my pocket. For the moment though, my most immediate priority was to make contact with a member of my family to see if they could put me up for a couple of weeks till I found a proper place to live. Thankfully, the reunion with Auntie Phil and Uncle Albert went down extremely well.

The following Monday, after breakfast, Auntie Phil sent me off with a packed lunch, thinking I was going on a picnic, but little did she know what I was up too. (Gold, lovely gold) I decided to catch the 239 bus and get off at the top end of Garrets Lane. However, as the bus sped along I couldn't believe how many changes that had taken place in my absence. New buildings had sprung up. There were so many cars and so many people. It would seem everyone had got themselves into a mighty big hurry.

Sometime later the bus roared up to Gordon's garage, adjacent to St Ethelbert's church. I was trembling with excitement at the prospect of getting my hands on all that lovely loot I had buried all those years ago, but more worrying was the thought, would the gold still be there? As I made my way through the church grounds I was horrified to find the place in a state of neglect. For a second I couldn't believe my eyes. Many years ago St Ethelbert's was a thriving church with a huge congregation, so what on earth had happened in my absence?

However, my observations did not go down, for it was impossible to overstate the grief that came over me. Part of the problem was made more wretched by the general state of the church grounds. The graveyard itself was greatly overgrown with weeds and bramble that has almost obliterated many of the gravestones. The windows were boarded up and blow me there was a 'For Sale' sign, positioned at the front entrance. However, my sadness quickly turned to joy as I cast my eye on a particular spot that was very precious to me. For over yonder stood a huge oak tree and just a few metres from it were the proceeds from the robbery.

But first I would need the necessary tools and equipment to dig it up. Also, the work would have to be done at night so as to keep away prying eyes. So with this in mind I made for the nearest hardware store to purchase the necessary items for the job in hand. For a while I flirted with the idea of going back that very night but my senses came back to me, knowing a little more planning was needed.

The following evening I managed to borrow my brother's pick-up truck and had loaded it up with the appropriate tools and then set a course for St Ethelbert's. As I poodled along I felt like one of those prospectors in California who had the gumption and guts to go searching for gold in the 1800's. Just like them I was filled with the same hopes and aspirations. On my arrival St Ethelbert's I immediately set about the task of pacing out the following measurements from the great oak tree. Twelve paces to the left, turn, then ten paces to the right.

Thankfully it was a moonless night which would help me no end. With the enthusiasm of a mule on heat I began the daunting task of digging, just like one of those Irish navvies. It must have taken me all of two hours to reap the rewards of my labour. There I was some six meters down and was momentarily gripped by fear of what might be down there, when I came across a rather ghoulish sight. There was a column of worms and maggots scurrying about, wallowing in a thick pile of mud. I proceeded to make good headway after my little scare when finally I struck something solid. Scraping away the loose bits of earth a big black box appeared before my very eyes. Well bless my soul. There it was my big black box. The very same box I had buried all those years ago. With great endeavour I grabbed hold of the handles and with a mighty heave I pulled it on to the grass verge. I immediately laid into it with my crowbar like a man possessed. Damn, the ruddy thing wouldn't open. The hinges were rusted solid. After two attempts with my crowbar it finally gave way and thus sprung open. What happened next filled me with an abundance of sheer joy. With gaping mouth I looked on in awe at the sight of beautiful, sparkling, gold bars, neatly laid out in rows of ten. It was my lovely gold as new as the day they were made. They were just lying there in bed, waiting for daddy to come along and tuck them up. In today's market the gold would probably fetch a small fortune. Boy, my head was going dizzy with excitement. What shall I do with all that money? I could buy myself a yacht, a big mansion, cars, tarts and even more tarts. But I must keep a clear head. Luckily, my brother's pick-up truck had a winch on the back of it. Ten minutes later the box was safely on board and without any further ado I made for the nearest exit point as fast as possible.

A few days later I contacted a middle man in the East End of London to dispose of the gold through his many contacts. Of course he'd take his usually 10% from the deal but I could cope with that. Once the necessary readies were converted into cash it had an estimated value of £800,000. One will get awfully bored counting all that lovely lolly out. No chance my old son, I gonna be rich and just loving it.

The following weeks were taken up with somewhat of waiting game; whereby I sat back, nervously biting my nails for the transaction of the gold to be eventually processed into cash. However, I had ample time to contemplate on what I was going to do with all that money. Then it hit me like a ton of bricks - the derelict church of St Ethelbert's. This could be the answer to my prayers. A flash of brilliance had suddenly shot through the ex jailbirds head. Cyril was able to ascertain that his main objective at this point of his good fortune was to buy the church in its entirety. He could thereby go about and have it thoroughly renovated to the highest standards possible. But here comes the whammy. Not only does Cyril intend to purchase the church but in addition his main objective is to become a fully fledged Vicar. Of course he would have to change his name due to his previous form, but he intends to call himself the very reverend, Cyril Harold Crumpington, minister of the cloth and the vicar of St Ethelbert's Church.

The poor punters will never know the difference," Cyril chuckled to himself.

Naturally I'll have to have elocution lessons in order to lose my cockney accent, but hey, my dream is finally coming true. At last I'm going to become a respectable citizen in life. I wasted no time in getting in touch with the estate agents (Griffin and Archer) who were handling the sale of the property. The asking price was £200,000, and being a bit of a wheeler-dealer in me time I offered them £180,000. A few days later my offer was accepted on behalf of the local council who owned the site. Once the appropriate paperwork had been signed I was in business. Anyway, having got the necessary quotes for the restoration work to be done, all I had to do was to sit back and bide my time till the work was completed. In the meantime I am going to live life to the full, buy me a new car, a house and all the trimmings that go with it.

It was six months later when I was sitting at home downing a double gin and tonic when the phone rang. It was the estate agents.

"Ah good morning Mr Saunders, or should I say, good morning you're Reverence. Griffin and Archer here, as you know we're the estate agents handling the sale of St Ethelbert's Church. I am pleased to inform that the restoration work has now been fully completed. The contractors are tying up a few loose ends but the good news is you can move in next Monday."

"Absolutely brilliant, my old china." Cyril chuckled.

It was by an incredible stroke of good fortune that the rest of my jailbird friends had managed to get themselves paroled. So consequently as a result of this welcoming news my immediate reaction was to make immediate contact with them. The reason for my sentimentality was this; I intended to make my brave band of villains an offer they couldn't refuse. More to the point, I was quite prepared to give my fellow inmates the chance to redeem themselves from their wicked and evil ways. Therefore I decided to offer them a position within the Church. Just think of the frightening implications. We'd have an assortment of burglars, con-men, pick-pockets and safe-blowers that would be the backbone of St Ethelbert's.

"Watch your handbags and purses ladies!"

At last, the day had finally dawned for the grand opening of St Ethelbert's Church and there was Cyril standing by the front entrance, fully rigged out in a vicars outfit and looking a right old twat if it may be told. With his new bucked teeth clanking away like a good-un, there he waited in eager anticipation to receive his congregation which indeed was most commendable. One by one they filed by till finally the church was packed to the rafters. But there was one late arrival.

"Ah, good morning my son," Cyril smiled.

"Good morning Vicar, sorry I'm late. What a lovely turn out. It's so nice to meet you. Bye the way my names George. I'm a retired policeman."

Gulp!!

As they stood there shaking hands George's face suddenly turned to a look of shock- horror.

"Excuse me for saying this Reverend but your face has a striking resemblance to a man I once arrested for armed robbery way back in 1959. Nasty bit of work if I may say so."

"Good gawd George, have I got a double lurking about, but I can assure you inspector I was cutting the cloth at that particular time."

Having taken in George's unwelcoming bit of dialogue we both managed to have a really good laugh at his silly bit of spiel, but deep down I was shaking in my boots, for I knew he was one of the policeman who had previously been on my case.

With the grace and dignity of a true vicar Cyril slowly but surely made his way down the aisle to the sound of an old fogey banging away on the organ, accompanied by the ghastly sound of highly strung choirboys who were singing as though their vocal cords had just been squeezed through a high-powered shredding machine. Holding a bible in one hand and a copy of the horse-racing journal in the other Cyril had noted with immense pride the abundance of people who had come to see their vicar in all his glory. Before he knew it he was standing on the pulpit about to address his congregation.

"Good morning everyone" Cyril smiled. "I would like to welcome you to St Ethelbert's Church. Glory be, for I am delighted to say I am your new vicar, Cyril Harold Crumpington, vicar of St Ethelbert's Church. My opening sermon is a text taken from the obscure book of nobbled horses and bent trainers, which in parts has been written in Latin and tongues which some of you may not perhaps be too familiar with so I'll let you have it in full verse.

(With fire in his belly and a gale force wind to match Cyril began his service)

"And so it came to Khyber Pass that a band of unscrupulous clergymen lay in wait in the stables of Babylon. Snorting vigorously was a handful of pedigree fillies owned by a God-fearing king called Marcus Bilious. (Bilious by name and bilious by nature) The king thus ordered that all his horses be trained by three foreign trainers who hailed from England, Ireland and Scotland. However, it was decreed by the King that all three foreigners were to be throw to the lions for their unscrupulous dealings with several members of the Jehovah Witness community, better known in the trade as the JW's, as well as more serious crimes, notably, for placing bogus bets on knobbed horses along with the more disgraceful practice of doping his horses, so as to lose the race. Just before the soldiers were about to throw the first of the trainers into the Coliseum there was a cry from the Englander, whereby he shouted, "Avalanche!" There was an immediate response among the soldiers of Babylon. In their panic to get away the Englander jumped over the wall and escaped to safety. However, the Scotsman and Irishman remained tied up and ready to be eaten by the lions - which by now were getting very hungry. The soldiers soon realised they had been thoroughly deceived by these people from a far off land. The soldiers thus returned to their positions and hence the Scotsman was frogmarched before the king. The soldiers pointed their spears at the Scotsman whereby King Bilious immediately ordered the kilted clansman was to be eaten by the lions, forthwith. But just before he was about to throw the Scotsman over the side the kilted clansman pointed to the skies and shouted "Flood." To avoid being drowned the entire garrison fled in panic. Thereby, the Scotsman jumpeth over the wall and escaped. After much debate the soldiers returned to their posts, infuriated they had been deceived for the second time by the fiendish cunningness of these people from far off lands. Hence, the Irishman was to have the full wroth of King Bilious. Once again the soldiers were just about to push the Irishman over the top to the starving lions when the Irishman shouted in a strong Irish brogue. "Fire you bloody heathens." And so thereafter the Irishman created a reduction in the earth's population by one mortal soul.

(The congregation were in raptures with Cyril's opening shot)

"The second part of my sermon is about the evils of betting and gambling. And I say unto you dear brethren, oh heavenly bookmakers and gentlemen of the turf, we thy servants of your mighty kingdom, sacrifice our praise and thanksgiving and most humbly beseech thee. Grant us the fruits and glory of your noble horse racing empire so that we may indulge in the occasional flutter at the bookmakers. Go forth my children and may your wallets be filled with lots of lovely wedge. We the undersigned beseech thee oh mighty God. We plead with you that our lottery ticket will come up trumps on a Wednesday and Saturday and may a few of us be filled up with the joyous spirit of the duty free wine and baccy from across the channel? Give heed to our prayers dear lord for I say unto you dear brethren, may the Holy Scriptures lift us to great heights - and least we forget one member of our church who goes by the name of Fred the Tread. I call upon this man to come clean about the disgraceful practice of selling dodgy remoulds to the unexpected motorist. And I say unto him, repent your sins or be castrated. He must enter the divine road to salvation and redeem himself. On a more happier note, dearly beloved, I say unto you dear children go forth and be blessed oh happy punters for the blinkers shall be worn at the three-thirty race at Newmarket, ridden no less, by Sir Galahad, and hopefully fellow Christians you may come away with a Pony or indeed a Monkey. Oh great father in that wonderful establishment called Broadmoor. May you be well and truly sectioned and strapped down in a strait jacket of that noble place? Forgive us oh heavenly father on the dole for we have sinned whilst sitting on the toilet smoking a dirty great reefer and glued to page three of the Daily Standard while frothing at the mouth and gloating at skimpy tarts flaunting their bits and pieces about. Oh Lordly, Lordly, Lordly, please look more favourably on thy whole church and let us leave with some urgency by the side entrance of Parkhurst Prison, and of course making sure you leave the keys to our salvation."

"And finally it gives me great pleasure that we are gathered here today to bring forth together two members of our congregation who wish to be joined together in holy matrimony, namely Julian the bent hairdresser and Simon the transvestite ballet dancer."

(A hushed silence fell through the church as the bride and groom appeared heavenly scented and beautifully attired)

"Dear Lord, I call upon you to commit this couple to a lifetime of vigour, strength and companionship, coupled with mature love. But I must stress to you dear parishioners that Julian wishes Simon to bear him a child, with some difficulty I might add. Lord, I therefore call upon you to lift up their vital organs to the greatest of heights, and may the marriage be enriched by a forthcoming baby in the presence of the Lord."

"Julian, do you promise faithfully to have and to hold, to love and cherish Simon's Hampton Court. And do you also swear by the grace of God that you will consume the marriage by giving Simon a baby."

"I say this you Simon and Julian." Cyril began with a cynical smile, "May you filthy pair of cross-eyed shysters have your cherries popped in the most gruesome way possible, and may your giblets be squeezed through a mincing machine at full speed with your unmentionables hanging on for dear life. Furthermore, your ring of confidence is to be painstakingly inserted with a dirty great red hot poker, thereby, vigorously twisting it till you scream out in pain, and lastly, may you both have the great pleasure of being well and truly "Rogered".

Julian trembled with a look of astonishment and said: "Well really dear and the price of butter."

"But who'll give the happy couple away? Will he please step forward?" The vicar asked.

From the rear of the church a man appeared. He slowly but surely made his way down the aisle towards the bride and groom. The man is question began to walk with a swagger and a wiggle; one hand was firmly placed on his hip while the other ran his hand through his shaggy brown hair. Standing there before the vicar was a stout middle-aged man who wore a lilac-coloured suit, pink shirt and a multi-coloured tie, and to top that lot, cemented firmly on his head was a motley brown toupee, better known in the trade as a Syrup. He then had the audacity to pirouette round and round like a floating ballerina as though he was about to break into a Swan Lake dance routine. In the background the congregation could hear the delicate rustle of nylon silk stockings that crackled majestically against the underside of his trousers, made more worrying by the constant twang of knicker elastic that slapped against the bareness of his skin, in addition to the overbearing reek of perfume that prevailed lavishly about his person.

The congregation couldn't believe their eyes. Was the man this way or that way they wondered, or was he one of the shirt-lifter brigade?

The man's voice then broke into a high-pitched feminine whisper at the same time feeling rather unsteady on his feet.

"Oh, hello reverend, my names Timothy Tucker but most people call me 'Fluffy-Bum'. Ere, I don't like to moan Rev, but I don't half feel queer."

"Are we ready to receive the rings?" Cyril smiled. A bony hand slithered out from a finely cut jacket followed by a long scraggy finger that pointed out in readiness for the big occasion. Simon and Julian's well-manicured hands had an almost a feminine look about them.

"Julie,Julie,Julie!" Cyril cried out with great passion. "Do you take this queen, I mean man, I mean queer to be your lawful bedded wife. Will you have and to hold, to love and cherish him, and do you Simon, swear that you will faithfully uphold and thereby play with Julie's Wurlitzer organ to the raucous tune of Great Balls of Fire. And do you both swear on the good book that your offspring will both follow in the same footsteps as bent bishops and defrocked clergymen who go about their business in a debauched and filthy manner?"

"Oh, we do, we do, we do, ducky," cried the happy couple."

"I now pronounce you man and midwife," Cyril sniggered.

The wedding ceremony itself was a rather splendid affair. The happy couple kissed passionately and lined up for the photos to be done. But then a rather disturbing thought had crossed the vicar's mind. Could this band of brazen, good-for-nothing hussies be wearing the latest streamlined pantyhose girdles - the very same girdles that incorporate such breath-taking features as the adjustable super strength side-panels, but not forgetting of course the reinforced gussets that are blessed with super-duper elasticised ribs that encapsulates ones vital parts to one of magnificent proportions?

(Cyril mutters under his breath) "Oh dear Lordly, it looks as though I've got a right load of ruddy whoofters on me hands - bent as ruddy cucumbers, the lot of em. But I must confess Julian had quite an impressive piece of machinery protruding from the lower parts of his abdomen, Simon however seemingly a bit on the lameness side. God knows what the buggers will get up to later on? I bet there're off for a good old threesome."

(Cyril continued) "And so ladies and gentlemen our service reaches its climax which I am delighted to say finishes on a high note. For you see the Lord moves in mysterious ways by working his purpose for his beloved worshipers. But what is that purpose you might ask yourselves? For only the good Lord knows."

Summing up the service: the congregation thus rallied to the aid of their new vicar by giving him a thunderous good handclap, simply intoxicated by his bazaar, if not eccentric teachings, especially with his outrageous theme.

(Cyril) "And so brethren it is with great pleasure I leave you with one last thought. Go forth my children and do not forget to go strictly kosher on your next shopping trip."

The vicar, battle weary but highly intoxicated with his bazaar sermon gave his final thoughts and summing up. "Personally, I thought things had gone magnificently well, apart from a good old moan from the mayor who was not very happy about the toilet arrangements."

"Reverend!" He fumed. "I must protest about the inadequate toilet facilities at St Ethelbert's. Urgent action must be taken about the high admissions of obnoxious smells we had to put up with during the service. I have taken the liberty of placing a small device inside cubicle two of the gent's toilet to measure the amount of melodiousness and polyvalence vapours.

"Oh poo wee," Cyril sniggered.

Later on Cyril I was joined by the Millington's and Mrs Rendlesham who were both parish councillors, who I must say, had a lovely pairs of rocks about her person. Both ladies had generously laid on a splendid array of sandwiches, cakes and tea in the church grounds. However, there was one burning question I wanted to ask Mrs Rendlesham.

"Tell me Mrs Rendlesham" Cyril began, "I've heard you've had the great distinction of singing with our church queers, I mean choir."

"Ah, but only occasionally vicar, but of course making sure that my back-side is facing in a north easterly direction and that the queers, I mean choir, have been fully defrocked and checking that their sceptres are pointing in a fully erect position, hence joining the choir."

"Well, thank goodness for that my child." Cyril heaved with a sigh of relief.

There in the far corner of the church stood the shadowy figure of our policeman friend, George, who by the look on face was still giving me the evil eye. Thus it seemed, George was still not totally convinced about my authenticity. The one burning question I had imprinted on my mind, would George through his many years on the force eventually find out about my true identity?

"For Gawd's sake leave it out Squire."

The Mystery of the Vanishing Inn

The geographical location for our story is set in the delightful town of Ashford in Kent. Here live two married couples who go by the names of Mike and Julie Taylor along with Dorothy and David Robinson. It must be said of the two couples that their warm outgoing personalities made them the centre of attraction and, gradually, folks became to realise what marvellous people they were. Let's face it, when you're in the prime of life, some folks like to put their feet up. Not so for these good people for they had one thing in common, the satisfaction and gratification of long term careers, and yet the most striking feature about the four friends was their everlasting ongoing friendship. Coupled with this amazing bond they had adopted the customary ritual of going on annual holidays together. Although established as nine to five, white collar workers, they had of course the usual ups and downs of modern day life, especially at having to endure the maddening routine of commuting to work each day. Over a period of time however it had become rapidly clear that their lives were dull, boring, and downright monotonous. They were fed up with the same old mundane routine. They wanted to try something a little different from their nine to five routine - something a bit more exciting and adventurous perhaps, but weren't quite sure on how to go about it. The moment of truth came in the form of a phone call.

Perhaps the most admirable quality about Dorothy Robinson was her organisation skills being she worked for a well-known travel company. Anyway, one day from out of the blue and for no apparent reason Julie received a phone call from her good friend Dorothy. So imagine Julie's surprise when further into the conversation a rather pleasant surprise unfolded which surprisingly came in the form of a holiday to Europe. This would take in a variety of countries that would include France, Spain and Andorra, and thus incorporating the wonderful cities of Paris, Toulouse and Barcelona, before finally finishing up with a lengthy stay in Gibraltar. The only thing required of Julie and her husband was to put down a small deposit and wait for the summer holidays to come along. And so, after much debate and haggardly between the two different parties a final decision was reached to go ahead with Dorothy's plans. All things considered it was altogether a thoroughly satisfying arrangement and indeed a lovely holiday to look forward to.

So it came to pass on a beautiful summer's morning their long awaited trip had dawned. In their desperation to get packed they spent the majority of the morning madly dashing about, trying to get themselves sorted out and flinging the last bits of remaining items in their travel bags at the same time going dizzy with excitement. Just as dawn was breaking the sound of a car horn heralded the arrival of a mini-bus, blasting its horn with maddening regularity.

"Good grief, that looks like Mike and Julie," Dorothy moaned. "Crickey, he's a bit early, its six o'clock in the morning for God's sake, what's the man thinking of."

It was indeed Mike and Julie beckoning them to get a move on.

"Just coming folks," David yelled from the upstairs window at the same time giving his two buddies a big wave followed by a two fingered gesture. Shoving the last bits of knick-knacks in their travel bags; they quickly made a bee-line for Mike's vehicle. Having satisfied themselves that everyone was of sound body and mind they set off in search of the M20 motorway, getting on at junction nine and then sailing past a multitude of towns and villages before finally catching sight of the sea and the Port of Dover.

Once on board the cross-channel ferry with their vehicle safely stowed below deck, they made a beeline to the forward section of the ship. From there they watched the English Coastline gradually fade away into the distance. France lay ahead and it wasn't long before Mike's minibus was rolling off the ramps and on to French soil. There was just enough time to grab a coffee and fill up with petrol, thereafter it was on to Paris and beyond.

The hours and miles had rumbled on with remarkable speed and before they knew it the four happy holidaymakers found themselves pulling into the small town of Foix, just south of Toulouse. Although it was originally decided to take the more direct route via Perpignan, and thus avoiding the mountains, Dorothy however had a sneaky little trick up her sleeve. Whether for this reason or another she decided to try something a bit more adventurous. Her plan was to veer off from the main drag and take the smaller single track road which according to the map had a special place of interest in store for them. It was a decision however they would bitterly regret.

Leaving Foix on a westerly direction the route goes up and through the mighty Pyrenees. Progress through the mountains was slow and difficult, and for much of the way the road got more menacingly as they journeyed through a series of tight hairpin bends and unyielding roads that were lined on one side by sheer granite rock. To make matters worse there were no crash barriers to protect them. One false move and they'd be careening over the side. The road twisted and turned in more abundance as they climbed higher and higher. Negotiating these twisty narrow roads was getting trickier by the minute; in fact the going was much tougher than they had anticipated.

Their only companions it would seem were the mountain goats that drifted in and out of the landscape. The scariest aspect of it all was the remoteness of the place. As if to emphasize the isolation of the area, all communications such as mobile signals had completely abandoned them. Being it was getting late and being the night was drawing in Julie suggested they should start thinking about finding somewhere to stop for the night. After driving for what seemed like hours and without any proper navigation equipment they began to wonder if they had accidentally drifted over the border to Spain.

"But don't they have border guards or such things?" Dorothy joked.

"I'm not really sure about that," David replied. "Now we're going out of the European Union I'm not really sure whether we're in France or Spain, but I'm not too bothered as long as we can find somewhere that's got nice clean sheets but without the bed bugs."

The four friends were quite happy to stay in the area for as long as possible so as to enjoy all the spectacular scenery.

The others pleaded with Mike to hit the gas pedal with a bit more urgency in order to find somewhere to stop. As they rounded a particularly sharp bend in the road a sign indicated of what lay ahead. Their pace quickened with feverish excitement as the four weary Brits came to a beautiful old ramshackle inn. Almost at once their spirits rose to unpredictable levels at the thought of nice warm beds and hot food. Their luck was in, a hanging sign indicated that hot food and accommodation was available. The inn to their amazement had all the characteristics of a fifteenth century coaching inn. 'La Couperin'.

"Must be French," David eagerly said, "look there's a French flag outside, let's go see if they've got any room?"

With suitcases at the ready and with an appetite like a hungry pack of dogs it was full speed on to the reception area. However, it began to dawn on the two couples that all was not what it should be. To begin with there was some sort of historical pageant going on. To their amazement there were lots of people milling about in strange costumes. Dorothy thought it rather strange that such an establishment in the middle of nowhere had managed to pull in so many people? The real surprise came when they further discovered there were no cars about, not even a telephone or a mobile phone. It was like being a time warp from another era.

Mike said he would take the mini-bus round the back and park it near some stables. Eager to try out his French vocabulary he thereby asked the stable boy if it was ok to leave his vehicle overnight.

"Ally vous a la cuppa," Mike joked.

"Vez-vous deux chambers double, pour un nuit s'il vous plait, monsieur," was the reply.

That's funny Mike thought, I don't recall that dialect?

Back at reception the others were trying desperately to get checked in, but no such luck. Thus the fact remained they found it nigh-on impossible to communicate with anyone. In the end they used the tried and tested method of sign language. In any event it was enough to convince the receptionist that these strange people from over the water wanted two separate rooms for the night. However, the receptionist's dreams were shattered in two split seconds when Dorothy began to holler at someone down the hallway.

"Now look here frogy old boy, Dorothy bellowed, "I want you with immediate effect to carry my two heavy suitcases up to my room. Come on man, get it together. For God's sake get a move on.

You know your work rate is absolutely appalling. You really do need to put a bit more oomph in your work." Dorothy shouted in a commanding voice which clearly revealed experience and expertise in giving orders to the working classes.

A man approached with a sword in his hand and by the look on his face he was about to chop someone's head off, namely Dorothy's. He was just about to whip his sword out when Dorothy did the most sensible thing. She did a runner.

"What a horrid man," Julie sighed.

A grand stairway led to the upper part of the inn. The rooms they found were clean if not antiquated, apart from a beautiful old four poster bed. Then in one bout of sheer madness, Julie, Mike, Dorothy and David decided to leapfrog from a standing position and launch themselves on the bed.

Just when things were looking up there was bad news.

"You're not going to believe this," David frowned. "There's no hot water, just a big jug, and to top it all there's no proper toilet facilities, just a great big lavabo bowl."

"Blimey, it's bit primitive round here," Dorothy moaned. "But nevertheless the beds look quite accommodating, if antiquated, but I suppose it makes it all the more charming and colourful. Let's face it, it's a welcoming change from the plush and expensive hotels back in dear old blighty."

"This pageant or whatever it is seems a bit weird," Julie puzzled, as if there's some sort of re-enactment going on."

"Yes, I agree, even more puzzling, it seems to fit in with the accommodation as there doesn't appear to have any proper toilet facilities, but I'm sure there's got to be a satisfactory explanation." Mike emphasised.

"Just as well I opened my bowels back there in the mountains," David joked. "I had the great pleasure of dropping something quite heavy and extremely smelly from a great height. You see folks," David began to explain. "In the fifteenth century the lowest of the low used to bung their waste out of the window, whereby it would land up into the courtyard below."

Dorothy held her nose and said. "Good grief!"

Later that evening the two couples ended the day with a hot meal served with all the trimmings. But the fact remained the inn had become somewhat of a pantomime. More and more had turned up at the inn and even more puzzling they were all dressed in fifteenth century costume - even the local Gendarmerie was not wearing clothes of the present era. Their suspicion's was interrupted by the arrival of the bill. The waiter hovered about for a few moments in hope of a tip, thus with some force he threw down the loose change. On the reverse side of the coinage was the figurehead of Louis the Seventh who presumably was the reigning monarch at the time. From that moment an unexplainable situation had developed. The whole atmosphere had suddenly changed to disbelief. The inn it seemed was not of the real world. The circumstances behind these strange occurrences did not escape comment. The four friends had come to the conclusion that the waiter had mistakenly given them the wrong coinage.

"Come to think of it, "David puzzled, even the dialect has no bearing on present times and yet the most striking thing about the place was how thoroughly charming and accommodating it appeared."

Undoughtedly, their main objective at the point of their holiday was to press on regardless with their travel plans. This was the assumption upon which everyone wholeheartedly agreed. The four friends would have happily stayed much longer in the area but obviously they had to make tracks.

The following morning they decided to enjoy a leisurely French breakfast coupled with a strong desire to gulp down as many coffees as possible. After breakfast they headed east, though the magnificence of Andorra, and thereafter cutting through a rugged mountainous area called Cadi-Moixero. The pleasant two-hour drive from Andorra took them through a timely introduction to Spain's changing landscape. For as they drove along they realised that their journey would be virtually indistinguishable from the day before, and once again this particular part of the world was filled with spectacular scenery. All traces of mountains had since disappeared as they treaded their through the openness of the Spanish countryside.

New images emerged of pleasantly rounded hills and fields filled with an abundance of olives and orange groves.

Sometime later, Mike's mini-bus rather reluctantly chugged its way into the magnificence of Barcelona having endured its epic journey across the Spanish mainland. After a quick sightseeing tour of the city it was full steam on to Gibraltar. They motored south via the coast road and thus passing through such places as Alicante, Malaga and Marbella.

It was a whisker away from twenty two hundred hours when the four weary Brits finally arrived in the confinements of Gibraltar. At the Spanish border crossing they were greeted by two English customs officials who politely asked for their passports. However, their passports reflected a look of great surprise on the officials face.

"Ere, I don't believe it", the officer said with some surprise. "Aren't you that lot that's appearing in "Babes in the Wood" at the Golders Green Hippodrome," he smiled.

"Good lord no officer," we're from the East Grinstead "Carrot Crunchers Club," Mike replied back with a cheeky little grin.

"Welcome to Gibraltar," the customs man smiled.

An agreement had been reached between the Robinson's and the Taylor's. As from now on they'd be doing anything along the line that took their fancy, so having said that, their stay in Gibraltar was characterised by the incredible number of attractions that were on offer. Therefore, the remaining part of their holiday would be taken up with a multitude of exciting activities. Hence they hiked the hills and walked the walks. Biked here and biked there. Surfed the surf and swam the swam - climbed the rock and saw the docks. Hit the highlife and done the pubs - intermingled with a day trip to Tangiers.

However, it goes without saying that their time in Gibraltar had flowed by with remarkable speed and the fact remained their holiday to this part of the world was coming to an end. It must be said however that no one wanted it to end, but like all good things in life their love affair with Europe had abruptly peaked. It was time to head back to dear old blighty. The night before they were due to leave Dorothy summoned everyone together for a farewell drink. In the final summing up of their trip Mike took upon himself to say his little party piece after downing several bottles of cheap wine.

"A toast ladies and gentlemen," as Mike staggered forward, hardly managing to stand up. "Here's to absent friends, past and present."

"I would also like to give a toast," David said, as he chinked his wineglass against the others. "Here's to all my fluffy and furry friends back in dear old blighty."

"I'll certainly drink to that," Julie said, as the others raised their glasses in approval.

In the course of their celebrations Dorothy had come up with another one of her brainwaves ideas. She suggested they pay a return visit to that lovely old inn they stayed at in the Pyrenees.

The following morning the two couples bore all the hallmarks of a thumping great hangover. Eager to retrace their steps it was once more to the wandering road. Leaving the delights of Gibraltar behind it was onwards oh great adventurers. The hours and miles had passed by with remarkably speed as the four weary Brit's had finally reached their objective - the sight of the old inn. Or so they thought. For almost at once a wary look of numbness had crept into the equation for their observations did not go down well, in fact they were struggling to come to terms with the situation. For reasons unknown the inn to their displeasure had completely vanished without trace.

In conclusion to this intriguing mystery and on the face of it there seemed to be a perfectly reasonable assumption that something that resembled an old inn had definitely been there and not by any stretch of the imagination could they have foreseen the events that lay ahead. As the night wore on a decision was reached to make camp for the night next to a crumbling old ruin. Perhaps tomorrow would throw some light on the matter.

In the early hours of the morning things began to go frightfully wrong. They were awakened by the sudden crack of a whip and the thunderous sound of horses. Peering through an opening of their tent the four friends were stunned to catch a glimpse of something quite extraordinary. From their vantage point they witnessed a procession of white transparent figures that floated majestically through the night air. It heralded the arrival of a coach that was being pulled along by a team of horses. The coach or whatever it was had drawn up at an old coaching inn. The head coachman jumped down and politely opened the carriage door to which revealed a beautiful young lady who was dressed to the nines in full regal costume as though she was going to a grand gala ball.

"What on earth's going on?" David scarily asked.

It was plainly obvious that some sort of strange macabre phenomenon had occurred. There could be only one possible explanation to their nightmarish ordeal. What they had witnessed in fact was clearly a ghostly presence from the past, perhaps a throwback in time. The figures they saw looked for real. Thoughts flashed through their minds for an explanation. The scantily lit darkness of the night seemed to extinguish all traces of their encounter. Meanwhile, when everything went back to normality the two couples dozed off to a peaceful sleep. How long they had slept no one knows, but their sleep must have lasted long for they woke refreshed but nevertheless clearly shaking from the previous night's occurrences. Subsequently, as a result of their harrowing ordeal they decided to seek help in a nearby village and there pay a visit to the local Gendarmerie.

Sometime later they arrived at a nearby police station, whereby, Dorothy painstakingly explained to the Gendarme the terrifying events that had taken place the previous night. He listened carefully to her story but then rather disbelievingly shook his head. Dorothy showed the constable the exact spot on the map where the incident had taken place.

The constable's lips curled with a cynical smile and listened sympathetically.

"I can understand your concern Madame, but you see there is no inn there, just an old ruin. What you have shown me on the map doesn't exist. You see, Madame, there was an old inn there some five hundred years ago but it was completely destroyed by fire, all you'll find up there is a crumbling ruin."

Dorothy was not satisfied with the constable's explanation. She therefore made further inquiries at the local tourist information office. There, Dorothy received the exactly the same news - for it was just like the constable had said, there was absolutely nothing there apart from a crumbling old ruin and to this day no one could throw any meaningful explanation as to the mysterious chain of events that took place in France on that fateful night.

(Footnote) This particular story is based on true facts.

The Amazing Adventures of Freddie Frobisher

Our story begins at the headquarters of MI6 in London, home to counter intelligence. The hierarchy have the unenviable task of finding a new recruit for a very important mission. That mission is to send an agent to RAF Felmersham in Lincolnshire and there to escort a rocket to the breakers yard for decommissioning. After hours of sifting through a mountain of CV's, the top brass were still undecided on whom to pick until they came to the bottom of the pile.
"I say, Alex old boy, what about this chap."
"Mmm, I don't know, if you ask me he looks a bit on the peculiar side. Personally, I think we need someone of top quality, someone brave, commanding; someone not afraid to show his metal!"
"But Alex, we've tried every possible agent in the book!"
"Well," Charles sighed, "we have one more candidate to look at."
"What's his name old boy? "
"He's called special agent Freddie Stanley Frobisher.
"That's our man." Charles points on seeing his CV.
(Alex looks truly horrified)
"You want that idiot! For God's sake man he looks daft as a brush. To say he looks mad is an understatement? Furthermore, the man's obviously off his rocker."
"But Alex, look how fearless he looks. You've got to realise old sport that good agents are hard to come by! Don't be fooled by his rather odd appearance for behind that genial mask lies a ruthless mean operator."
(Frobisher's pride and reputation was at stake here. However, a spy was one thing but being a complete twerp was another)
"Are you stark raving bonkers Charles? This chap according to his CV hasn't worked for the last couple of years! Apparently, he had to give up work because he was hooked on giant gob-stoppers. In fact, it says here, after graduating from Oxford (municipal bus

company) he turned his attention to the more serious business of Winkle Picking in the Thames Estuary."

"Oh, for heaven's sake Alex, don't be such a spoilsport. Look, let's give the man a break. I've never been so sure in all my life. I bet if we throw in a few gob-stoppers he'll be a complete success."

After further consultation Alex and Charles agree to bring in special agent Frobisher for an interview. The following week Freddie is summoned before MI6 in London. There standing before the top brass was a man looking totally bemused with himself. But like a true blooded agent, Freddie throws his bowler hat at the coat stand, misses, and almost knocks out one of his superior officers, along with Miss-Spend-a-Penny. In charge of the operation was a man called 'The Commander'. All eyes were focused on the Commander. The Commander's chair swivelled round and round, thereafter, to reveal a man of his later years and bizarrely dressed in an old boiler suit as though he'd been doing an oil change on an old jalopy.

"Ah, Frobisher, you've arrived at last". The Commander smiled. "My dear boy, do please come in and I must apologise for having disturbed your afternoon nap." the Commander blasted. "Right, let's get the preliminaries out of the way. I order there be marching music of the most military kind," he insisted. The Commander's orders were duly carried out. With a true taste of British eccentricity, the top brass stood to attention; click the heel of their boots together, accompanied by the deafening sound of regimental marching music.

"Atten-shon! Everyone face south with fingers in ears and salute our beloved leader The Commander."

(At the end of this bazaar ritual Freddie's mind begins to wander and begins to scratch himself)

"Now look here Frobisher, pay attention! I've got a very important assignment for you. I want you to get your back-side up to RAF Felmesham in Lincolnshire and there you are to take charge of the mighty Thunderbolt Rocket. Your job is quite simple. You are to escort the rocket to the breakers yard for decommissioning. Is that clear," the Commander shouted loudly. The Commander then pointed to a picture of a rocket. On seeing the sight of a dirty great rocket, Freddie prefers to hide in the closet and there to indulge in a jar of gob-stoppers.

"Come, come Frobisher, don't be frightened! What are you; a man or a mouse?"

(Freddie gives a confused look and immediately checks down his trousers to make thoroughly sure he's a man)

"For God's sake man, you're secret agent Freddie Frobisher, commonly known as 006 and a half. The Commander insisted, and don't you forget it. By the way Frobisher, they tell you've laid everything from here to Timbuktu. Is that true? And I do believe you like it shaken, not stirred."

(From his briefcase Freddie pulls out a brickies trowel)

"Pa-pa put it this way ga-ga-guv, I've done so much, la-la-laying, me pa-poor old trowels worn out!"

"What! What the hell are you mumbling about Frobisher? Look, all I want to know is whether you can do the job?"

(In sheer frustration Freddie is compelled to break wind)

"Ah, well-spoken Frobisher." The Commander smiled.

(The Commander then beholds a set of keys in his hand)

"Here Frobisher, as a special treat you can take the Ardly Canardly."

"The Ardly Canardly guv."

"Yes, that's right; she can get down hills, but can-ardly get up em."

(Parked outside was the sight of a dustcart)

But dirty dealings are afoot - because quite oblivious to MI6, lying in wait in a block of offices across the road was the evil pair Moriarty and Jockstrap whose sole intention was to kill Frobisher in the most gruesome way possible. By way of binoculars and a concealed microphone, the evil pair was busily casting their beady eyes towards MI6's building.

"Look Jockstrap, I can see him; that bumbling fool, Frobisher!"

"Yes, yes, I can hear him Moriarty, there're coming through loud and clear."

"What are they talking about?"

"Apparently the top brass are about to give Frobisher a very important mission. There're sending him to RAF Felmersham and there to escort a rocket to the breakers yard would you believe."

"Where is he? Let me see him! I'm going shoot him. Come on let's get it over with!"

"For heaven's sake Jockstrap, don't do it like that. It's too good for that half-witted fool! I want to make him suffer. I want to gouge his eyes out one by one and then slap him round the face with a wet fish. I want to see him fry in a tub of boiling hot fat. I then want to cut him into tiny little pieces and serve him up to my cats!"

"I can see the baboon. Let him have it, kill him now Moriarty!"

(Jockstrap and Moriarty begin fighting over the gun)

Don't be a fool Moriarty, give me the gun!"

"No, you can't have it!"

"Give me the bloody thing before it goes off."

In the scuffle that follows the gun accidentally goes off with an almighty bang which causes the bullet to ricochet off of MI6's window. It thereby hits a power cable which plunges the building into complete darkness.

(Jockstrap and Moriarty look horrified)

"I told you so Jockstrap; every time we try and kill that bumbling idiot it always ends up in disaster. We need to finish him off once and for all!"

Therefore, having failed to kill their arch enemy the evil pair decide to pack up and head for RAF Felmersham. But before Freddie had the chance to leave MI6's building he was being issued with the latest gadgetry that would make his mission go off with a bang.

And so it came to pass for an hour and more the dustcart sped happily through the open countryside and encountered a series of tight hairpin bends, followed by the ghastly sight of huge pot-holes that were in great abundance. This brings things to a grinding halt outside the local sewage works - whereby the Ardly Canardly wallowed in a sea of great splendour, amid the stench and smell of raw sewage which left an awful lot to be desired. With nerves of steel the bumbling agent pressed on regardless and was rewarded by the sight of a military establishment. It was none other than the perimeter fence of RAF Felmesham. But just as Freddie was about to drop his load of council waste the inevitable happened. The dustcart hit a dirty great manhole in the middle of the road which caused the dust-cart to buck wildly like a horse. To all in the vicinity it sent out a clear message of a -'neigh-noddy-neigh-noddy-neigh-noddy-neigh'.

The moment of truth came when the Ardly Canardly let out a cry of great anguish as Freddie tried to negotiate first gear. Not knowing what to do the haphazard agent decided to pull a number of knobs and levers. The dustcart let out more dirt and dust but in greater volumes. The Ardly Canardly was much harder to operate than Freddie had anticipated. He opted to shove the thing into reverse gear which had the desired effect of sending the beast bombing down the road at a top speed of 20mph. Two policemen who were standing by the roadside with their note-books at the ready watched in horror as the Ardly Canardly went zooming by.

"Ello ello ello, who the ruddy hell was that?"

"Blimey Sarge, the idiots in reverse gear."

"He's driving like a bloomin maniac!"

"Hey wait a minute, I recognise that face. It's that half-witted fool who works for MI6 called Freddie Frobisher."

"Yes, I've heard all about him. The man's a walking time bomb!"

"He's probably on an assignment."

"I'm going to make an arrest!"

"No, you better not do that otherwise you'll have MI6 on our case. Best let him carry on."

But as luck would have it the dustcart suddenly breaks down just as Freddie was beginning to get the hang of things. By a stroke of luck a flashy sports car pulls up which revealed a beautiful young lady.

"Is something wrong," the girl asks?

"My ca-ca-cart's ba-abroken down," Freddie stutters. (The girl looks confused.)

"You're what! What did you say?"

"My ca-ca-cart's ba-broken!" Freddie pleads. (She looks sad and sympathetic.)

"Oh, your heart's broken?"

"No, me ruuddy ca-cart's ba-broken! Ca-can't you ruddy un-undersstand English?"

"Oh, you don't understand English, Herr Fonggruggler?" she jokes.

(Freddie begins sucking a giant gobstopper.)
"No, I da-da-don't understand English!" Slurp, slurp.
"Do you need a lift darling?"
Oh, yes please, I've got to get to report to RAF Felmersham in a hurry!" Freddie pleads.
"That shouldn't be a problem. You seem like a nice man. What's your name?"
"My name's fa-fa-fa-Freddie."
"Oh Teddy; I like that name!"
"No, no, it's fa-fa-fa-fa-Freddie, not Teddy?"
"What was that you said? You're ready?"
"No, I'm, fa-fa-Freddie."
"Oh never mind that now. My name's Sally G!"
"Cor, Sally G. Is it short for anything?"
"It's short for Sally G. String, but you can call me Sal."

The passenger door is abruptly pushed open which enables the haphazard agent to jump in. Once inside Sally smartly pulls up her skimpy mini-skirt, there to reveal a gorgeous pair of thundering great thighs. Hot and flustered by the sight of Sal's legs, Freddie tugs at her mini-skirt in a desperate attempt to wipe his snot infested nose on it. Sal's mini-skirt went higher and higher to her midrib area, and thus portraying the tiniest of throngs. Sally talks seductively. "You realise I'm going to take you all the way honey."

Overcome by emotion, Freddie wipes his forehead in nervous anticipation with his usual chat-up line: "Ere, I tell you what darling, I don't like to brag, but I ain't half got a biggen," Freddie chuckled. Sally licks her lips at the very thought. However, the only thing on Freddie's mind at this moment in time was to do some laying with his faithful old trowel. Sally looks on in frustration, as Freddie prefers to suck a giant gobstopper. "Slurrrrp, slurrrrp."

A little way due west of Lincolnshire's fenland lies RAF Felmesham the reputed home to the largest selection of alcoholics, whoofters, and work-shy lay-abouts. Following the Commanders directions to a tee, Sally's car finally draws up to the entrance of a military establishment. Waiting outside was the sight of three government officials, eccentrically dressed in black evening dress, bowler hated and top-tailed. Their job is to make Freddie's mission go off with a bang - and by gad, that it certainly does.

The car door opens and out step the happy couple. From Freddie's back pocket a pair of ladies briefs suddenly appear. To make matters worse his flies were undone. Totally encapsulated by all the excitement Freddie wipes his forehead with the briefs, thinking them to be a handkerchief, but soon realises what they are. To add to insult, a bra falls precariously from his briefcase. Without any further ado, Freddie is introduced to all three of his new colleagues, who strangely go under the name of Reggie.

"Good grief, that must be that bumbling idiot Frobisher, and by George, the lucky bounders got a beautiful girl with him," one of the officials points out.

"Oh hello," Freddie smiles, as he mumbles something to himself. "That's the last ba-ba-bloody time I da-do a sa-service on her!" Freddie moans as he beholds a set of spanners together with a pair of nylon silk stockings.

"Ah, you must be the famous Freddie Frobisher; the one they claim is the one short of a full pack of dolly-mixtures. Please, allow me to introduce myself; I'm Reggie, and this is my other two colleagues called, Reggie and Reggie."

(Freddie goes to shake Reggie's hand, but discovers there's a pair of ladies panties protruding out from his inside pocket)

"I don't know how they got there."

(There is more confusion, as the three officials stare intensely towards Freddie's flies)

"Flies!" Reggie1 points.

"Flies!" Reggie 2 shouts loudly.

"Your flies!" Reggie 3 persists.

"There aren't any flies round here," Freddie smiled.

"Your flies!" Reggie 2 repeats.

(Again the officials' point in the direction of Freddie's flies, and yet again Freddie tries to work out what they are saying)

"Do your flies up man!"

(Sally comes to his rescue in the nick of time as agent Freddie suddenly realises his flies were undone)

"I knew the man was a ruddy pervert!" Reggie 1 informs his two other counterparts.

"Now where was I before I was so ruddy interrupted? Ah yes, I would like to introduce myself, along with my two other colleagues. This is fellow agent Reggie. Reggie-Freddie-Freddie-Reggie-Reggie Freddie."

(In total confusion, Freddie shakes the hand of all three Reggie's)
"Reggie-Freddie-Freddie-Reggie-Freddie-Reggie."
"On, and don't forget me, my names Sally."
"Sally-Reggie-Reggie-Sally-Reggie-Sally-Reggie."
Finally, Sally shakes the hand of all three agents.
"Reggie-Sally-Sally-Reggie-Sally-Reggie-Reggie-Sally."
"See you later Alligator in a while Crocodile". Sally joked, as she zooms off in her car and so leaves Freddie to get on with his work.

"Right Frobisher, let's get down to business, the rocket's this way," Reggie 1 points.

But dirty dealings are afoot, because hidden from view were the evil pair Moriarty and Jockstrap who are getting ready to pounce.

(The scene is a rocket sitting on its launch pad, whereby Reggie 1 begins to demonstrate the workings of the rocket)

"Here we are Frobisher, do please step inside the rocket and make yourself comfortable. I'll start by showing you the display sequence."

"Cor it's nice and comfy in here! What are all these instruments for?" Freddie asks.

"Never mind what they're for. All you have to do is stay with the rocket while it's being transported to the breakers yard. Now whatever you do, don't touch any of the switches on the control panel or you'll end up pushing daisies!"

"Da-da-da-don't wo-worry governor, I wo-wo-won't touch it."
"What did he say?" Reggie 3 frowns.
"I don't know what he said?" said Reggie 2.
"I can't understand a word the man's saying!" Reggie 1 moans.

Freddie's mission seemed perfectly straightforward till his curiosity got the better of him. To Freddie's delight the rocket was blessed with all the latest gadgetry that will make his mission go off with an almighty bang. Inside the cockpit area Freddie wallowed with idle curiosity at the extraordinary mass of equipment on board. Not knowing what to do Freddie decides to press one of the numerous switches on the control panel. This unfortunate act of madness manages to ignite the rockets firing mechanism which causes the rocket to spring into life. The Thunderbolt gave a triumphant hoot of its horn, accompanied by a thick column of black smoke together with a mighty roar of its mighty engines.

The Thunderbolt was now fully operational which had the desired effect of sending the beast haring down the launch pad. Under the force of tremendous acceleration it pushed the rocket nearer and nearer towards the abyss. It was indeed a truly magnificent sight to behold as the Thunderbolt headed to the far reaches of outer space. Intermingled with all this frantic activity Freddie was busily amusing himself with the two-way radio on board. As luck would have it, the bubbling agent found himself on a mission to Mars as he is blasted into space. Suddenly the world was put on high alert as governments around the world were forced to go on red alert, fearing an international incident was seconds away from disaster, whereby a rocket was crazily out of control, packed with TNT and being self-propelled by a mad-man who was high as a kite on rocket fuel. From every corner of the globe planes were rolling down the tarmac in hot pursuit of a runaway rocket. In the aftermath of this amazing feat the Thunderbolt had managed to reach the magical height of 60,000ft. That's when Freddie noticed a formation of unidentified planes that were hot on his heels. If he didn't watch out he'd be on the receiving end of a damn good tonking. But before they could get a fix on the rockets position the Thunderbolt had managed to leave the earth's atmosphere and had entered into a state of blissful weightlessness. Having failed to destroy the out of control rocket the aircraft returned to their respective bases.

"Tally ho chaps here I come!" Freddie yelled as he is blasted into space.
Meanwhile back at the ministry the boffins were somewhat mystified by the complete disappearance of their prized possession

which had mysteriously vanished into thin air. From a safe distance Moriarty and Jockstrap looked on in awe as their archenemy had managed to escape, yet again.

"I don't believe it Jockstrap! He's managed to launch the ruddy rocket!"

"That bumbling fool has done it again! He's a menace to society!"

"Come Jockstrap; we will follow him in our own rocket and go after him"

"Are you crazy, we haven't got a rocket?"

"You wanna bet; look over there, there's another rocket sitting in its silo just waiting to burn some rubber. I'm gonna kill that scumbag Freddie Frobisher! I'm gonna kill him!"

"No I'm gonna kill him"

"No I'm gonna kill him Jockstrap!"

(The evil pair began to fight on whose going to fly the rocket as they try in desperation to ring each other's neck s, when finally they come back to their senses)

"Don't kill me you fool. It's Frobisher we want to kill!"

"I've hated Frobisher ever since we were in science class together."

"Yes, I can still remember that terrible incident you encountered. It was when Frobisher mixed up all the wrong chemicals in your test tube. To put it in a nutshell there was a terrible reaction which resulted in a massive explosion. In fact didn't it blow your vitals off, old boy?"

"Yes, it's quite true Jockstrap. As I recall the doctor told me I'd be impotent for the rest of my life."

"Don't rub it in Moriarty. I hate Freddie Frobisher. If it wasn't for him I could have been a success in life. I could have been somebody; a guardian of the peace; a figure of renown; a leader of men! In other words, a man's man!"

"Well really dear, don't rub it in." Jockstrap replied with a sense of embarrassment.

"Just think of it, if it hadn't been for your accident, weren't in line for promotion as science master? But tragically, Frobisher took that away from you."

(Moriarty begins to cry)

"Yes, it's true Jockstrap. Shortly after this dreadful business had transpired I was invited to attend a fancy dress ball that was being held in London. In attendance would be the dreaded Freddie Frobisher along with other high raking dignitaries from all walks of life. I was well informed that Frobisher would be dressed up as the famous Henry VIII. This was my big chance to eliminate the bugger once and for all. I therefore decided to go there dressed as a policeman. With my trusty truncheon at the ready my mission was to plant one on Frobisher's head with the greatest of force.

Anyway, while in the course of my duties I had managed to dish out several parking tickets, when all of a sudden I caught sight of Frobisher's ugly bonce. I immediately dashed across the banqueting hall and thus withdrew my truncheon, and, in true policeman style I thereby whacked it over the head of the said person.

However, to my horror my observations confirmed it was none other than the Archbishop of Canterbury's head. I was immediately escorted from the venue and thrown out on to the streets with compliments from the management that I would be receiving a court summons from the archbishop.

Meanwhile, while travelling through space at an unrelenting speed the second stage of the rockets breaks away from the main fuselage, leaving the Thunderbolt to carry on with its mission - destination Mars. Meanwhile back on earth, the Commander's feelings were running pretty high and was feeling increasingly frustrated by his inability to contact his bungling agent. In fact he was plainly in the mood to cut off Frobisher's head and thereby feed it to his cats. But to his gratification Freddie receives a communiqué from MI6 which brings bad news.

(A vacuum cleaner (UFO) comes into view)

"Frobisher! We've just picked up a signal on our satellite equipment and apparently you've got a vacuum cleaner, hot on your tail.

"I've got what on my tail?" Freddie inquisitively asked.

"That's right, a vacuum cleaner. We firmly believe it's the Hoover upright model, the one with the bag at the side. You know, the one that beats as it sweeps as it cleans."

"Ere, leave it out Gov, you're having me on."

(Freddie receives another message from the Commander.)

"After further investigation we've managed to identify the mystery object. We're not so sure if it's a vacuum cleaner after all but we've come to the conclusion that it's definitely a UFO. So for God's sake man, get the hell out of there before it's too late."

Tension mounts as the two probes are dangerously out of control and are heading straight for each other, teetering on the edge of disaster. In an attempt to avoid a collision with the weird-like vehicle, Freddie tries to manoeuvre the rocket away from the oncoming probe. But should he manoeuvre the rocket to his port or starboard side, he thought? However, peering out from the mysterious vacuum cleaner were eerie, grey-like creatures who were busily studying their monitor screens and watching the rockets every move. However, little did Freddie know that the alien powerhouse had the capability of penetrating deep inside the main hub the rockets interior which enabled their sensors to pick-up any life forms?

While the Thunderbolt maintained a constant orbit around the Moon it was being carefully being monitored by a dedicated team of top scientists back on earth. On the bridge of the strange shaped UFO (vacuum cleaner) was their leader along with the rest of the alien crew, whereby the Captain of the vessel was busily conferring with his crew.

(The Captain) "We seem to be on collision course with a runaway rocket. Are there any signs of intelligent life?"

"None Captain! There doesn't seem to be any detectable life forms or energy source.

(The scanners continue to pump out vital information about the Thunderbolts support system which according to their monitoring equipment has revealed the presence of a strange mumbling sound)

"Hey, wait a minute," a confused alien announces. "There seems to be a minuet blimp coming up from the sensors. There appears to be a humanoid but without a brain."

(The aliens looked at each other in astonishment and were somewhat mystified by this unusual statement which was fast developing into somewhat of a mystery)

"No brain! Why that's incredible! His technology must be far superior to ours. Send the following communiqué."

"Didip-didip-didip-didip-didip" came the signal from the vacuum cleaner to the rocket.

Within seconds the Thunderbolt was pouring out a stream of unintelligible messages.

"Bing-bong-bing-ping-bong-bing."

There was a moment of deadly silence before the sound of a rip-roaring belch was heard. Aghast by what they heard, a groan of terror then ran through the alien probe.

"Did you hear that fellow aliens? The brainless one has spoken in a strange sort of secret code which is totally unrecognisable to us. We have received you message oh great superior being! Bring the intrusive creature up on the screen and let's see what it looks like," the Captain hastily orders.

(Here's where the real surprise comes in as Freddie appears on the aliens monitor screen. The aliens are truly flummoxed. Before them was the vision of a really ugly looking android that appeared to be thick as two planks?)

"Great Scott, what a hideous sight!" The Captain shrieked in horror.

(With some amusement Freddie slides the window back from his cramped cockpit)

"Oh hello, I wa-wa- wonder if I ca-ca-can use your toil-tol-toilet?"

"What was that he said," one of the aliens asks?

"I'm not sure," the second in command replied. "The brainless one seems to mumble something."

(Danger mounts as the two craft come dangerously close to impact. In desperation Freddie tries to manoeuvre the rocket away from the oncoming probe)

"Too late we've collided!" The Captain yells, as he is thrown from his seat.

Here's when things get really exciting. In the mayhem and confusion of the collision several pieces of apparatus break away from the rockets main instrumentation panel and land on Freddie's head, which amazingly, resembles a regal crown. Stunned by what they see the aliens are transfixed to their monitor screens – whereby the apparition of a man could be seen wearing a royal crown on his head that was embedded with bright glowing lights.

"Hell's bells! I don't believe it," the Captain looks on in euphoria. "It's the King of ruddy Jupiter!"

"Oh, but surely not oh masterful leader."

"Just our luck to meet another bloody royal."

The Captain orders the intrusive humanoid to be brought before him for interrogation. Moments later, Freddie emerges from the tele transportation room whereby his human remains have been completely demolecularized and reassembled at the flick of a switch, thereby, having gone through a procedure of being thoroughly regenerated to a mortal human being once again. Waiting eagerly to greet the bungling agent was the Captain of the vessel along with the rest of the alien crew. What happened next was beyond comprehension. Once safely on board the UFO the Captain immediately points to a giant tapestry which depicts aliens bowing down at the feet of a God-like image and whose features are identical to that of Freddie's. Ironically, the God is called 'Zonk the Plonk' and written beneath the tapestry were the words: 'Love thy Plonker'. By an incredible twist of fate (and seeing the likes of Freddie) the aliens believe that their beloved God has returned.

"Rejoice! Fellow aliens for our beloved God, 'Zonk the Plonk' has returned."

"Did you hear that everyone, 'Zonk the Plonk' has returned?"

There was an immediate reaction from within the vacuum cleaner which quickly turned to sheer elation. Overcome with emotion the alien crew danced in jubilation at the news, whereby; a red carpet was prepared in gratitude for their beloved God who has returned to the fold. Overwhelmed by the good news the aliens knelt down in honour of their returning saviour. The jubilation continued as the delirious keyed up aliens revelled to the sounds of rock and roll hits of the 1950's, while chanting: "Plonker--Plonker--Plonker." Hence the 'Plonker' was given a standing ovation.

(It's impossible to overstate at this point the influence Freddie Stanley Frobisher will have on the crew of the vacuum cleaner)

"Forgive me oh Great Plonker!" The Captain bowed in honour. "We greet you most humbly. We have waited many millennia for your return, but where have you been all this time, oh great brainless one?"

(Freddie is clutching his privates in desperate need of the toilet) However, through his remarkable psychic powers of communication he immediately strikes up an instant rapport with the aliens.

"Well, if you really ma-ma-must know fellow aliens, I was on my way to Pluto for a le-leak. You see, I was in ur-urgent need of the toilet. In fact, I was nigh-on ca-close to wetting my pa-pa-pants. There wa-wasn't even a ba-ba-bog-board. In fact you kind gentlemen came just along just in the na-na-nick of time, I might add."

"What did he say?" the Captain queries, looking totally bemused.

"I'm not sure Captain. He seems to mumble something?"

"I think he said he wants to be placed on the colon board?"

"Well come along then, quickly! Do as the Plonker says; let's give the man a full colon, at once!"

"Oh, goody goody! I do love doing a full colon. One gets so much pleasure at shoving a dirty great instrument up a nice round bum."

In super speed the aliens quickly change into their operating gowns in readiness to perform their delicate operation. On the front of their operating gowns was the insignia of a God-like creature, and written beneath was the words: 'Love thy Plonker'. Suddenly the room was filled with an eerie dense vapour. The alien's stare intensely into the Plonker's mind for it was not a pretty sight. They see images of naked earthlings being subjected to seductive goings on, downing pints of cheap booze, while men and women were indulging in sexual acts of pleasure.

"These androids are a queer old lot," the Captain bemoaned. "There only function in life it would seem is to reproduce and consume vast amounts of food and drink themselves stupid by indulging in great volumes of intoxicating liquor! They're nothing more than a race of brain-dead morons. In fact we have here fellow aliens a classic example of a dirty old android at his most evil and wicked ways.

"Continue with the full colon!" The Captain insists. "We need more bowel movement, I urge you to give the Plonker more bowel movement!"

A silvery blanket is placed over Freddie's body, whereby rude prolonged noises could be heard. The aliens then stick their heads under the covers to see what's going on.

(Meanwhile, back at MI6 headquarters in London, the Commander was beginning to crack up under the strain and was feeling somewhat frustrated and indeed angry at not being able to contact his man-on-the-job, Freddie Frobisher)

"Where the hell are you agent Frobisher? Please come in and for God's sake give us back our rocket back, I beseech you!"

(Fed-up with his bundling agent's incompetence the hierarchy begin fighting amongst themselves on whose going to kill him)

"Will you please stop fighting?" The Commander screamed. "I'm going kill him and that's final!" Again, the commander tries to contact Freddie. "Come in agent Frobisher! Have you regained entry yet? I repeat; have you regained entry?"

(It was by now firmly established that Frobisher's popularity ratings have soared to the sensational height of zero. In fact the Commander's nerves were shot to pieces)

(Meanwhile Freddie was still receiving his full colon)

"How's the patient doing?" The Captain gingerly asked.

"He seems to be in full remission oh masterful leader. Sedimentation is normal. Electrocardiogram is within borderline limits; although I must point out a possible hardening of the Mitre Valve is highly likely. But more surprisingly Captain, there is definitely no joint movement."

"No joint movement. Why that's incredible."

"And not only is that Captain, his brain seems to be on par with a highly strung Brazilian dormouse."

"Holy Martian rocks, what a truly Great Plonker we have here!" The Captain rubs his hands with glee.

"However Captain, there is a slight complication regarding his mental state of health. My diagnostic assessment is that he is suffering from a combination of a psychological disturbing phenomenon which is brought on by an acute state of

Hyperventilation. Furthermore Captain, it seems the driving force behind his condition is a deep rooted fear of female cats which often results in sweaty palpitations and hot flushes."

"My word, the poor Plonk is in a bad way."

"In conclusion Captain his case illustrates many of the features that are found in 'Mad Cow' Disorder".

"Are you trying to tell me that me that our beloved leader is suffering from a condition known as 'Hereford Bull Syndrome'.

"Yes, I'm afraid so Captain."

The Captain was now faced with an almost insuperable situation. Should he continue with the experiment or cut his losses, therefore nip it in the bud before it's too late. He obviously had some serious decisions to make.

"Enie Minnie minney mow - shall we let the Plonker go?"

(Sod it the Captain thought as he rubbed his hands with glee)

"To hell with it, let's have another experiment."

Now strapped down, his jerking; twisted body was undergoing some serious treatment. With deft touches the alien surgeon drew a faint line across the Plonkers head in readiness for good old fashioned nip and tuck. Finally, the hour of deliverance had finally arrived when the aliens sent a bolt of high velocity energy that went surging through the Plonkers brain, thereafter, an electrode was carefully placed on the Plonker's private bits and pieces. The aliens watched with bated breath as they encountered the frightful sight of a man's genitals being amazingly transformed to the biggest pair of ghoulies they had ever seen. Rather reluctantly Freddie further received a series of powerful laser beams to his bottom. The pain was absolutely excruciating but of magnificent proportions. Overcome with emotion an alien cries out.

"Yippee, what a cracking day we're having! "

"Have you managed to extract the deadly gas from his rear end?" The Captain inquired. "Fear not Captain, for the K-Y jelly we picked up at 'Boots the Chemist' back on earth, really works wonders on these vile bums," a fellow alien sniggered. "In fact Captain we are on our way to a place of no return!"

"Good work fellow alien, but I really must insist we open up his bowels with a bit more urgency, come on let's see what the man's made of? An almighty cheer came from the alien crew as they managed with great difficulty to extract a horrible smelly substance called – Poo-Pong-Poo." (A big cheer came from the alien crew as their immaculate uniforms had dramatically been transformed to a chocolate brown colour)

"Captain! I must be quite frank with you sir," the second in command confronts his Captain. "I really do think we've given our beloved leader a bit of a bum steer."

"Nonsense! I've heard these humanoids are at each other's rear-ends like raging bulls on heat."

(Freddie mutters something to himself) "Oh I am enjoying myself; it's not often one gets the chance to have a full colon!" Never in his wildest dreams did the Plonker believe that one day he'll be sitting on the throne, basking in glory.

Freddie at once realised that his life from now on would take on a whole new meaning. It must be remembered however that the bundling agent was in complete control of his facilities, apart from a sore rectum. It's also worth remembering that the Plonker's bravery throughout the ceremony was one of suburb dignity. Grim faced and now powerless he awaited the full wroth of the ships dentist.

Many extractions later and now practically toothless, Freddie lay there in the recovery room as he emerged from his terrifying ordeal. He was thereby greeted by the delightful sound of heart warming music. However, the poor chap's vital parts had unfortunately been squeezed to the bone in the most undignified manner. This act brilliantly accomplished Freddie found himself being miraculously transformed to a truly invigorated and restored man; whereby he remained cool calm and self-composed. Therefore, he took tremendous care to choose his words very carefully but managed to let out a cry of sheer anguish. "Infamy, Infamy, the buggers have got it in for me!"

(Just then the Commander comes through on his mobile phone)

"For God's sake Frobisher, cut out the crap and get your backside down here, you're in big trouble!"

(More drama was about to unfold when an unidentified probe appears on the aliens monitor screen that was coming in at a tremendous speed)

"Captain! The sensors have picked up another probe to our rear."

"Who would dare to violate our rear space? Bring it up on the scanners and let me see."

(Sure enough an image materialises on the aliens monitor screen)

"Is there anyone on board the craft?" The Captain asks.

The aliens focus in on the runaway rocket. It's the gruesome twosome, Moriarty and Jockstrap. Inside the rocket there is hectic activity going on. A man's head could be seen bobbing about in an uncompromising position. It appears that Jockstrap was giving Moriarty head.

"Oh that's great Jockstrap! Just what was needed after a hard day in the saddle? A little bit more is needed Jockstrap. Oh no, not too much or it'll fall off! For heaven's sake Jockstrap, take your false teeth out first, I'll have stretch marks round me vitals."

(In that instant Moriarty and Jockstrap's rocket comes into focus)

"These two give me the willies!" the Captain shrieked.

"It appears it's not just their rear end they're probing!"

"Who are they?"

"I'm not sure Captain."

"They're a horrible looking pair."

(This devious act of skulduggery was completely taken out of context by the aliens who totally misinterpreted what the evil pair was up too)

"It's disgusting! The Captain cried. "A chill runs down my spine just watching their debauchery! I think I'm going be sick!"

(We cut back to Moriarty and Jockstrap)

"Oh that's much better Jockstrap. My rear end was beginning to go numb!"

"We should be fully operational now Moriarty!"

(Back inside the UFO)

"Enough!" The Captain yells. "Beam that disgusting pair before me."

"Yes at once Captain."

(One of the aliens works the transporter and within seconds

Moriarty and Jockstrap are brought on board the vacuum cleaner)

"Where are we Jockstrap?"

"Crickey! We've been abducted Moriarty, look aliens!"

"We saw you on our monitor screens you despicable pair of humanoids!" the Captain angrily declares.

"What do you mean?" Jockstrap groaned.

"What were you doing in our rear space?" the Captain asked.

"We weren't doing anything," Moriarty pleads?

"That's perfectly correct." Jockstrap declares. "We're looking for an evil looking man called Freddie Frobisher, that's all!"

"Oh you were, were you? I've heard that one before. Take them away! The Plonker shall decide what to do with them!"

(Moriarty and Jockstrap are taken before the Plonker and there he sat in a seat of stately splendour like a bishop that was about to address his congregation that were scattered haphazardly in sparsely populated pews. However, the sound of footsteps and human voices led to the Plonker making his first official proclamation)

"I don't believe it; Moriarty, it's that bumbling fool Freddie Frobisher!"

"Yes, you're right Jockstrap! But what in hell is he doing here and why is he wearing those ridiculous clothes?"

"Yes, why are you wearing those ridiculous clothes!"

(Moriarty and Jockstrap are understandably surprised by what they see)

"Oh mighty leader;" (The Captain bowed in honour) "We found this despicable pair of humanoids invading our rear space. What shall we do with them?

(This is obviously a decision for the Plonker)

"Those two twits again? They give me nothing but trouble wherever I go. Fa fa, all I care you can send them to Uranus."

"What did the Plonker say?"

"I'm not sure Captain?"

"I didn't catch a word of it?"

"His language is obviously too superior for our delicate ears. Please repeat yourself oh Great Plonker!"

(The aliens kneel down at Freddie's feet and wait on his every word)

"I sa-sa-said, for all I care you can send the bu-bu-bu buggers to Uranus!"

"I think he said the buggers are from Uranus, Captain."

"Well, do as the Plonker says, send them back to Uranus! We don't want this despicable pair on board our ship! Put them in the dromonitor and transport them to Uranus, at once!"

(Moriarty and Jockstrap look horrified.)

"But we don't want to go to Uranus! I'm gonna kill you for this Frobisher!"

"No I'm gonna kill him!"

(Jockstrap and Moriarty begin ringing each other's necks, arguing whose going to kill their arch enemy)

"They're a pair of maniacs. Take them away!" The Captain forcefully orders.

Moriarty and Jockstrap are eventually taken away, kicking and screaming, before finally being placed in the dromonitor. Meanwhile back on his throne Freddie is busily tucking into a true alien lunch and like all good heads of state he reaches under his cloak and pulls out a hard-boiled egg, taps it on the side and begins peeling off the shell. (But there's something missing?) He reaches inside his cloak and pulls out a salt sprinkler, carefully giving his egg the full treatment. Rounding off a splendid lunch of tea and toast he reaches inside his gown and so produces a book - entitled, 'The Thing from Outer Space'.

With our new sung hero safely installed on his throne, Freddie was feeling like a true born leader.

(When all was done and dusted the aliens finally reveal their plans to Freddie)

"Oh Great Plonker, now that you have revealed yourself to be our true God of purpose our existence is almost complete, for soon we shall enslaved all the peoples of the universe with our superior technology and science. No one shall block our passage. We shall therefore enforce colonic irrigation upon all who stand in our way."

"Cor blimey, that's a bit of a tall order,"Freddie smiles. In readiness for the big occasion Freddie produces several rolls of toilet paper.

"Oh great Plonker you must now go and inform the earthlings of their forthcoming fate!"

The aliens bring up photos of world leaders on their monitor screen to whom they think will make ideal candidates for Freddie to contact on earth. They stop however when they see a picture of a well-known Politian called John Thomas to where the aliens burst out laughing.

"My God I don't believe it," one of the alien's points out. "It's Wee Willy Winkle!"

"He he he!" The aliens laugh loudly.

"Wee Willy Winkle; who the hell's he?"

Ah, well, he's the one our earth people call Little Willie," Freddie explains.

"In fact, talking of willies oh masterful leader." (A fellow grey informs his captain) "Did you know that down on earth, several members of the legal profession refer to John Thomas a two-timing android? Furthermore, his fellow MP's claim he has the tiniest of tiniest of manhood's."

"Never!"

"It's true!"

"No wonder he's called Wee Willy Winkle."

(The aliens bring up more photos of world leaders whereupon the picture of a rather large woman appears)

"Holy Martian rocks he's far too scary for the likes of us. We need a bigger man than that!" This is a job for the almighty Plonker to sort out."

(When at last the aliens make the necessary preparations for their journey to earth)

"Oh great Plonker we are ready to send you on a mission of great importance. You shall meet with the Queen of England and inform her we are invading at once! But first you are to receive the official inauguration ceremony where you will be given the highest award bestowed on to you by the alien community."

"Ere, does that mean I'll be teaming up with Scullery and Mouldy of the X-Piles?" Freddie joked.

"Not on this occasion oh mighty leader," the Captain confirms.

"Transfer the Plonker to the mother ship. He shall go to earth in style in one of our top-notch, central heated, five-star ships," the Captain demanded.

Fredrick Stanley Frobisher was on the brink of discovering his true vocation which seemed a far cry from his days at MI6, and seldom has a man earned his corn so magnificently as that of good old Freddie.

And so, when all was done and dusted the almighty 'Plonker' was finally on his way back to earth along with the rest of his alien's cronies, fully rigged out in his true royal regalia.

As with most journeys through space it was littered with major obstacles. However, as the UFO passed by the planet Uranus their sensors homed in on a couple of undesirable characters, namely Jockstrap and Moriarty, whose exploits had landed them being banished to that particular planet.

The data which had been accumulated on the evil pair confirmed that they were living in a hippy commune in a far off place called Nokidoki. Moriarty and Jockstrap could be seen working frantically on a rocket which they had managed to steel from a military establishment, but there was no time to make contact with the gruesome twosome. The Captain and his crew had more pressing matters to attend to. Therefore, it was full steam on to earth. In lightning speed the UFO had entered the outer limits of the earth's gravitational pull. Soon, the mighty Plonker would be amongst his own people, and he certainly hoped the waiting public would not suspect for one moment the panic he will cause by his sudden appearance. Surprisingly, the UFO was a little late for the Christmas festivities, but its bright pulsating lights made the seasons illuminations seem rather dull. Scant attention was paid to the hundreds of onlookers as they observed a circular shaped object hovering in the vicinity of St Paul's Cathedral. Though incredibly it may seem, it will be the Plonker's first public appearance since his heroics at RAF Rendelsham. But just as Freddie was about to land a rather disturbing thought had crossed the aliens mind. What if the Plonker in all his wisdom was welcomed into the Royal Family? It would be inconceivable if he failed to gain the Queen's admiration, for the evidence was quite clear. The silly twat really believed he was of true royal blood and therefore nothing could stand in his way of getting ordained. But surely the Queen's confidence would be totally shattered when she discovers that she is about to welcome the man-of-the-moment, otherwise known as the Plonker into her kingdom. However, a man of low intelligence he might be but as far as complete burkes go there is no one to touch him. Of course we're talking about special agent Fredrick Stanley Frobisher, more commonly known as the Plonker. And may God have mercy on the good people of England should he ever become the future King of England?

At long last the Plonker has landed and there to greet his fellow countrymen Freddie came up with these well chosen words. "Good morning fellow earthlings how's your bum off for spots!"

Freddie's mission at this point seemed perfectly straightforward. He is about to become a highly respected lollipop man, escorting frail old ladies and snotty little brats across the road. However, it's impossible to overstate the upheaval that will follow from his arrival. His presence could last for days, if not weeks, but in that time, squads of heavily armed police, bomb-disposal units, to say nothing of the military presence and not to mention the scores of onlookers. Meanwhile the story unfolds: an unidentified flying object has suddenly descended from outer space and is hovering thereabouts in London, whereupon people have been gathering all morning to witness this incredible event. Meanwhile, euphoria has erupted at a television studio where breaking news has just come in.

(Newscaster) "Reports are coming in that an unidentified flying object has just landed in the grounds of St Paul's Cathedral in London. Crowds have been gathering all morning and we've just heard in the last few minutes that a door has opened from the craft. We go live to St Paul's where our man on the spot, Mark Austin Ruby, where he hopes to obtain an interview the occupants of the strange craft.

(Newscaster) "What's happening down there Mark?"

"Well John, here I am by the spacecraft. As you can imagine people have been flocking here all morning to witness this amazing spectacle. I would describe the object as about fifty meters in diameter and has a metallic look appearance. It rotates like a spinning top and there is a strange humming sound. But just a moment do my eyes deceive me for I can see a number of grey-like creatures peering through circular portholes. Good heavens a door has opened up and something grotesque is wriggling its way towards us. It's some sort of hideous creature, dressed silver-gowned and oddly enough wearing a pair of thick rimmed spectacles.

(Newscaster) "You say the creature is wearing spectacles, Mark."

(Mark) "Yes, that's right John but I'm not entirely sure how it came about them."

(Newscaster) "Bye the way what does the creature looks like?"

"Physically, it resembles something out of a science fiction horror movie. Appearance wise it has mad saucer shaped eyes that stare behind thick rimmed spectacles. One of its eyes hangs precariously from its socket while the other one faces north with a twist of madness about it. Both of its eyes light up as though fuelled by liquid oxygen and any movement is painfully slow. Crickey, the creature is on the move. No, no, it's stopped. Heavens above, the damn thing is undoing its tunic. Ere, I don't like the look of this. Good grief, I don't believe it, the creature has produced a copy of the 'Gardner's Weekly' magazine."

(Newscaster) "Oh come off it Mark, how on earth would the creature get a copy of the 'Gardner's Weekly' on the likes of say Pluto."

"I don't know but get this: the creature is pointing to the page on how to cultivate exotic gardens by using high-powered rotivators."

(Newscaster) "Do you except me to believe that the creature has the means of cultivating Martian type landscapes?"

"Something else and quite amazing has happened. The creature has now produced a copy of the Lancet, the medical journal, and has opened it up to the page on face-lifts, where the prominent figure of a doctor Nasher, better known in the trade as Nasher the Slasher, whose giving his views on plastic surgery".

(Newscaster) "Do you think the creature has come to earth pacifically for a nose job?"

"Yes, without question John! Good grief the creature is going berserk; the thing is pointing to the Lancet again and yelling: - "nip-tuc-nip-tuc-nip-tuc".

Dear of dear of dear, the creature has now unzipped his flies and pulled out something which resembles a bottle of bleach. But get this, the creature has now the audacity to tell us that his bowels are fully operational and used on a regular basis. It further claims that in order to keep them in tip-top condition it uses a cheap lavatory cleaner, which by alien standards, gives it more Ooomp!!"

(The creature 'Freddie' begins drinking a bottle of lavatory cleaner followed by a big burp)

(Newscaster) "Did I hear you right; you say the creature uses a cheap lavatory cleaner? Good grief has it no shame. Look here; it's imperative that we keep all channels of communication open with the damn thing."

"You can't be serious old boy, let's face it, the ruddy thing is about to wipe us off the face of the earth."

(Newscaster) "Well, for heaven's sake man, don't just stand there or you'll be a dead duck."

"What's happening now, Mark?"

"Hold on, there seems to be some sort of movement. I do believe there's something is building up."

(The creature cocks his leg up and breaks wind)

"Ah, at last the creature has produced some sort meaningful lingo. Yes, it looks as though he is about to speak to us."

(Little by little the creature edged it way forward to the waiting crowd)

"Yikes, the thing is on the move again and making its way towards the press box, revealing to us a document of some importance and what looks like a long prepared speech. Yes, yes, he's about to address the nation John."

(There is mass panic as the creature unzips his flies. In sheer desperation the police try to hold back the crowd, fearing a stampede)

(Policeman) "Ello ello ello, what's he up too, I definitely don't like of him. Come on; move back, looks as though we've got another ruddy perv on our hands."

"Don't worry everyone, we're dealing with it!" Another policeman pleads.

(A group of armed officers rush forward to try and capture the creature, better still, blow its brains out. One of the reporters asks the creature to identify himself)

"Mark Austin Ruby of London News."
"Do you have anything to say?
"Why are you here?"
"Which planet do you represent?"
"Do you have a message for us?"
"Who are you?"
"What are you?"
"Are you an alien minister without a portfolio?"

(There was a moment's pause as silence engulfs the waiting crowd. Freddie removes his robe and the crowd wait in awe for something to happen. The silence was unbearable as the creature begins scratching himself and fiddling with his flies)

"I'm a ma-ma-man!" Freddie pleads.

(The media people by this time were going berserk for some answers. The press begin firing questions at the creature)

"Speak to us in proper English; we can't understand a thing you're saying?"
"What language do you speak?"
"Are you from the Spanish Inquisition?"
"Are you an alien?"

(We go back to the Correspondent on the job)

"Well, the creature has at last spoken, but I'm not sure if anyone can understand a thing the beast is saying. I think it may be speaking in a strange sort alien dialogue. I can just about make out a few words. Heavens above! I've managed to pick something up. The creature has in fact made the most outrageous statement. He stubbornly insists he's from the East Dulwich area of London and is employed by the local council as a Lollipop Man."

"What!"
"That's right."

(Newscaster) "Oh come off it Mark, I've heard that one before. Listen! He's from Pluto along with the rest of his alien cronies, I'm totally convinced of that. Not only that, I do believe the creatures has brought a deadly bug with him from outer space."

(Newscaster) "How do you make that out?

"Well, put it this way, every time the thing breaks wind the creature releases a hideous substance called 'poo-pong-poo'.

(Newscaster) "Are you sure it's not a gas leak or maybe rotten eggs?"

"Of course not, I tell you he's dropped something that resembles a cross between a sewage plant and dodgy cesspit."

(We cut back to the crowd who inch their way forward in hope of getting a glimpse of the thing from beyond, whereby a man in the crowd makes his point of view)

"I do believe we've got some sort of prehistoric monster on our hands here, maybe of the Neolithic age."

"You've all got it wrong," a heckler shouts. "He's neither prehistoric nor Neolithic, but a man, I tell you!"

(In frustration the crowd begin to chant)

"He's not a man."

"Oh yes he is, he's a man."

"My God, the creature intends to prove it. He's damn-well undoing his flies."

"Of course I'm a ba-ba-bloody ma-man!" Freddie angrily fumes.

(A sense of urgency ran through the waiting crowd as they begin to chant obscenities)

"Prove it then!"

(Just at that precise moment Sally G-string turns up in her sports car and quickly goes to the aid of our beleaguered hero)

"He's a man and I can prove it!" Sally categorically pleads.

(An Australian couple who were standing close-by were somewhat shocked by the creatures antics)

"Struth Madge, the ruddy thing's got no strides on!!!"

(Sally breaks in) "Oh Freddie, what have you up to now since I last saw you!"

"Well, Sally, you're not going believe this, but I've been well and truly colonised. Not only that, I've had me ba-ba-brain removed along with my teeth pulled out. I've had my bu-bum interfered with along with me ghoulies knocked out of place."

"You've had what? Oh never mind, there's no time for that now! Now tell everyone that you're a man, do you think you can do that for me Freddie?"

"Cor, not half Sal."

(Sally kisses Freddie passionately on the lips, which of course gets Freddie all hot and flustered. Sally carefully unzips Freddie's flies and there to her amazement, hung proud, half a pound of the finest Lincolnshire sausages)

(Several policemen immediately respond to the incident)

"Ere, I don't like the look of them sausages! Bit on the limpish side if you ask me."

"You see, I told you I was a man," Freddie smiles.

(The crowd cheer with delight.)

"I'm a ma- ma-ma-man!"

"Now Freddie, what on earth were you doing on board that UFO?" Sally asks.

"Well, you see it's like this Sally. I was on my way to Pluto when these ka-ka-kind gentlemen took me in," pointing towards the aliens.

"What on earth is he talking about?" a reporter asks.

"I can't understand a thing he's saying?"

"I think the creatures got a speech impediment."

"I've got a very important message to tell you," Freddie states, "so stand back and give me plenty of room!" Freddie clears his throat whereby he takes hold of a microphone and begins to read a long prepared speech.

"Dear e-e-earthlings, I a-a-address you on baa-half of an e-e-exteeerritorial sp-species, ca-ca-called (microphone breaks up - crackling sound) from a fa-fa-from the ga-gal-laxalaxies of (feedback-sound) w-who ha-ve tra-travelled a-across the u-uni-verse ta-ta make you aware of your fa-fa-forthcoming fa-fate. The p-people of (crackle sound*)* ar-ar-are going to (crackle sound) if you da-da-don't (feedback sound*)* wa-what they sa-say (crackle) the en-entire pa-pa-planet waaaa (crackle-crackle) fa-fa-frazzeled"

Having hopefully got his message across Freddie decides to break wind with great force. So great was the impact that the crowd begin running for their lives.

Through his vast superior technology Freddie has unknowingly released a highly sensitive substance from his rear end. Thereby the bundling agent has taken upon himself to eliminate the entire human race with a blend of highly intoxicating gases that contain a copious amount of rejuvenating fluid, found exclusively in residential homes and old fogey institutions. Once these chemicals were released it had the desired effect of transforming the earthlings into brain-starved zombies. Spurred on by this exciting prospect, Freddie drops another one of his thunderous great farts. The crowd by this time were worn out physically, as well as mentally, overcome with fear that this brutal monster who had zoomed in from outer space had managed to drop his guts with some vigour. Fearing for their lives the crowd move back in panic, sensing the creature was quite capable of producing more deadly gases. In the frenzied activity that followed, Freddie had unknowingly mislaid his speech, whereby; a gentleman from the crowd picked it up and began to read its contents. To his sheer horror the document was an indication of the alien's intention. They were about to invade the earth and perform Colonlonic Irrigation on the entire human race. Just then a hatch opens up from the UFO. One by one the aliens come out in their droves and trudged their way forward like lost zombies. Holding in their hands was the gruesome sight of funnels, tubes and surgical equipment, which had the desired effect of a 'Dyno-Rod' advert.

You shall be our slave's you nasty little earthlings!" The Captain said forcefully."

(People begin to panic at the very thought of being subjected to Colonlonic Irrigation. While all this is going on Freddie senses a sneeze coming on)

"Atishu, atishu, atishu." The mucus from his nostrils forms a deadly spray, commonly known as the common cold. This unfortunately proves too much for the aliens who start dropping like flies. In fear of becoming another statistic in the Guinness book of Records the rest of the aliens run for the safety of the mother ship. Now, with the entire crew safely on board the Captain gave his final command. In his final summing up of their trip he thereby addressed his crew.

"Our work is done oh fellow aliens. Rejoice, for the mighty Plonker has delivered our message to the earthlings! I fear there is nothing left for us to do. We shall return to our own planet and leave the humanoids to their miserable fate. Our beloved Plonker has fulfilled his mission. Close the doors and fire up the retros." The Captain ordered.

Gradually, the UFO lifted gently away and out of sight, leaving the earth behind and, as it did so the Captain commented: "I told you our beloved Plonker would wipe out the human race and drop something obnoxious."

Rebuffed by his efforts to warn the earthlings of their forthcoming fete, and based on this assumption, there was no questioning the creature's uncanny implications which was to devour the whole human race, thus allowing the aliens to continue with their total annihilation of the earth. A groan of mass hysteria rumbled through the uneasy crowd of onlookers who were petrified by fear, sensing the aliens would return and carry out their plans to destroy the earth. Faced with this prospect the creature (Freddie) is pursued by a howling mob of hysterical people, screaming for the creature to be destroyed. In his desperate attempt to get away, Freddie raced through the darkness of the London night and as he did so he relinquished all traces of his existence with exception of his royal regalia and then vanished into the obscurity of the London night.

But who should turn up in stately splendour, leading a procession of highly polished limos? Low and behold it was her Majesty the Queen of England. Inside the leading vehicle The Queen was busily working on her maiden speech for a new ship that was being launched later that day. Accompanying the Queen was Prince Charles and Prince Philip. In one hand the Queen holds her speech while in the other a bottle of the finest Chardonnay wine. (But then something amazing happens) The royal party were somewhat bewildered by what they see, for a man (lunatic) was running alongside their car with his face flat up against the window and madly banging on the window with his fist. It's our Freddie would you believe.

"I say Charles whose that idiot," the Queen fumes.

(Freddie brings the entourage to an abrupt halt)

"Any cha-ance of a lift ma-alady," Freddie asks. "I've got to get a-a-cross London in a hurry."

"I say mumsie old girl he looks a bit on the peculiar side. His clothes are odd, and by George his wearing a stately crown on his head." (Prince Charles looks on with disbelief)

"Good gawd, he must be one of our lot," the Queen smiles.

"Come off it me old thunder-horse of a wife, he's one of those Loony Left lot, I shouldn't wonder." Prince Phillip scowls.

(After further deliberation the Queen kindly offers Freddie a lift. While driving though London the Queen practices her speech)

"How does this sound Charles and Philip? It gives me great pleasure to name this ship the Black Hole of Calcutta. May all who sail in her have their intestines fouled up to a rapturous concoction of the bends, dodgy food, and unscrupulous chefs who pick their noses and fling big black bogeys and snot into the cooking utensils?" The Queen then turns to Prince Charles and cracks a bottle of Chardonnay over his head as though it was a ship.

"I say, steady on Mumsie old girl. Bit strong on the Chardonnay, aren't we?"

The Queen cracks another bottle over Charles' head, and as a result knocks Charles unconscious, while bird noises were busily buzzing through Charles's head and so begins mumbling to himself, while merrily singing to a chorus of…"One talks to the Trees."

(Charles regains consciousness)

"Now look here Mater," Prince Charles sighs, holding his head in pain. "I've got a bit of a confession to make old girl. I desperately want to go out and get a job just like the lower classes do."

"A job," the Queen looks on in aghast. "Are you mad Charles? Only the lowest of the low get jobs."

"But mummy, I've got my heart set on becoming a coalman."

"Now look here Charles; you know that coal is bad for the environment - anyway we're royalty for God's sake, we have all the money we want!" The Queen pleads.

"Oh don't be such a spoilsport mummy! Look, let me clarify my position to you. I must confess old girl that since I was a little nipper I've had this burning ambition to become a fully-fledged coalman.

You see for years now I've had visions of getting myself blackened up and do some serious humping. It's therefore imperative I do some humping. Please mummy let me some humping. All I want from you and daddy is a shagged out old mare, a horse and cart, plus twenty bags of the finest nutty slag coal."

"Do you mean to tell me Charles, you'll be gallivanting round the back streets of London, dressed like a ragamuffin man, at the same time shouting obscenities at your horse while whipping the living daylights at the poor fellow?" The Queens eyes widened in disbelief and then snared disapprovingly at her son. The sheer thought of Charles becoming a coalman was too much for Her Majesty to take in. There was only one thing for it. She picked up the last bottle of Chardonnay and cracked it over Charles's head.

"On your edd be it, chum", she said with great passion

The Duke then jumped into the fray. "For God's sake Charles, haven't you done enough humping in your life and getting yourself blackened up indeed? Before you know it me lad, you'll end up looking like that newscaster chappy - Trevor McDonnut. What would Camilla think of all this nonsense?"

"Will you please leave Camilla out of this daddy?"

"Humping indeed! What you need my lad is a good douse of liver salts: gets the old bowels opened up." The Duke snarls with a cynical smile.

(Just then Freddie's mobile phone rings. It's the Commander.)

"Frobisher! I've got fresh orders for you. Get yourself across to Battersea Park in London and there make your way to the Beijing State Circus. You are to contact one of our agents called Jeffrey. But I warn you, he'll be in cognito - craftily disguised as a gorilla. The last we heard of Jeffrey was in cage number six, eating his daily quota of bananas. Jeffrey will give you precise instructions in secret code. Have you got that Frobisher and for heaven's sake don't mess this one up or it'll be curtains!"

The commander cursed disapprovingly with words to the effect: "Damn incompetent twit. I'll have his guts for garters if he messes this one up."

(In response, Freddie bows his head with a toothless grin)

"Da-da-don't worry Gov, by the time I've finished with him he'll be eating out of my hand. Oh, and by the way Gov, does Jeffrey like Pork Pies? If so, I'm quite prepared to throw in a bottle of the finest navy rum to swill it down."

"In heaven's name man, you'll have poor old Jeffrey well and truly plastered. Furthermore, do get a move on, poor old Jeffrey's nuts will be frozen stiff."

The scene is Battersea Park, London, home to the Beijing State Circus. One by one Freddie inspects each of the cages which house huge hairy gorillas. Upon reaching cage number six, Freddie comes face to face with undercover agent Jeffrey.

(With nerves of steel Freddie's draws near to the metal bars of the cage) "Pssst, pssst. Oi, it's me, Freddie Frobisher. Now look here old boy what are my orders?"

Sitting quietly in his cage was the frightening figure of a fully grown gorilla. An undesirable character, whose only purpose in life was to unzip bananas, grunt, and crap on the floor in the most undignified manner.

"Ugggh, ugggh," cried the gorilla, banging his enormous fists on his chest. In his desperation for further orders Freddie quickly takes out his note-pad and hastily writes down the gorillas every word.

"Ugggh, ugggh, ugggh," the gorilla bellowed in a savage rage.

"Yes, yes, I've got that. My orders are to go immediately to the centre ring of the circus and there I am to take to the high-wire. My objective at this point is to meet double agent Ivanish Romanoff who is part of the act. Once I have made contact with him I am to go directly to the trapeze act, where I will meet the flying Boretto Brothers whose main objective is to drop me from a great height. Furthermore, I am to participate in a series of spectacular daredevil manoeuvres that incorporate the loop-de-loop, triple somersault, and if I am still alive, ending with the double shasham. Ere, the buggers are trying to kill me."

In no time at all Freddie immediately changes into the appropriate attire that consists of skimpy leotards, heavily reinforced jockstrap and thick woolly gaiters. It wasn't long before Freddie found himself hurtling through the air, hundreds of feet up, looking down towards the crowd. The band struck as the crowd were put on tenterhooks.

He flies through the air with the greatest of ease, the daring old twat on the flying trapeze, his movements and actions so graceful above, his equipment bent, and so disgracefully dislodged.

Whilst doing a series of death defying manoeuvres, Freddie comes face to face with double agent Romanoff, who issues precise instructions for a rendezvous meeting for his next contact, whereby, Freddie is duly ordered to go to a place of capital punishment, thereafter, he is to be placed in a dirty great cannon and hence blasted into space.

"Ere just a minute that sounds a bit dodgy." Freddie thinks.

Having managed to gather his composure our hapless hero finally reaches ground level again where he receives a rapturous applause. The ringmaster takes hold of the microphone and makes an important announcement.

"And finally ladies and gentlemen we come to the finale of the show. You are about to witness the most daring act of all time. A man is to be placed in a cannon whereby the subject will be dressed in full military attire, thereafter he will be well and truly obliterated and hence, blasted into to darkness of the London night sky and with precise and meticulous aiming, he should by all accounts, land up in the vicinity of West London."

As the minutes ticked by the audience waited in eager anticipation as the cannon is duly loaded up. The moment of truth comes when Big Bertha's fuse is lit. Suddenly the silence was broken by the deafening sound of an almighty explosion that ripped through the circus like a bolt of lightning. Our hapless hero suddenly finds himself hurtling through the air as he is blasted into space.

Meanwhile the scene is Oxford Street in London's West End. Waiting patiently for a bus was a little boy with his mother. The little boy happened to look up when he saw something quite extraordinary.

"Mummy, mummy, what's that thing flying through the air. Is it a bird, is it a plane. What is it mummy?"

"It's neither a bird nor a plane, darling. In fact it looks like the famous 'Prat-Man'. The very same 'Prat-Man' who I dare to say is one short of a loose cannon. He's probably on his way to meet-up with his old friend and side-kick called 'Dobbin'.

To put things in perspective: picture for a moment a man dressed in full military attire. Thereby place a sign on his back to indicate he's completely mad. Shove him in a cannon. Light the blue touch paper. Prepare for detonation and then blast the scallywag to kingdom come. If that's not enough, let him frantically wander about, screaming and yelling, asking people, where the hell am I? Anyway, having been shot out of a cannon our beleaguered hero finds himself outside the main BBC Television Centre in Sheppard's Bush, London. Waiting by the main gate were two uniformed commissionaires who were somewhat mystified as to the sudden appearance of a man zooming in from outer space.

"Hey George, get a load of this weirdo."

"Regular Army, I fancy."

"Never, he's Royal Fusiliers – Queen's Own, if I'm not mistaken."

"Hey, wait a minute George, he must be one of those contestants from the Broadmore Institution, you know, them lot on the Universal Challenge show."

"You know what, I think you may be right George, better get him up to the theatre before the show starts."

(Eager to turn out another gritty performance, Freddie is immediately ushered up to studio 502, to where the grand final of the Universal Challenge show was about to start)

(Voiceover) "Please welcome ladies and gentleman to another popular edition of 'Universal Challenge'. In the chair for tonight's show is our quiz master Dimbo Gasgroin, better known for his thesis on the methodology of grouse shooting late at night."

Dimbo begins……………..

"Tonight's academic institutionalized teams are made up of the Old Lags, who for many years have been long standing inmates at the permanent halls of residents at Parkhurst Prison. And I welcome with great affection to our other team who are commonly known as the Nutters, who themselves are long standing residents at the Broadmoor Institution.

(Dimbo kicks off the show)

"Right teams, here are the rules. You get ten points if you get three correct questions in a row. You can confer on questions. I'll give you five bonus points if you get the first one right. Hands on buzzers please. Here's your started for ten points."

"Who was the Scottish man who claimed to have eyes of liquid gold, ruby red lips, soft speaking voice, took a size twelve dress, and regularly went under the knife?"

(Buzzer goes)

"Yes Broadmore." Was it John Thomas?"

"Wrong! It was Phillip McCavity, the transvestite dentist from Dundee. Here's your starter for ten points. Which Irishman won the Nobel Prize posthumously for his heroic efforts in reducing cement mixers into high-powered sports cars?

(Buzzer goes)

Dimbo glanced round the crowed television studio, noting with some displeasure that the contestants were busily engaged in various activities of unsavoury behaviour.

"Oh do stop picking your noses Broadmore, and for God's sake Parkhurst, stop scratching your bums. Your starter for ten points. In the 1955 movie (The Creature from Outer Space) what was the stick-like insect that later turned to human form."

Both teams dither.

"Oh do hurry up teams; I've got a bus to catch."

(Buzzer goes to Old Lags)

"Was it Vincent Price?"

"Don't be daft," Dimbo laughs.

"Five bonus points if you get this one right. What revolutionary scientific discovery did Count Frankenstein put forward when he induced an immense beam of high velocity electrodes through a stiffs body.

(Broadmore) "He used the concept to wake up a man without the use of an alarm clock."

"Wrong, but near enough."

"Here's an interesting one – which tool of theology do Anthropologists use in their universal quest for the repatriation of Nigerian dentists?"

"Yes Broadmoor!"

"Was it that man Fillet McCavity?"

"Oh come off Broadmore."

"Your starter for ten points. Which leading politician played the hunchback of Notre Dame in the TV presentation of Short and Curlies?"

(Buzzer goes)

"Was it our old friend John Thomas," the Nutters said.

"Don't be pathetic. It was of course John Nutcracker."

"Here's a question that will blow your minds away." Dimbo sneakily smiled. "What did Henry VIII give Jane Seymour on their wedding night?"

(Buzzers go mad and jam)

"A good seeing too!"

"Naughty, naughty teams, it was in fact Hampton Court."

"Here's an interesting one, teams. What's red, throbs between your legs and has the capability of reaching up to speeds of 50mph."

(Buzzers go to the Parkhurst)

"We believe it was a 1950's GPO motorbike."

"Oh yes, well done Nutters."

"At this point in the show, you have five points each. Here's an easy one teams. Name me the Pakistan businessman whose sales of non-flush lavatories sold throughout the Indian subcontinent, and who later became known as the 'Crapper from Clapham'."

(Buzzer goes to Broadmore)

"We know this one. The gentleman in question is called the Shyster from Shitoo."

"Oh yes, well done Broadmore."

"In police termology what did Chief Inspector Phillip Condom refer to when he said: I've got a lovely bunch of coconuts?"

(Buzzer goes)

"Yes Broadmoor.

"Bollocks!"

"Oh, yes, well remembered Broadmoor."

"Next question. In what year was the Geneva Convention first ratified?"

(Both teams dither)

"Oh for God's sake you must know this one. What a bunch of loonies I've got on my hands. Here's an easy one. Who in Greek

mythology was depicted on nude paintings as a fine young athlete, and known to the local gentry as Gorgeous George?"
(Buzzer goes to the Parkhurst)
"We believe it was Napoleon."
"Don't be daft Parkhurst. Napoleon was a famous composer. Your starter for ten points. Name me the Irish long distance runner who broke the world record by jumping every single fence in the Grand National, blindfolded, and without the use of a horse?"
(Buzzer goes to the Broadmore)
"Was it our friend Paddy MacGinty?"
"I'm afraid you're wrong yet again. It was in fact Shamus O' Malloy, the foolhardy alcoholic from County Tyrone."
"Which eccentric English poet wrote this rhythm whilst in prison?
There was a young man from East Cheam, who invented an odd machine. On the nineteenth stroke, the bloody broke, and whipped his walnuts to cream.
"Don't know."
"Name me the famous politician who said: I'll show you mine if you show me yours."
(Buzzer goes to Parkhurst)
"Harold Wilson."
"Wrong! It was in fact an MP addressing the House of Commons in a debate over the Conservative Party manifesto policy."
"Here's a toughie teams. What is a Pathologist?"
(Buzzer goes to Broadmore)
"We believe it's a man who walks through a series of well-defined trails."
"Absolutely, spot on. Well done."
(Buzzer goes)
"Which 'sectioned' Irish novelist, believed he had the divine gift of talking to traumatized horses, who themselves have been sectioned?"
"We believe he was one of us – a bloody Nutter!"
"Name me the man who drunk himself death while driving a cement mixer on his way to a beer fest."

"We strongly believe the man in question was apparently a forty six year old, white male, aptly named two-pint-Harry. His remains however were found in a gigantic barrel of authentic German larger."

"Oh, yes, well done Broadmore."

"Can you name me the species of insect that lives up a hippo's bottom?"

(Buzzer goes to Broadmore)

"We believe its 'Simon' the slimy snail who slipped his way up the slippery slope of a shite infested bottom."

"Oh yes, spot on Broadmore! My God it doesn't get much better than this."

(The gong goes for the end of the show)

"Right teams, you have managed to accumulate a total of twelve points each, making it a draw. So with that it's goodnight from me and goodnight teams.

(Just then Dimbo's phone rings)

"Good evening Mr Dumbo or is it Dimbo?"

"Please call me Dimbo!"

"Did you say Dumbo?"

Dimbo-Dumbo, who the hell cares? Look, it's the Commander of MI6 here. I do believe you've got one of our agents on your show, masquerading as a contestant."

"Ah, yes, you must mean Frobisher, the man with the brain of a deranged caterpillar."

(Dimbo passes the phone over to Freddie)

"Hello governor, its Freddie here."

"Listen very carefully Frobisher, I've got a very important assignment for you which is right up your street. So impressed was Her Majesty the Queen with you, she has requested that you are to look after her pet parrot called 'General Gordon' while she is away on a weekend trip to Balmoral. Muck this one up Frobisher and I'll have you hung drawn and quartered. You're to start first thing in the morning at eight sharp – is that clear!"

"Cor, thanks a lot governor, it's just what the doctor ordered. In gratitude, Freddie bears his customary toothless grin and nods his head in approval.

(The Scene is Windsor Castle)
There is no more magnificent sight then that of the mighty structure of Windsor Castle. It's hard to believe that this awesome building was built over eight hundred years ago. Windsor Castle covers a huge area and it is much larger than people imagine. So big in fact that it covers more than twelve acre's that takes a good half a day to walk round it. The main attractions are the State Apartments and St George's Chapel. Historically, Windsor Castle is believed to be the oldest inhabited castle in the world and dates back to 1070 and is thought to have been built by William the Conqueror. Earliest references of the castle are entered in the Doomsday Survey in 1086. However, it was Edward III who was the main man responsible for the present day layout of the castle. Later on, King Henry VIII completed the final touches to the place. As one proceeds through the endless wards and terraces, one can take in the breath-taking views of the Round Tower with its various fortifications, and of course the beautiful countryside which includes Eton and the River Thames. But for today our attention must turn to our hapless hero, Freddie Frobisher.

On a bright summers morning Freddie duly arrives at Windsor Castle where he is immediately greeted by a member of the royal household. The Queen in all her wisdom had drawn up a list of duties that were to be carried out with the utmost urgency. But first Freddie is to be given a grand tour of the place. His tour kicks off with a leisurely walk through the magnificent and beautiful St George's Chapel. Apparently, the work began on the Chapel in 1475 by Edward IV and later completed some fifty years later by Henry VIII. The chapel is ranked one of the finest examples of late medieval architecture in England.

In the course of Freddie's tour the guide pointed out that beneath the marbled floor lays the remains of a multitude of monarchs and Knights of the Garter. Apparently, each Knight has his own resting place, and, to mark their fine achievements, hangs the crests, helm, mantling, swords and banners of each Knight. Freddie's interpretation of this mind blowing news was once a night is enough. Clearly shaken by this worrying news that a party of stiffs was lying beneath his feet, Freddie proceeded to make his way into the State

Apartment Rooms. Here, our hapless hero encountered the most wonderful works of art on display. Freddie was finally led into the throne room which housed the Queen's lovable pet parrot called General Gordon.

Having completed his tour of Winsor Castle Freddie found himself in urgent need of the toilet, as ever. With some urgency he made a quick dash to the lavatory and as he did so he entrusted General Gordon with his royal crown, sceptre, mitre, and gown, and wow, the parrot looked like a true blooded royal.

Meanwhile, a trillion light years away, the aliens were returning back to their planet, recovering from the Plonker's reign of terror. Tucked up in bed, fast asleep, was the Captain who was annoyingly woken up from a deep sleep, covered in a cold sweat, and moreover recovering from a series of deeply disturbing nightmares brought on by the vision of a man wearing a royal crown on his head, dressed silver-gowned and spectacled.

"Yikes, it's the ruddy Plonker," the Captain shuddered with fear. To steady his nerves the Captain made himself a drink, equivalent to a Martian gin and tonic. "I wonder where the bugger is at this very moment," the Captain pondered in deep thought.

Eager to retrace the Plonker's whereabouts the aliens homed in at one of England's finest tourist attractions - Windsor Castle. The entire crew gather round a giant monitor screen as their sensors homed in on a rather strange looking object. For their perched on the royal throne was the sight of a parrot, magnificently turned out in true royal regalia?

"Holy Jupiter rocks!" the Captain shrieked in horror. "Behold fellow aliens for our beloved leader has turned into a stick-like creature. (On seeing the likes of General Gordon) The alien's were mortified as they got their first glimpse of something quite extraordinary.

(The Captain tries to communicate with the parrot thinking it's the Plonker)

"Oh mighty Plonker are you of sound body and mind? Do you have the means to communicate with us?"

(Hence came a reply) "Cooooooooooooooooooooooooooooooor - not half! Pieces of eight - pieces of eight - show us ya knickers – who's a cleaver boy then. "

I must point out to you good people out there that General Gordon is one hell of a remarkable bird. Though incredible it may seem, the General to his credit has undoughtedly mastered the art of impersonating people? The parrot was more than capable of holding talks on intelligent matters; he could reel off nursery rhymes, tell dirty jokes, and swear like a trooper, and so on.

(Meanwhile back on board the UFO the Captain was conferring with his crew)

"I don't believe it fellow aliens our beloved leader is talking in a dialect which is neither known to man or reptile. It's blatantly obvious that our beloved Plonker is communicating in a dialect which is spoken on the planet Nebularius".

(The biggest surprise comes when the versatile parrot begins to break out in speech, whereby, General Gordon does its best to impersonate the famous American President - Ronald Regan. The parrot's inspiration came when President Regan first took up office and did his rather dodgy, inauguration speech.)

At first, General Gordon screeched, ruffled his feathers, and then jumped on the PA system and began to break out in the finest American brogue.

"Fellow Americans," General Gordon began. "Have I got one humdinger of a speech for you guys out there? Let me see now, how does it go. Ah yes. A rummadudum-e-dum- a rummadedoo-e-do. No, no I think it went more like, a-diddle-e-diddle-dum-a-diddly-diddly-doo, or was it, ah-tiddily-tiddily tum – ah-piddily-piddily-poo."

It began to dawn on the aliens that the Plonker (stick like creature cum parrot) must immediately be brought on board their craft and taken back to Nebularius where it rightfully belonged)

(Yet more drama was about to unfold)

The unexpected sound of barking dogs was accompanied by the clatter of jewellery which brought forth the arrival of the Queen. It was Her Majesty returning back from her weekend trip to Balmoral.

Eager to be reunited with her beloved parrot the Queen immediately makes her way to the throne room only to find the cage empty.

In his desperate attempt to clarify the situation Freddie does his best to explain the circumstances behind the mystery. His explanation was this: General Gordon, while munching his way through a pile of nuts and bird seed, notices another parrot perched precariously on the window ledge. Low and behold it was General Gordon's old soldier friend, one eyed Percy, the African Grey parrot. General Gordon couldn't believe his eyes at the sight of another parrot in his midst. In his desperation to see his old friend again he thereby asked Percy if he fancied going on a three-day bender with him. The response from Percy was met with sheer jubilation. Furthermore, Percy informed his old chum that his most cherished wish was to re-join the General's old regiment. The Queens 'very own' Foot and Mouth. In true military fashion, both parrots saluted each other and thereafter took flight and thus disappeared through an open window.

The Queen meanwhile was not amused by such a feeble excuse and the sheer incompetence of the man. In fact her exact words were: "a likely story" she said. "Off with the bugger's edd," she cried out in rage, and thereby requested that the bungling agent should stand trial for his complete incompetence.

(Meanwhile, General Gordon was taken on board the UFO and on his way to Nebularius with the rest of the aliens)

It was the day of Freddie's trail at the Old Bailey. In the final summing up of his trial the prosecution rested its case and it seemed the scales of justice was about to be tipped in favour of the crown. In fact the evidence against him was clearly overwhelming and left no shadow of doubt that he was guilty as hell. Therefore, his case was a foregone conclusion as to the outcome.

The judge, a well respected man called Lord Chief Justice Chaffney Brown, read out a list of charges and then asked: how does the plaintiff plead?

"Not guilty m'lud," Freddie smiled.

"Freddie Stanley Frobisher I hereby incite you with a list of charges which has been brought before me by Her Majesty the Queen. That on the afternoon of the 19th July you did wilfully let

General Gordon escape from the throne room. The second charge that has been brought before me is that on the 21st August, you did wilfully capture one of the Queens feathered friends called Gentleman Jim, a highly desirable plump chicken. You just couldn't resist the temptation, could you Frobisher? Without any feeling for poor old Jim you did wilfully pluck his feathers till he was stark bollock naked. You then had the audacity to stick a generous amount of Aunt Bessie's pork stuffing which was then, forcefully shove up his bottom. Finally, Gentleman Jim was then placed in a pre-heated oven, gas mark 8. The facts then speak for themselves. Subsequently, as a result of your barbaric act you did thus eat 'Gentleman Jim' and thereafter you had the Gaul to gulp his remains down with a huge mug of tea.

"May it please your honour; the plaintiff would like to point out that the chicken was most delicious." The clerk informed the court.

(Summing up the case) "Frobisher! You are a menace to civilised society and therefore, you shall be hence taken to a place of tranquillity, namely to the nearest mental institution. There you are to reap the rewards of your bungling ways. I therefore invite you to indulge in state of the art décor, excellent wine, good food, accompanied by satellite television and adult movie channels together with lots of dirty magazines. Furthermore, I therefore sentence you to be detained at her Majesties pleasure. And may God have mercy on your tackle."

"Cor blimey, thanks a lot, m'lud," Freddie smiled, and thus bowed his head.

The Queen, by this time was cock-a-hoop at the outcome of the trial. In fact her exact words were....."Yippeeeeeee!!"

However, the most intriguing aspect of the case was the complete absence of the evidence, namely, General Gordon along with Gentleman Jim.

The climax to our story ends on a happier note. General Gordon to his credit has meanwhile taken up full residence on the planet Nebularius, whereupon the talkative parrot is in complete control of an alien species known as the Greys: in fact the General to his credit has the audacity to be masquerading as the Plonker. The parrot was however particularly valued for his contribution in scoffing an endless supply of nuts and bird seed. Meanwhile the real Plonker, otherwise known as special agent Freddie Frobisher was regrettably serving out his sentence. However, there's one remaining question that still puzzles MI6? Where the ruddy hell was their rocket?

The Lost Treasure of the Nazis Gold

The year is 1945 and the Second World War had thankfully come to an end. It seemed inconceivable that so soon after this dreadful business had transpired, people began to wonder what on earth had happened to the lost treasure of the Nazis Gold which Hitler and band of generals had managed to stash away somewhere in the outback of the Bavaria Alps. The story goes that wagons loaded with gold bullion, money, and priceless art collections were loaded on to trucks and taken to Berlin. From there the priceless cargo was then transported to a small village in Bavaria. Eye witness accounts had testified they had seen a procession of mules and soldiers leaving the safety of a village called Garmisch and making their way towards a vast wilderness area, somewhere in the outback of the Bavaria Alps. And that was the very last time the soldiers and mules were ever seen again. So what happened to the consignment of gold, one might ask?

Meanwhile our story takes place at an establishment in the heart of London's West End. One evening, two friends were having a few drinks after doing a hard day's work. Peter and his pal Richard had been the best of buddies for most of their working lives. They had this regular thing going for them. Work all week; do the odd bit of overtime, and then on Friday night it was off to central London for a meal and a few beers. In terms of employment both lads had extremely good jobs as researchers for a well-known pharmaceutical company. As far as their recreational activities go, it was pubs, football and girls. However, their great passion in life was Archeology and, having been on several digs over the years they found it got quite infectious. This interest of theirs (archeology) will have a strong bearing on our story.

As the night wore on a mysterious stranger who was sitting directly opposite began to stare at the two friends with an inquiring look of despondency. The man looked somewhat troubled, and several times the two pals caught the stranger casting speculative eyes in their direction. Unannounced, the stranger allowed himself to make his presence felt by joining the two lads by parking his large framed rump next to theirs. He looked a decent enough chap I would say, though he had a look of sternness about him. There was a moment of awkward silence till finally the stranger broke his silence. It then transpired that the person in question was called Karl who hailed from the town of Heidelberg in Germany. Once a few facts had been established, intermingled with a few more drinks, Karl allowed himself to be heard. The fact remained that Karl was in London on very important business. He made it quite clear that the discussion that was about to follow would get more and more intense with each passing moment.

"Perhaps I should come clean as to why I am here?" Karl took a deep breath and began to give an account of his actions. "Well, first of all, what I am about to reveal to you must be kept in the strictest confidence, so therefore, I must ask you, not to repeat a word I say, to anyone." Karl politely asked.

"Right, I'll start from the very beginning. The reason I came to London was indeed a tragic one. The truth of the matter, alas, was one of great sadness. You see, my uncle passed away several weeks ago, here in London. He was an officer who served in the German Army in the Second World War. His unit of Tiger tanks was sent to the Russian front with devastating consequences. Eventually, the Russians gained the upper hand and pushed his unit back into Germany. Anyway, having eventually made it back to Berlin my uncle found himself being hemmed in on all fronts with the Russians storming in from the East and the Allies from the West. Which brings me to the next bit of the story?

When I was clearing out my uncle's house I had the melancholy task of sifting through a pile of documents that were scattered about. Therefore, it was instrumental that I made an attempt to sort out his affairs, but more importantly, to find the long lost map my uncle always seemed to go on about. Among the items I found was a trove of important papers which included a number of manuscripts and piles of old papers. It then transpired when opening a chest of drawers I found a letter plus a number of old maps which according to my uncle in his self-proclaimed introduction letter, told of a surprising secret. One of these maps gentlemen relates to the long lost treasure of the Third Reich or better known as Hitler's Gold. In the course of my observations I came across a document that showed the precise location of the treasure. Apparently, it was hidden in an old disused mine at the foot of a mountain.

"Anyway, on with my story and back to Berlin," Karl continued. "My uncle was thus given fresh orders with immediate effect from the hierarchy. Those orders were to escort a shipment of gold that was being dispatched to a secret location in southern Germany. However, just before my uncle died his last words were: "Karl, he said, within the confinements of my house you'll find a metal box which contains a number of notes and documents along with a detailed map. The map will show you the precise location to where the treasure is located. Study them carefully Karl," he said, "for I know with your knowledge and resolve you'll find the treasure."

"I know what's going through your minds," Karl sighed, "it all sounds too farfetched. You see, for my plan to succeed the necessary equipment will have to be purchased, such as mules and supplies etc. What I desperately need are people who I can trust. I cannot do something like this by myself. For the last hour or so I've been sitting here watching you two guys with intense interest. I'm a good judge of character; furthermore, I strongly believe you are both honest and trustworthy. I also think you'll be just sort of people who will be a great asset to me and indeed the expedition."

A picture surfaced of Karl's immediate plans. "In a nutshell," Karl began: "I would dearly like you both to come on board and join me. It's not going to be easy. You'll have to put up with the freezing conditions and spend days riding on mules, humping up and down mountains, but I promise you both the adventure of a lifetime. I intend to call the expedition, 'Operation Treasure Trove'.

Karl continued, "Over the years many books and documentaries programs have been put forward to the whereabouts of the treasure, but to this day no one has managed to find a scrap of evidence. As I've previously mentioned, there have been numerous stories on the subject, and contrary to certain beliefs, the gold will never relinquish itself to any mortal human. In my wanderings through the Bavarian Alps, I've enjoyed the real treasures, the sheer beauty of the place with its forests, flora, streams and mountains, and of course the solitude of the place. Just think of it, if it's found, the gold I mean, the lucky so-and-so's will become stinking rich overnight. So what I am prepared to do is offer you a piece of the action. In addition, I'm willing to give you both a quarter of the proceeds. Just think of it, here's your chance to become men of wealth."

"There's one thing that puzzles me," Richard butted in. "How on earth did your uncle manage to land up in England?"

"That's a good question. When my uncle realised the war was all but over he fled from Bavaria and landed up in France. He was later captured by the British and interrogated by the military police. He was eventually shipped off to England and spent the remaining part of the war in a prison camp in Kent. The funny thing is, having got himself acclimatized to the British way of life he liked it here so much he decided to stay, hence the reason for living in London."

The response from Peter and Richard was of course met with deep suspicion and mistrust which had crept into the equation as to why a complete stranger would make such an outlandish offer?

"Look, don't make your minds up straight away," Karl announced, "chew it over the weekend and give me a call with a yes or no. I'll be staying at the Carlton Hotel here in London. Let me know by Monday what your answer will be?" Karl said.

Finally, the three men shook hands and went their separate ways. Later, as they made their home Peter and Richard began to reflex on the night's extraordinary events.

Richard began. "You know its funny Peter, it's not the treasure that intrigues me but the sheer adventure of it all, and you realise old sport we start our annual holiday in a week's time - three glorious weeks!"
"Yes, that would fit in perfectly with Karl's expedition plans. What say we give it a go and tell Karl that we're up for it?"

The following Monday Karl received a communiqué by way of a telephone call from Richard and Peter who confirmed they were giving Karl the green light to go ahead and make the necessary arrangements on their behalf. Meanwhile, Karl flew back to Bavaria to make the final arrangements for their forthcoming expedition, such as purchasing the appropriate tools and equipment etc.

The initial plan was for Peter and Richard to join Karl in Garmisch the following week. In accepting Karl's invitation they would initially be making up to a party of four people in total. Meanwhile, time had passed by with relative speed and by now the boys were getting very excited at the prospect of their forthcoming adventure taking shape.

Karl's expedition party would consist of Karl, Peter, Richard, along with Max; a friend of Karl's who would be their guide. Meanwhile, in Garmisch itself, news had spread like wild-fire that a party of potential prospectors were about to embark on an expedition to find the long lost treasure of the Nazis Gold, which according to the locals Karl had been busily purchasing masses of equipment in readiness for a long drawn out spell which had produced quite a stir among the local inhabitants. However, unbeknown to Karl and his entourage, lying in wait was a man called Hans Stroller. He was the son of a former Nazis officer. Hans's father was the man responsible for the shipment of the gold once it had been delivered to Garmisch. More importantly; Stoller senior was the very last person to every see the gold again or know of its whereabouts. More to the point, Hans Stroller bore a deep grudge against Karl due to a long drawn out family feud between the two fathers. Hans Stroller had a cunning plan up his sleeve. Knowing of Karl's expedition plans and knowing of the gold, he decided to follow Karl from a safe distance and when the opportunity presented itself his plan was to keep the gold for himself. In fact he had a partiality for exterminating his arch enemy. Therefore, the problem could only be resolved by killing Karl.

In the days that followed a few loose ends were tied up before everything was up and raring to go. Karl decided to make his own observations for the journey such as making notes and sketches etc, or at least keep a record on what they found and saw. It was indeed a perilous journey upon which they were about to embark on.

At last the day had dawned of their long awaited expedition into the great unknown. On a bright sunny morning abundant with a sharp chilly frost, Karl's party was at last ready to set off on a journey to a vast wilderness area, and, for the next few days it would be spent alone, amidst a vast expanse of snow-capped mountains, stunning vistas and magnificent scenery. The moment of truth came when a posse of men and mules could be seen leaving the safety of Garmisch and making its way towards the Bavarian outback.

The first bit of their hazardous journey took them through a valley carpeted in a thick blanket of fir trees, before eventually connecting up to a network of well-defined trails that would take them over and beyond. In front of them was their first mountain to negotiate. A path led them tenuously along a series of cliff edges and high ridges before climbing higher and higher, taking them on a route along the eastern flank and then picking up another trail that twisted and turned in tight zigzag patterns. The going was tough and for hours their toiled in the freezing conditions.

Upon reaching a position of some height Richard had become somewhat shell-shocked as he peered down to an over-hang on the valley floor below.

"I'm afraid I can't go on," Richard said in a distraught voice. "I feel absolutely exhausted. I'm tired and drained of energy. I want to push forward but my heavy rucksack and equipment dictate otherwise.

Peter on the other hand had disappeared into oblivion which had caused much concern.

"Come on you lot," Karl screamed, keep going, for God's sake keep going or we'll all freeze to death up here."

"For the first time in my life," Richard moaned, "I now know what it feels like to be totally encapsulated in total isolation, away from the human race with all its vulgarity.

Their journey was hindered however by the severe weather conditions as they trekked through blizzards by day and having to put up with freezing temperatures at night. Exhausted, they eventually reached a high plateau where they stopped for a rest and a water break. But just then something quite unexpected happened. From the corner of his eye Max saw something glisten from the valley floor below. He immediately jumped off his mule and from his saddlebag produced a pair of high-powered binoculars where he began to scan the valley floor to throw some light on the matter. Judging by the expression on Max's face he had seen something of immense interest - for their hidden amongst a clump of trees was pieces of wreckage that was haphazardly strewn about. Tensions ran rife as the four adventures stood there gazing down towards an unknown crash site.

"My God," Max gasped, "it's a plane."

Karl grabbed the binoculars out of Max's hand in disbelief.

"Good heavens you're right Max. It looks like an old Dakota, circa around the 1940's. I can just about make out some markings. It seems to have broken up in two different sections," Karl announced.

"There's some letterings stamped on the side of the fuselage, marked USA."

"Let's go and investigate," Richard and Peter asked.

"OK," Karl said with a look of trepidation, "but I'll warn you this will put us out by a day or two, I'm afraid."

Slowly but surely they descended from whence to ground level again, twisting and turning down a series of dangerous rocky slopes that one false slip would send the entire party over the precipice. Upon reaching ground level again it was decided to make camp for the night and then at first light their objective was to go and investigate the mysterious plane.

The next morning, Max was already up and raring to go. With the necessary tools at the ready they began to cut their way through the dense undergrowth which had overgrown with bracken and foliage. The turning point came when Karl's party came face to face with the mangled wreck of a plane. It was without doubt, a Dakota that belonged to the United States Air Force. With no time to lose Max and Karl began to prize open the cargo door. To their astonishment the Dakota still had its full complement of cargo on board. Grates and equipment were tightly packed together with ropes and chains. The flight deck itself was littered with a stream of debris. There was a deafening silence as Max approached the cockpit area and there sitting at the controls were the grizzly remains of the crew, now reduced to skeleton form. Eerily, the Captain, Co-Pilot and Navigator were still sitting at their posts, and amazingly, still wearing their dog-tags. Karl made a desperate attempt to find out some hidden truths about the plane as to what happened? Almost at once they began to search for hidden clues. Tucked away, next to the co-pilot was a briefcase containing the planes logbook accompanied by the planes manifest? Scant attention was paid to the documents which contained orders from the high command of the United States Air Force, dated 1942 and marked '*most secret*'. Karl delved further and further into the paperwork when it hit him like a ton of bricks. Apparently, the

Dakota was carrying a shipment of armaments and ammunition which according to the manifest list was on their way to the American combat troops in Germany. As one can imagine the scene was one of stunned silence by their find. Acting on impulse, Max began to break open the crates. The real surprise came when the boxes revealed an amazing assortment of rifles, machine guns, ammo, mortars and grenades.

"Well my friends, we've certainly hit the jackpot," Karl smiled.

"Yes, that's all very well and good," Richard frowned. "But what the hell are we going to do with all this stuff; we can't take it with us, so what next?"

"This gentleman is a job for either the German or US authorities to sort out," Karl said. "No doubt we'll get a very substantial reward for our efforts. Look, as soon as we get back to Garmisch I'll inform the authorities about the planes position and its contents. That's all we can really do for now, but hey you guys this is what we've come for, adventure!"

With little more to do Karl gathered his brave band of troops together for a briefing.

"Right gentlemen; let's get down to the real business as to why we are here, and that is my friends to find the long lost treasure of the Nazis Gold. First of all I'm going to consult my map to get a bearing on our present position."

From his satchel Karl produced an assortment of maps and charts which included his uncle's priceless map. It was by an incredible coincidence that his uncle's map seemed to coincide with their present position. The mine it seemed was just a stone's throw away.

However, Richard had a more pressing matters. The call of nature had annoyingly manifested itself. Over yonder was a clump of bushes, whereby Richard decided to use it as a public convenience.

But just as he was utilizing some nasty looking weeds he noticed a rather inconspicuous opening. Acting on impulse he began to cut away the loose bracken which revealed an opening to an old derelict mine. Quite determined to throw some light on the matter he then proceeded to make further headway to satisfy his curiosity. But he would first need help.

"Hey everyone, come quick, you'll never guess what I've found?" Richard shouted in a loud voice.

The others rushed over to see what Richard wanted. Further inspection revealed it was an entrance to an old disused mine.

"Hey, what say we become miners for the day," Peter said with great enthusiasm.

"This gentleman I am pleased to say is the long lost mine my uncle talked about," Karl beamed with a broad smile.

"I've got to admit Karl, you may be right," exclaimed Max, as he pondered over the map.

"It just so happens we've got the gear with us to do the job, so why don't we get changed into our overalls and start doing a little prospecting?" Max beamed with excitement.

(Happily everyone agreed)

Karl's party wasted no time in putting together a plan of action which first meant clearing the entrance to the mine. With their torches at the ready they were about to enter the mine at their own peril for they had no idea how deep the mine went or where it would lead? A warning sign greeted them at the entrance…………………..

(Achtung Auchtung Eintritt Verboten)

However, it was nonetheless imperative they continued on. Once they had established themselves within the mine they had barely scratched the surface when they soon discovered the conditions were indeed treacherous. The piercing cold was unbearable - however the adrenaline and excitement that they had accumulated certainly made up for it. But more dangers lay ahead. Part of the problem was made more hazardous by the twisted support beams which looked as though they were about to give way at any moment. Little by little they ploughed their way through a complex of abandoned coal wagons that sat on narrow gauge tracks. Another obstacle to overcome was the fallen masonry which had accumulated on the surface which made it treacherous with each step. To make matters worse things had become frightfully spooky. The atmosphere had suddenly changed to a spine chilling coldness, as though someone was watching them. But who? Could it have been a ghostly presence from the past that had come back through the ages to haunt them? Then without warning their torches had suddenly died of an early death. How weird? Miraculously, they came back on again. The mine was becoming spookier by the minute. Richard acted as though he had seen a ghost lurking about.

The mine indeed was a dark and forbidding place hidden with perilous dangers. But what lay at the core on the mine? It appeared that the mine was made up with a vast honeycomb of tunnels and shafts that split and confusingly went their separate ways. It was a case of which one to take? By a twist of fate the four adventures had by chance stumbled across a rather amazingly discovery. For their scrolled on a support beam were chalk marks that depicted tiny little arrows that pointed in a horizontal position - this was further accompanied by German graffiti.

"Are you thinking what I'm thinking?" Karl said with a look of suspicion.

"This gentlemen I am pleased to say is clear evidence of previous Nazis occupation." Max confessed.

Then without any warning they began to notice a strong acrid smell that got more and more intense - when suddenly there was a violent rumble, followed by an almighty blast that ripped through the mine like a tornado and in its wake obliterated everything in its path. To make matters worse the present shaft they were in had been pulverized by the sheer force of the blast which had developed into a sea of whirling dust and debris. Their forward and rear guard was now completely blocked. It was indeed a most precarious predicament that they found themselves in. It was difficult to establish how bad things were? They would have to act quickly or it was curtains for them. Karl noticed a pick and shovel, resting against one of the support beams. It was all hands to the pump as they began to dig like mad at the mass of rubble that had accumulated. It was backbreaking work and indeed unforgiving. Everything had to be pushed aside to make way for a clearing. So there was Max on his hands and knees, furiously scrapping away the last bits of remaining debris that had formed into a pile of rubble. When at last, there was now just enough room for a man to squeeze through. Their efforts were rewarded by the joyous sound of laughter as the last member of the team finally emerged from their nightmarish hell. It was now a case of establishing which of the tunnels they were in or indeed which one to take? There was a lot riding on their predicament. It was nonetheless imperative they soldiered on regardless in hope of finding a way out. However, their fears quickly turned to one of joy as they encountered a bright beam of intense light that shone brightly from a far off distance.

Karl at this point had a driving ambition - to stay alive and to keep moving. Clearly shaken from their nightmarish experience they huddled together and contemplated on the task of what lay ahead. Whoever or whatever was responsible for the blast had probably been blown to smithereens. Indeed, quite unbeknown to Karl and his party it was none other than the work of Hans Stroller who had foolishly dynamited the mine in the hope of killing his arch enemy. For a split second the very thought of the mine being dynamited was unthinkable.

Having struggled to come to terms with the situation they realised there was no going back. In fact they became more cautious and resolved by the minute and under these circumstances and considering their precarious position their only option it would seem was to push forward.

Typically, Karl jokingly remarked. "There is nothing more satisfying gentlemen than that of a mine being blown apart from a person or persons unknown, which hopefully sends the blighters to kingdom come, moreover, down an unfathomable hole, thus dispatching the culprit to his maker."

By a bazaar twist of fate, the strangest and most amazing thing happened next. For almost once their spirits began to rally when that bright beam of white light got more and more intense. By now their adrenaline levels were pumped up to unbelievable levels as they continued to soldier on. Sometime later they came to a section of the mine which had completely eroded away. The erosion had caused a massive recess to appear. The opening led to a high-domed central chamber. Inside was an accumulation of broken-up slag and iron ore lying about? Panning the chamber with their torches they delved deeper and deeper into an unforgotten world of previous habitation. But what happened next was something out of an archeologists dream, for there tucked away in the far corner was a number of wooden boxes, piled up, two high. Further investigation revealed their origin. Clearly visible was the insignia of the Third Reich accompanied by swastikas. Feverish activity followed. Karl, Max, Peter and Richard began to break open the boxes like men possessed. The turning point came when all was revealed. In the stunned silence that followed the four adventurers were somewhat bedazzled by their find. For their stacked in neat rows of eight was the sight of gold ingot bars as new as the day they were made.

"Well gentlemen!" Karl beamed. "This is it; this is the treasure my uncle talked about. We've found it, my God, we've found it." Karl jumped in the air with delight.

"Yes, that's all very well and good." Peter butted in. "But how on earth are we going to get this stuff out of here, and how the hell do we get out of this place? Don't forget we're trapped in here."

"Yes, you've got a point, Peter. I'm afraid I got carried away."

"There's got to be a way out of the mine," Max butted in. Our only salvation is to follow that bright beam of light."

Begrudgingly, they left their treasure trove behind and pressed on regardless in their quest for salvation, moreover, to find a way out of their present position. At last, after fighting their way through a sea of rubble and obstacles they reached the bright beam of light. To their surprise the imposing light came from a vertical shaft. The sides were made up of solid rock which had niches carved in both sides for footholds. Karl gestured with his finger, thus pointing upwards. Max had no hesitation in climbing up first. Little by little they made their way up. Their efforts brought them to another level which led to a second story and yet another vertical shaft. The beam of light was getting more and more intense as they continued to make good headway. The whole party was hanging by a thread as they searched for a way out - when at last the welcoming smell of fresh air and brightly lit sunlight greeted them. The last man to emerge from their hell-hole was Richard who was perched precariously on a rather unstable footing. But just as he was about to climb to safety the footing gave way. The result of this little mishap was a complete cave in. The shaft had given way and had collapsed before their very eyes, making it impossible for anyone to return. Their miraculous escape had brought them to the foot a mountain. Now, with the whole team safely established it was a matter of making their way back down to ground level again to pick up their mules and equipment.

Later on, back in the safety of Garmisch, Karl's brave band of adventurers was still recovering from their nightmarish ordeal. That evening Karl called for an urgent meeting, presumably to go over everything and how the expedition had gone.

"First of all gentlemen," Karl began, "I would like to thank you all for your heroic efforts during the course of the week, and I might add, your magnificent display of courage and bravery. Our objective was to find gold, which indeed we did. However, I am also aware that people will begin hounding us for clues as to the whereabouts of the mine. So therefore, I must ask you never to reveal the location to anyone. Look at it this way. There is no possible way we could ever gain entry to that mine, seeing that all the entrances are completely blocked. It would take a small army of men and machines to re-open it. It has also come to my attention that the person responsible for the explosion in the mine was our old friend Hans Stroller, who should by now be with his maker. It was a little unfortunate perhaps that he had succumbed to his devious and evil ways, but the one thing we can look forward to gentlemen is a very substantial reward for finding the crashed Dakota, so all is not lost. The main thing is we had one hell of a good time together with a most successful expedition. Looking back on it gentlemen I am obviously overwhelmed by the experiences we shared together. In the meantime I give you a toast." Karl smiled as he raised his glass in the air.

"Gentlemen! Here's to our next expedition!"

Richard almost choked on his drink) "Oh, no, not another one!"

Esmeralda the Duck

The following deeply disturbing events contain all the classical symptoms which quite frankly border on the edge of insanity. To put it more bluntly, there are certain fundamental principles that must be observed in relation to dealing with screwball type characters. In fact this particular story is entirely devoted to my good friend David. He is without doubt a most trusted friend and travelling companion. However, the one thing that concerns me is his extraordinary odd behaviour. You see for some time now I've had this very uneasy feeling about the fellow and I strongly believed he was not of the full shilling.

My theory's based on the assumption that the poor man's gone completely round the bend and stark raving bonkers. My fears were quickly brought to fruit one fine summer's day in the Royal County of Reading, Berkshire. Strolling along by the embankment next to the Kennet River, my friend told me this remarkable story about an old flame called Esmeralda. Finding a seat to rest our weary legs, my oddball of a friend unexpectedly broke down in tears, which resulted in a quick delve into his far-flung past. David's story went a long way back, to the days of his youth, when he was a fine handsome young man, and full of it, the ego bit I mean. You see quite by chance he had met this beautiful young lady called Esmeralda way back in his Merchant Navy days.

It was love at first sight and after a brief courtship period they decided it was time to settle down and get married. But just after the wedding Esmeralda was unexpectedly taken ill with a mysterious illness. Sadly, she never recovered and died several weeks later. This devastated poor old David. But there was far worse to come. Far from drawing his troubles to a close, there were only just beginning. David told me in complete confidence that he had this sensational theory as to her whereabouts. He strongly believed that his beloved Esmeralda had been reincarnated in the form of a duck. Yes, I did say a duck, and apparently this duck lived on the River Kennet, just a stone's throw away from the city centre. Oh yes, it's completely true.

More to the point, David had seen her on numerous occasions and had even savoured the pleasure of her company. Apparently they whiled away the hours talking about the state of the economy, stocks and shares, and would you believe it, politics. He even sang her one of his sea-faring songs to her, entitled, 'A Life on the Ocean Wave'. The one burning question they both had strong views on was the European Union situation. Should we or should we not go for a hard or a soft Brexit?

How did my friend recognise Esmeralda, one might ask? Well, the duck in question had distinctive marks around her neck and at the base of her head, making her instantly recognisable. We carried on walking to where the rivers parted company and went their separate ways by Blake's Lock pumping station. Thereupon, David froze to the spot and was looking a trifle startled. There bobbling about in the water sat this beautiful coloured duck, pleasantly plucking away at her feathers and getting herself nicely tarted up for a male duck to come along and sweep her off her feet. In between the pruning and posing there was lots of quacking noises, going on. On seeing us the duck decided to jump on to the embankment and flash off her vitals in the hope of picking up a few snippets of food. She seemed a friendly little duck as her head began to sway from side and her tail began to wiggle as though she liked us.

"Ah!" we sighed.

"My God! There she is, my beautiful Esmeralda," David bellowed as he dropped to his knees like a sack of potatoes.

"Are you sure it's her?" I inquisitively asked.

"For God's man, look at her plumage and those beautiful brown eyes. Observe the way the sassy little bugger swings her hips to and fro, and by George, look at the way she wiggles her bottom. By Gad, that's my Esmeralda all right. I've a good mind to give her a great big kiss."

David left me like a bullet from a gun, racing down the embankment towards his quarry. It was at this point I began to have strong reservations about the fellow. The poor chap's sanity seemed to disappear in one flash of a second. Then in a bout of uncontrollable madness he acted like a maniac who had just escaped from an asylum.

For whatever reason, my friend had become mentally stimulated by the duck's quacking. Never before had I seen the sight of a human being, thrusting himself into a Third Reich Goosestep, along with the harder task of trying to impersonate a flock of finely read chickens and singing to a chorus of cock-a-doddle-doodle tunes. The little duck, or Esmeralda as we'll call her, started to pick up speed. The sight of a raving mad lunatic, racing down the embankment was far too much for the poor little duck to take in. Her podgy little body swayed and fluttered from side to side as she hardly managed to keep up pace with this monster of a man whose sole intention was to accost her. Then painfully from the top of his voice, David began to ask the duck a few inquisitive questions?

"My dearest, my darling, Esmeralda, where have you been all this time, my precious, I haven't seen you in ages, my little angel cake," David cried in a passionate plea.

The duck responded with a raffling of her feathers together with a cheeky little grin.

"Quaaack, quack, quack," was the animated cry from the duck.

"Yes, yes, it is I my beloved, David, you're once intended."

"Quack – quack - quack."

"Mmm, what was that you said my sweetest, I didn't quite grab what you said?"

"Quack, quack, quack."

"Well bless my soul, are you trying to tell me you were living in the Balls Pond Road area of London, in between Burt the Butchers shop and Julian the Hairdressers."

"Quack – quack – quack!" was the reply.

"On my poor darling, it must have been quite dreadful for you."

"Quack – quack – quack."

"And what was that you said my beloved, you say you then moved round the corner to an Indian take-away establishment called Taj Mahal."

"Quack – quack – quack."

"Please carry on my sweetest it's getting quite intriguing."

"Quack – quack – quack."

"You would further like point out that the proprietor of the establishment, a formidable character by the name of Mr Singh, fed you on an endless supply of red hot Ruby Murray's, one so hot that you could neither sit nor stand for a solid week."

"Quaaaaaaaaaaaaaaaaaaaaaaaaaaaaaaaaaaaaaack!"

"Oh my poor little cupcake, your poor old Harris must feel like a red hot raging inferno. Here my little cherub, let me enlighten you with a dirty great, well-endowed Dildo, it really works wonders for dirty blocked up Harris's."

"Quack – quack – quack."

"There there, don't be silly, my little wonder flower, I won't hurt you, my precious."

"Quaaaaaaaaaaaaaaaaaaaack."

"Oppps! I think I've slipped up my little angel cake, it seems I've dropped you right in the shiiiiiiiiiiiiiiiiiiiiit, my beloved."

"Quack – quack – quaaaack."

"Now I realise my little dumpling you are communicating in highly sensitive duck dialect which is obviously a dialect that needs to be decoded into proper English grammar. But having said that my little wonder flower, I take your quacking very seriously and I assume my little petal cake, when you say, one quack means no, two quacks for yes, and presumably my bumpkin, three quacks means, sod off you demented bloody pervert, go get a clean Mac on."

It had been a rather sad day for the duck colony and by now a large crowd of people had gathered that were somewhat mystified by the hilarious antics that were going on. I believe our little duck friend was beginning to enjoy all this, as though she was winding David up. The more bazaar his questions and the more sillier his antics, then the more Esmeralda would quack, and so on. The end to the story is when Esmeralda finally took flight, leaving poor old David to ponder on his next move with his beloved Esmeralda, which I sure wouldn't be too long coming.

The good news is however that Doctor Goodworthy, David's shrink, has assured me that his patient is coming along just fine and is almost cured of his terrible affliction. Furthermore, in order to gain his release him from you know where, David must first pass a test. Dr Goodworthy's plan is to put his duck patient by the banks of the Serpentine in London to where thousands of our duck friends gather. All he has to do is to casually walk through them. He must not chase, harass or talk to the ducks. If he falters however, and does a wobbly, thereby, pretends to be cured but then goes completely bonkers, then unfortunately, it's back to the sanatorium once more.

In conclusion to this story: it has been made known by several members of the medical profession that the man in question is completely 'Quackers'.

Saved by Doctor Death

The more suave, intellectual type of reader, might well wonder what a chap like me was doing in between my swashbuckling adventures? Well, believe it or not, I was actually doing my utmost to find regular employment. Why, yes, it's completely true.

Since being made redundant the first thing I did was to sign on the dotted line down at the Jobcentre. I did everything that was asked of me to find a job. However, the Employment Services were getting a bit over zealous at this period of time. They demanded that I take any old job which I presumed was to get me off their books. They did to their credit send me to lots of job interviews at various locations scattered about all over the Home Counties. During these interviews I was given a number of IQ and personality tests plus a selection of technology exams along with all sorts of similar trivialities. But it was the same old story. Because of my age I found it nigh-on impossible to get to the interview stage.

"Oh we really want people in the 20 to 30 age group," the human resources people always seem to come up with.

It got quite frustrating at times and was beginning to get me down. I could tell you lots of funny little stories while on my job searches, but we'll leave that for another day.

The strain of not being able to find a job was beginning to take its toll, and to top it all the Employment Services stubbornly insisted that I was to sign on the dotted line every single day. Yes, every single day, and all this paraphernalia went on for well over a month. The strain of it all was truly unbearable. So consequently as a result of the enormous pressures being thrust upon me, I landed up having a complete mental breakdown in the end. How could the buggers do this to me - me a man of the world, suave, sophisticated and debonair? Therefore, I landed up seeing a shrink in the end at the funny farm. It was inside ward ten or better known as the Farringdon Wing I had the resounding pleasure of meeting a doctor who specialised in dealing with nervous disorders. He was known throughout the hospital as the dreaded Doctor Death.

So there I was lying down on the treatment table, eyes bulging from their sockets while frothing at the mouth and talking some gibberish about mad scientists and how to get a free shuttle ride to Pluto, and then outrageously singing to a rapturous chorus of God save the Queen, along with..."There're coming to take me away ha-ha-he-he-ho-ho - to the funny farm? Oh yes the funny farm - he-he-ho-ho-he-he".

Standing over me was a guy dressed in a white smock and bearing an uncanny resemblance to something out of a Frankenstein horror movie. His name was rather reluctantly whispered with fear and trepidation throughout the entire hospital, especially by staff and long-term inmates. For the life of me I couldn't figure out how this particular doctor got such a name, but it certainly had me worried. And such was the state of my health I was diagnosed to be suffering from a variety of sociological conditions which included, Delusions of Grandeur, Nausea, and Paranoia, along with the more serious condition of Ergasiohobia. In other words I was thereby cast as a complete nut. In my quest for answers to my long suffering systems, I grabbed hold of Doctor Death's lapels, and, with a mighty yank, I pulled him down towards me.

"Now look Doc, give it to me straight," I said, sweat pouring down my face. "Am I expecting a baby or not and if so will it be a boy or a girl? How long have I got before the delivery? Come on out with it man."

"There there, calm down laddie, I can assure you, it'll all be over soon, just lay back and take it like a woman," the Doc smiled in a reassuring manner.

"However, before we can proceed with matters I really need to do a diagnostic assessment of your condition. It's then imperative that you completely disrobe. You are then to bend over and touch your toes with your legs spread wide open. This will hopefully give me the full picture." The Doc demanded.

To my horror the Doc then shoved his stereoscope up my bottom and started fiddling about with my private bits and pieces. Judging by expression on the Doc's face his actions indicated he'd come face-to-face with something of an enormous magnitude.

"I must say old chap," the Doctor's face beamed with a look of astonishment. "For an up and coming Politian, you're marginal's I must point out are of the most magnificent proportions. But surely, with such enormous marginal's you would prefer to have a good old fashioned nip and tuck around your 'Sheik me Ghoulies'. The Doc smiled.

"Anyway, getting back to this so-called baby of yours, how you are going to support this brat, I mean baby. Do you have a regular job, and if so, what is it?" The Doc inquired.

"Of course I've got a job and a mighty good one at that. You see Doc I work down the local sewers," which was of course a great big fib.

"In the course of your work did you meet anyone interesting down there?" Doctor Death inquired with a concerned look on his face.

"Cor blimey, not half I did. It was whilst down there I had the great distinction of meeting Roger the cross-eyed rodent along with his friend Timothy the enormous turd."

To convince the Doc I was nutty as a fruitcake I thereby came up with a brilliant idea. It was an old trick used by several of the inmates in the 'Sectioned Unit'. The general idea was to look as Mad as a Hatter. I thereby went in search of the dirtiest pair of diapers I could find, and, with great care I placed them on top of my head at the same time I shoved a generous amount of cotton wool in my ears and up my nose.

The Doc then entered the room, accompanied by a nurse.

"How's my patient doing? Is he ready face the outside world?"

"Blub-a-lub-blub-a-lub-blub-a-lub." I replied with great enthusiasm. To make things more realistic I decided to use my two forefingers and positioned them at the side of my head to make it look like a TV aerial. I then twisted my head from side to side as though I was receiving a signal of some significance from outer space. This act of eccentric behaviour would hopefully convince the Doc I was well and truly bonkers.

"What on earth are you babbling about, man? It sounds as though you're doing a commercial ad for an oil company." The Doc enthused.

"Blub-ah-lub-blub-ah-lub-blub-ah-lub."

"Blub-ah-lub-blub-ah-lub-blub-ah-lub."

"I say sir; it could be your patient is trying to communicate with us in a broken type of Swahili." The nurse pointed out.

"My word, I think you may be right, nurse. Now why didn't I think of that?"

In response the Doc did his best to reply in Swahili.

"Hapana-Sizungumi-Kiswhili-Nanazungumza-Ninatoea-Kukujua."

I of course gave an immediate reaction to the doctor in Swahili. "Dear Doctor and members of the medical profession. Blub-a-lub-blub-a-lub-blub-a-lub. My name is Hamilton Smyth Caruthers, the honourable Member of Parliament for the North Finchley Constituency. I have on many occasions been asked to take on the role of Chief Whip - better known as the fearsome, Mr Whiplash. May I take this opportunity in conversing with you in my native Swahili tongue which I do believe is frequently spoken by several members of the Labour Party? I would also like to point out that my mother is a two-ton hippopotamus called Deirdre who had the outrageous audacity to have an enormous tattoo inscribed on her bottom with words to the effect: kiss my big fat smelly arse". As for my father, God bless him. He is a pipe-smoking, beer-swigging, smartly dressed Orangutan called Colin, whose sole function in life it would seem was to go on a number of three day benders with a few of his fellow apes."

"Blub-ah-lub-blub-ah-lub-blub-ah-lub."

The Doc hesitated for a moment and then asked me this question?

"Oh I see," Doctor Death smiled, "I take it you're father is a beer swigging Orangutan then? But tell me something else. Have you ever had the urge to join your Orangutan friends?"

"Like a true blooded ape I immediately jumped in the air and there went about scratching my bum, ghoulies and armpits, and in the process I bellowed out in true ape style, "Ugah, Ugah"

"Well then, let me ask you another question. Have you ever thought about taking up fox hunting?" The Doc inquired.

"Cor blimey, not half Doc," was my reply. "There's nothing more gratifying than the feel of the wind blowing through ones hair as one gallops across Wimbledon Common, downing a bottle of scotch whiskey and then to be greeted by the sound of horns beckoning up the hounds to whip up a chase. Even more gratifying is the sight of a horse's rump easing out a freshly made turd. God! You can't beat it Doc."

"Anyway, at the end of my rhetoric the Doc was having none of my endless bull-shit and outrageous behaviour. I then felt his hand on my tummy as he pushed and prodded me like a sack of potatoes. After a quick examination he gave me his rather disturbing verdict.

"Right, do you want the good news or the bad news," the Doc inquired.

"Blub-ah-lub-blub-ah-lub."

"Well, the good news I pleased to say is that you'll be dropping one quite soon now and indeed with great force. It would seem, because of your child-bearing hips, enlarging tummy and substantial sized breasts; a baby is truly on its way. But it is with the gravest concern I must inform you that your expected baby may not be in the form of the human kind. Furthermore, I strongly suspect that your baby could be the result of a biological nature. But which I have no idea. The bad news is, I'm afraid; I may have to perform a colonoscopy in conjunction along with a hysterectomy. We really need to get you up to theatre and get down to the bottom of things as to why you're having these so-called babies of yours?

"Thank God for that Doc, I've been dying to drop one for ages."

"Don't worry," Doctor Death smiled, "I'll all be over in a flash of a surgeon's knife."

I also overheard the doctor whisper to the nurse.

"Extremely sad case I'm afraid nurse, probably caused by a condition known as Lymphogranuloma, in conjunction with Chronic Constipation, accompanied by Hyperlipidaemias. However, this 'blub-a-lub' thing has certainly got me worried. Defiant signs of madness."

"If your patient's not having a baby does that mean the poor sod's got a touch of the Itchy-Twitches?" The nurse pointed out.

"Yes, I'm afraid so nurse, this poor bugger will never be able to work again, and not only that the man's obviously off his rocker. Babies indeed!!"

As far as the Doc was concerned his patient was nothing more than a raving mad lunatic.

On hearing Doctor Death's gratify words, I felt like going down on my knees and kissing his highly polished shoes. The explanation to my somewhat odd behaviour was this. The Doc to his credit was about to give me a new lease of life which indeed was music to my ears. In my uncontrollable state of hysteria I had the resounding pleasure of looking forward to an extended stay of one year or more on the tablets, and thereafter joining the mass ranks on the sick, in addition, no more signing on the dotted line, down at the Jobcentre.

So it came to pass, Doctor Death put me on a variety of medications and strongly advised me to keep away from circular saws and never ever go near men wearing long trench coats. I was beginning to wonder who really needed the treatment, me or Doctor Death. Sometime later I got myself down to the hospital pharmacy to pick up my prescribed boxes of Prozac, Thephorin, Glutaro and Normacol, and went back to a quiet and simple life in suburbia, happy as Larry.

Schizophrenia in F Sharp Major

Bernard Grodzinski was a renowned conductor of classical music throughout his entire working life, and being particularly highly praised by the music critics of the New York Times, Boston Globe and London Daily Telegraph for his 'beautiful inspired tranquil renditions' of the Symphonies of Tchaikovsky, Stravinsky and Shostakovich. In addition to his unique talents Bernard had the great distinction of conducting the L.S.O at the Henry Wood Proms in London as well as his highly esteemed exciting interpretations of the new orchestral works of Tavener, Lutoslawski and Glass at Carnegie Hall, New York City.

However, music lovers were deeply saddened to learn at the age of seventy five the famous conductor had suffered a complete mental breakdown and had been sent by his physician for diagnosis and convalescence at the Pine Oaks Psychiatric Hospital in the Catskill Mountain region of New York State. It was while inside this particular hospital that the famous conductor had the resounding pleasure of meeting a fellow inmate called Joey Rivera who had been assigned to look after him in a wheel-chair. Joey himself had been a patient at Pine Oaks for some considerable time now and had formally been diagnosed with a severe mental health problem, certified by the doctors as having an incurable condition known as DSM-IV and personality disorder. Further to this disturbing news Joey also suffered from the more serious condition of Schizophrenia which would often send him into a state of uncontrollable madness.

Rather amazingly it seemed the two inmates were almost identical looking as though they were twin brothers. It was also remarkable that these two elderly gentlemen seemed to have struck up a genuine friendship together. Anyway, as their friendship grew stronger Joey related to Bernard that his most cherished wish was to escape from Pine Oaks; thereafter to be admired by people of America for his wonderfulness and charisma, even if it was for just a short period of time. Bernard however was getting rather irritated by the constant presence of Joey in his life and had developed a strong desire for a period of relaxation and peacefulness in order to regain his composure by being left completely alone. It so came about that a brilliant idea had suddenly manifested itself into Bernard's brainstem.

"Look here Joey," Bernard began. "I've come up with a marvellous idea. Why don't you and I swap roles? It would be really great if you could take up my position in society and thereby take over my role at conducting orchestras while I sit back here and enjoy a bit of peace and quiet. I'd be really honoured if you finished up in Carnegie Hall or even Radio City. I always get applauded and shouts of 'encore' that sometimes goes on for five minutes or more after performing. It's because they love me so much. You see Joey; I could really do with a break from all the accolade. So what I am proposing is for you to find a way of escaping from Pine Oaks and then perhaps one day soon you'll turn up in New York and there go about conducting the New York Philharmonic Orchestra. The reason I say these things is because we look so much alike," Bernard pointed out. "In fact people will think it's really me. Believe me you'll be admired and applauded for the rest of your life for being such a wonderful and successful impresario.

"But Bern," Joey sighed. "I don't know nuttin about classical music or orchestral interpretation," Joey replied in a strong Brooklyn accent. "How the hell could I go about conducting orchestras?"

"Don't worry" Bernard replied. "I'll teach you all there is to know about conducting. Moreover, I'll show how to move your hands in the appropriate manner at the different sections of the orchestra just like I used to do. If it's contemporary music with discords, the strings, woodwind, brass and timpani performers all know how to play their instruments and make it sound really magnificent and impress those nerds from the New York tabloids who always seem to slag me off. Look its child's play, I don't want to hear another word, you're going and that's final," Bernard insisted.

In the ensuing days and weeks that followed a regular pattern had developed, whereby the two inmates would thus disappear into the boiler house and out of sight of prying eyes. The conditions they found were just perfect for making as much noise as possible. Whilst inside their steamy hideaway Bernard explained to Joey the different orchestral groupings to where each section of instruments was located.

"All you have to do" Bernard emphasised, "is to make each piece of music you are doing with the help of your baton and hand. The beat of the music is indicated with the conductor's left or right hand. The hand identifies each beat with a change of either an upward or downward motion. Move the baton up and down and don't forget the baton is an extension of your arm. Therefore you need to relax your fingers and wrist so it will give you just enough tension to control the speed. Once the orchestra kicks off your baton will do the talking for you. Furthermore, try to emulate the speed and tempo required, and don't forget preparatory beats should be given with the maximum of effort, and under no circumstances should you use your head. By focusing the tip of your baton your hand will get the orchestra to play louder or softer, or play faster or slower. Increase the beat with either your hand or your baton. So in other words conducting is a means of communicating artistic direction. Here, I'll show you how it's done." Bernard illustrated. It is so easy you can't possibly get it wrong."

Joey wondered if Bernard's teachings were indeed genuine or was he telling him a load of misleading rubbish. The thing was Joey knew all too well how wonderful he was and had gathered Bernard must have already come to the conclusion that his understudy must also be of the genius mould. Joey felt he was quite capable of learning any new skill in the world, especially at conducting orchestras. Meanwhile Bernard was doing some serious thinking, "I wish that nerd would just say he understands everything and go away and leave me in peace. It'll give me great pleasure if he is identified as a fraudster for making a complete a fool of himself, but who the hell cares. In fact, it will serve him right if he finishes up in a strait jacket."

And so after much thought and deliberation Joey came to the conclusion that he was definitely the right man for the job and so ruddy wonderful in fact, he felt certain he'd be a more brilliant conductor than Bernard. So the scene was set for Joey to depart from

Pine Oaks, forthwith, and thereby start a new life in the big city as the famous Bernard Grodzinski.

Meanwhile Bernard chuckled to himself. "Thank God he's finally decided to bugger off."

Joey's master plan was to sneak out of Pine Oaks in a laundry truck that arrived each Friday morning to pick up the dirty linen. His plan was to hide in a skip and there keep a low profile till the opportunity came along when he could break out and enter New York, proper. Anyway, to cut a long story short, Joey's escape went off without a hitch. At precisely two o'clock in the afternoon Joey duly arrived at the steps of Bernard's house in Upper New York, still dressed in his sanatorium attire. To Joey's delight he came face to face with a highly polished brass nameplate with an inscription. (The home of Bernard Grodzinski)

Feeling somewhat apprehensive about the whole thing Joey flirted with the idea of returning back to Pine Oaks, but there was no going back. After a brief moment of hesitation Joey finally plucked up the courage and rang the doorbell. Slowly but surely the door opened and there to be greeted by a distinguished looking man of his later years. It was Osborne-Bates, a rather refined English butler who on seeing Joey beamed with joy. However, judging by the expression on the butlers face he hesitated for a moment. Bates had obviously come to the conclusion that his masters distracted manner and dishevelled appearance, made him look rather odd.

"Oh master, welcome home sir," Bates beamed. "I must say sir the rest has certainly done you good and you look so much fitter and younger than you did."

Bates led the way through the house as the grandfather clock chimed the hour - much in the manner of a tourist being shown round a stately home.

"Pardon me for rushing you like this sir." Bates began. "But if I may be permitted. I would like to draw your attention to something of great importance that has materialised. There was a phone call this morning from the composer Otto Schweinhaund. He explicitly asked for you sir. Furthermore, he wanted to know if you were free to conduct his first performance of his latest work, Metamorphosis on the mountains of Tierra del Fuego in F Sharp Major with his favourite orchestra, the New York Philharmonic. Am I right in assuming you would like me to confirm your availability? I'm afraid there won't be time for rehearsals but I'm sure it won't be a problem for such an experienced conductor as your good self."

Giving a nervous little cough there was a moment of uncomfortable silence as Joey gave it much thought. "Of course I don't need to rehearse, Bates." Joey boasted and cheekily flexed his hand to and fro and articulating his most brilliant imitation of Bernard's voice and with an accent that became so familiar at Pine Oaks. However the butler thought to himself. "The master really does sound much weirder than before, but I suppose being banged up in the loony bin for so long does strange things to one."

Joey at this point was beaming like a Cheshire cat and not by any stretch of the imagination could he have foreseen the immense satisfaction he got at having pulled off this amazing deception, knowing full well the butler was totally unaware to the switch. He therefore concluded that his acting skills were of the highest standard.

The next morning after a good night's sleep, Joey first breakfasted and then was briefed about his moments for the day. Sometime later the sound of a car horn heralded the arrival of Joey's transport. On that fateful day of the concert Joey duly arrived at Carnegie Hall and allowed himself to be ushered in by the stage door entrance? A commissionaire manning the reception desk was amazed to see the great man in person and had not the slightest dought it was none other than the real Bernard Grodzinski.

Joey was duly escorted to his dressing where he was immediately introduced to the famous Otto Schweinhund. The very same Otto Schweinhund who was regarded as a highly celebrated man of classical musical and a composer of the highest esteem. To Joey's delight Otto greeted him like a long lost brother.

"Bernard! It is zo wunderbar to see you again. But first I must tell you I did not vant zat Pillock, I mean Trevor Dimmock conducting my music! Therefore, I am so delighted you were able to take up my offer for tonight's performance."

Bernard again hugged Joey rather like a soccer striker who had just scored a magnificent goal in a world cup match. Arm in arm both conductors made their way to the vast auditorium to take their positions. The vast hall thronged with a fine selection of well-dressed gentlemen, accompanied by fashionable attired ladies, eagerly waiting for the concert to begin.

The first performance would be taken up by the dreaded Trevor Dimmock who was conducting Rossini's Barber of Seville Overture, followed by Beethoven's Emperor Concerto with Daniel Barenboim as soloist. During the performance Joey watched intensely at the way Trevor Dimmock moved his hands in time with the music and hoped that when his chance came along he'd be able to swoon the audience with his own version at conducting orchestras and to the highest possible standard. In hindsight Joey felt pretty sure that he would bowl them over with his music and therefore concluded it was clearly going to be a piece of cake that was of course if he executes the very same tactics as the great Dimmock and by doing the exactly same things by way of moving his hands in such a way that the beautiful sounding music would come through and make the orchestra perform to the highest standards, not that he any idea of what the music was supposed to sound like.

Once Trevor Dimmock had finished doing his version of Beethoven's concerto it was Joey's turn to let rip with his piece of music. Otto duly escorted Joey to the rostrum where he faced the full wroth of the mighty orchestra. A buzz of expectation ran through the mighty hall as the bogus conductor gave the cue for the concert to begin. Joey remembered what Bernard had taught him back at Pine Oaks and was determined to raise the standard of conducting to unprecedented levels; so therefore, he was determined to lead by example. Complete with baton in hand and to the hysterical clapping from the New York audience he started off his performance with an exciting new contemporary work, which nobody in the hall apart from the orchestra and the toilet attendant had ever heard before. The situation was made more compelling when the patrons felt thoroughly reassured that the great Grodzinski was about to deliver a magnificently original interpretation, thereof.

Meanwhile back at Pine Oaks the real Bernard Grodzinski was monitoring the situation on his radio and was feverishly tuned in to the classical concert at Carnegie Hall where his understudy was performing. It began to dawn on Bernard from what he was hearing that his partner in crime had presumably mastered the art of conducting. However, an unfortunate development was about to unfold with devastating consequences.

Back to the concert and all seemed to be going well when some blithering idiot in the brass section uncharacteristically hit a bum note in 'F Sharp Major.' This provoked the bogus conductor into a state of uncontrollable madness. There was a momentary indefinable pause, when a man, holding, what looked like a baton in his hand, had suddenly decided to leap in the air like a frog on heat. As the music reached an almighty crescendo and, for, whatever reason, Joey had become mentally stimulated by the ear piercing note in 'F'. So much so in fact that his body twisted and turned like a demented contortionist. Never before had the good people of New York witnessed a man flapping his arms about whose soul intention was taking to the air like a jumbo jet at the same time trying in his desperation to impersonate a flock of finely feathered chickens. The conductor had thus lost the plot. Then in bout of barbaric madness the place turned to a scene of uproar. To accomplish his mission Joey raced down to the orchestra section and grouped his way about in search of the perpetrator who dared to give him a bum note. It was nothing short of a good old fashioned head-banging session. In the middle of this madness and mayhem was a section of the orchestra, who by the look on their faces were having the times of their lives. The outrageous sight of musicians, smashing their instruments against the rostrum was one of pure savagery. Never in a million years had music lovers witnessed such amazing scenes of utter carnage. Summing up these dreadful events it can only be described as a scene of sheer barbarism.

In the meantime more drama was yet to unfold when a bald headed guy in the string section had suddenly sprouted hair. A lady violinist had used her bow to fire with some vengeance at her ex-husband on the trombone. There were also strong overtones from the saxophone player who reeked of swamp gas. The man on the French horn stood up and declared: "Will someone please wipe my bottom; I seemed to have released something of enormous magnitude."

"Evolution baby, evolution!" cried the man on the symbols.

The plot deepened further when the guy on the trombone had the cheek to ram his Nelson's Column up the backside of a lady cello player.

(More drama followed)

"I say, what's that enormous thing the conductors waving about in his hand." A member of the orchestra looked on with distaste.

"Good grief, it's an absolute whopper," the lady violinist gasped in horror.

"My God, it's a dirty great German sausage." The man on the piano confirmed.

"What in Carnegie Hall - never."

"Filthy things - outrageous."

"Ah, you can't beat a good old Porker Snorker," Joey beamed, as he proudly carried on conducting while beholding a dirty great sausage in his hand.

I doubt if there is anything more gratifying than that of a man who had completely lost the plot. Fearing for his job and those of the orchestra, all concerned parties rallied round to the aid of their beleaguered conductor. For indeed, such was their situation, they trembled with fear that their P45's were in the post for their outrageous behaviour. To underline his position, Joey finally came to his senses and seemed conscious of the enormous blunders that he had made. He fumbled his way through a mumbled speech to which the audience listened impassively.

In the meantime, howls of outrage could be heard from one particular member of the audience.

"For God's sake," Otto Schweinhaund shouted. "Pull yourself together man."

Almost immediately there was a flurry of activity going on inside the mighty hall. The mayor of New York stood up and proclaimed........

"Ladies and gentlemen, I would like to say a few words of gratitude to our beloved conductor, Bernard Grodzinski. In recognition of your magnificent performance for tonight's concert I would therefore like to offer you the freedom of New York City - the smuck!"

Having exchanged numerous insults with certain members of the orchestra for their disgraceful behaviour, especially for the bum note someone had given him, Joey came to the conclusion that the concert had off with an almighty bang. That said, the bogus conductor was unceremoniously taken back to his dressing room, only to find a rather red-faced Otto Schweinhaund waiting there to greet him. However, far from being displeased with Joey he seemed quite happy about the situation.

"My dear Bernard," Otto smiled. "The effort and commitment you put into tonight's performance was truly Wunderbar! In fact your interpretation of a rather highly strung free range chicken was simply outstanding."

"Why gee thanks Otto, you're a real pal."

"Tell you what, Otto smiled "Why don't we have return concert sometime in the near future and hey, how about doing a concerto entitled, "Herbert the Frog."

Joey smiled, cleared his throat and began to speak with a deep husky voice.

"Quid-ip-quid-ip-quid-ip!!"

Joey left Carnegie Hall in a blaze of glory. The following day at the Pine Oaks sanatorium the real Bernard Grodzinski was reading the New York Times and was amazed to read the critics account of the previous night's concert at Carnegie Hall.

Bernard Grodzinski's interpretation of contemporary music composed by Otto Schweinhund achieved new realms of profundity, audacity and immortality, never previously attained, and even the experienced performers of the New York Philharmonic seemed discombobulated but still coped magnificently with Grodzinski's interpretation of the 'Funky Chicken'. Indeed, it was nonetheless a momentous accomplishment by the great conductor.

In the weeks that followed Joey had plenty of time to think about his future. Therefore he decided there was no going back to Pine Oaks; after all he had much work to do with his new role in life. There were the offers, the tours, and the concerts to attend. For all

Joey cared, Bernard could simply rot away in Pine Oaks. So In a nutshell Joey went on to become the most celebrated conductor in living memory.

Harry the 'Hamster' Hillier

As I recall, it was a lovely June evening in the summer of 1999, and there I was sitting in the garden with my feet up, relaxing, and taking the world in its stride. When from out of the blue my phone decides to ring. With pace I rushed inside, burning with curiosity as to who the mystery caller was? Low and behold it was good old Uncle George, asking me how things were going, followed by the usual chit-chat associated with long drawn out phone calls. Anyway, in the course of his conversation he said he had something of a pleasant surprise.

"Look, I'm going up to Lincolnshire tomorrow morning to visit an old RAF chum I once served with and I wondered if you fancy coming along with me for the ride. On the way back we could pop in and pay a visit to your father in Lincoln. What do you say?"

"Why yes, it sounds great."

"Right, I'll be with you tomorrow morning at eight hundred hours - synchronizing watches." Uncle George insisted.

It was actually eight thirty in the morning before he trudged his way up to the front door of my house, due to the same old problem of extracting his well-built frame from under the duvet covers and nodding off back to his sleep.

After the mandatory utilisation of my toilet we were soon on our way, taking an easterly route towards the town of Royston and then connecting up with the A1 trunk road. Well into our journey we reached an area, known as Grafham Water, where beautiful lakes surrounded us. Thereafter, Uncle George decided to fill me in about his friend who went by the bazaar name of Harry the 'Hamster' Hillier, who was working as an Electronics Engineer for the RAF.

"That's a rather unusual name I inquisitively asked. Did Harry manage a pet shop before going into the services?"

"Good Lord no, he hasn't got the mental capability or the organising skills to do anything as complex as that. No, he acquired the name when he was flying Wellington bombers. Incredible as it may seem the whole crazy business started when Harry decided to take his pet hamster on board his aircraft with his furry little friend locked inside his cage. Harry had this very strong belief that his beloved little hamster had the capability of locating and tracking down a Russian submarine's position by the uncanny extrasensory perception that these creatures are believed to possess."

"In his desperate attempt to see his popularity ratings soar to unimaginable levels, Harry's commanding officer was instrumental at getting the project off the ground and therefore gave his full blessing to try out Harry's amazing theory in the Western Approaches. Anyway, during the maiden flight the pilot deliberately did a mock dive somewhere over the Atlantic Ocean, just off Land's End. Once the plane had levelled itself out there was utter pandemonium, whereby panic set in. With gaping mouths the entire crew looked on with disbelief, because the door of the hamster's cage had mysteriously sprung open which resulted in the complete disappearance of his furry little friend."

"Oh where oh where is my beautiful little hamster," Harry sobbed with grief.

The crew searched every solitary inch of the aircraft but the hamster was nowhere to be found. Everyone had assumed the worse that the damn thing must have fallen through the bomb bay doors and had plummeted down to the depths of the Atlantic Ocean with the lovely little creature lost to the world forever.

Then on the return journey home the crew were somewhat preoccupied with what seemed like a major emergency. The co-pilot thought the left-hand tractor propeller had stopped working and began to work up a sweat, when all of a sudden a ghoulish but distinctive squeaking sound could be heard by several members of the crew. Apparently, the mysterious noise came from outside of the aircraft. Harry was just about to send out a mayday message and threatening to put the entire crew on a fizzer for neglect of duty in failing to lubricate the said equipment properly. Harry raged. "If we do manage to get back in one piece before the prop packs up, I'll put the lot of you on a month's Jankers."

However, it was the navigator plotter who pointed out to Harry that it wasn't the tractor propeller at fault; the sound was actually coming from the twin 0.303 machine gun, situated in the plane's nose. They soon discovered it was our furry little friend the hamster, stuck up the gun turret. It was just possible to make out the tiny fellows head which protruded out from the nozzle of the gun. The hamster looked quite happy in a hideous sort of way. His tiny head could be seen swivelling round and round as though he was on a day outing to Brighton. One of the crew suggested firing a few rounds of ammo so as to clear the gun and thereby obliterate anything that resembled nasty little rodents. When Harry heard of this he was outraged at the very thought of his poor little hamster being splattered all over the south coast of England. Anyway, to cut a long story short Harry decided to go up front all by himself and extracted the hamster, there from rearwards. Having managed to dismantle the gun, Harry found the little fellow alive and kicking.

This act brilliantly accomplished, Flying Officer Hillier was never ever decorated for his amazing act of bravery. Not even a DFC or a medal, but finished up with the name of Harry the 'Hamster' Hillier, which is entered folklore.

"What a truly amazing story," I told Uncle George.

Later on in the afternoon we arrived at the RAF base in Lincolnshire and drove straight to the officer's married quarters adjacent to the main barracks. Waiting there to greet us was the famous man himself, 'Harry the Hamster Hillier'. Once the niceties were out of the way there came a brief moment of true eccentricity when Harry and my uncle began hugging each other like long lost brothers at the same time breaking into some sort of crazy banter, cum wireless op lingo, with words to the effect:

"Prang ho Roger, old boy."

"Tally ho foxtrot Romeo."

What the two of them were babbling on about I hadn't the foggiest? Uncle George then introduced me to Harry, where it was immediately decided to have a look round the base.

"Mmm, but I'll need to get you both day passes," Harry sighed. "As they know I'm an officer, I'll tell the sergeant that you're both from the Air Ministry Ablutions Department, they will never know the difference," Harry beamed.

"Why that's perfect, Uncle George injected, my friend's an absolute whizo on lavatories."

"Top hole, old boy," I cheekily saluted Harry, at the same time trying to impress him with my RAF jargon.

Surprise came when Harry received a communiqué on his mobile phone. It was a message from his wife. The message confirmed that his wife had gone into Lincoln to do some shopping and got herself arrested by the police for using abusive language to a traffic warden who nicked her for parking on a double yellow line.

"Sorry old chaps got to go down and bail the stupid cow out. God! Why on earth did I ever get married?" Harry moaned.

Harry duly apologised for taking off in such a hurry and was quick to point out that another meeting was definitely on the cards, but on a less hectic day. As an alternative we drove us to a nearby village pub for a quick one, where we sat and listened to a couple of RAF nerds who done nothing but complain about the station warrant officer - with comments about what a damn rotten bounder he was. Our final mission was to pay a visit to my father in Lincoln. All in all a most revealing but nevertheless hilarious day's outing. I was certainly was ready for bed when Uncle George dropped me off.

Hello Boyo

The first time I clapped eyes on Taffy was when I was living in a run-down Victorian house in the heart of Luton, Bedfordshire. The place was mainly made up with an assortment of grotty old bed-sitters and endless squalled rooms. Luckily, my bedsit had the luxury of full cooking facilities. I would describe the patrons as a mix bag of drop-outs and those who'd been living rough on the streets. On most nights we would gather round the sitting room and there indulge in lots of hilarious banter. The conversation would usually go on for hours and would continue on the subject of their heroic adventures and those unfortunate enough to be living rough.

One particular evening the owner of the place informed us that a new arrival was about to descend upon us with immediate effect. Anyway, during the course of the evening the sitting room door swung open to which revealed a man of ill repute. There was nothing notable about him except for a visible contrast between the drabness of his clothes and the solemn look on his face. Let's face it, his clothes could scarcely be described as being flamboyant or even upmarket, although I must say he seemed to be a man of a simple and harmless disposition. He was in my opinion a person who belonged to the hippie sect. What had also come to my attention that the person in question had about him a most unusual feature? For it seemed that both his eyes were not focused properly, thus pointing in different directions. To put it another way, he was well and truly cock-eyed. Scary as it may sound they had an almost sinister look about them. Anyway, once the introductions were out of the way I was then introduced to our new inmate with a: "nice to meet you". He returned the compliment by politely saying: "Hello Boyo."

A few days later I invited one of the inmates to join me for a spot of lunch. I can remember the occasion quite vividly. It was the day of the Grand National at Aintree and feeling like a little flutter, I put a bet on a horse with odds at 30/1, and with a name like Flash Harry, I thought it was a dead cert. Anyway, putting that aside, I decided to knock us up a bit lunch before the race started. Calamity struck, when I soon discovered I was practically out of food with not a morsel of food to be had. The order of the day was to totally replenish the pantry cupboard back to its former glory. But in order to do so a visit was needed to a handily placed supermarket. In our desperation for food we set off along the Luton to Bedford road, or the A6, as its better known.

Having eventually parked up at the back of the Arndale Shopping Centre in central Luton we proceeded to walk the short distance to a handily placed supermarket. But just as we turned into Bute Street there was deafening crash of thunder which resulted in a heavy deluge of rain - thus completely soaking us. So to seek refuge we rapidly agreed to enter the first building that came along which funnily enough turned out to be the local Jobcentre. Once inside we began to study the vast amount of jobs on display. Glancing at one particular job I called a member of staff over and quibbled: "Madame! I feel like an Irish navvy visiting Gestapo headquarters. Bejasus Pat! You vill take a job or be reprimanded - Ja Woh!"

As the place was quite busy we decided to make for a quiet corner where we could sit down till the rain stopped. What happened next was beyond comprehension. From nowhere this chap suddenly materialised. When I took a closer look at him, I at once realised it was the new guy from the digs where I was staying. He looked us up and down in the most critical way possible, grinned, and then had the cheek to plonk himself down with hardly a whisker to spare. Considering the state of his appearance I adjudged him to be an aging rock star or some well trodden hippie. You know the sort of thing. Long shaggy hair, unshaven, beaten up clothes and complete with the shades.

As luck would have it we managed to strike up a note of bright conversation and by far the most striking feature about the man was his amazing vocabulary. For his every second word seemed to be 'Boyo'. The punch line came when he asked us how long we'd been on the 'Rock and Roll'. In a state of giddy indecision I became somewhat flustered by his bazaar statement.

"Well actually I'm into jazz music," I proudly boasted.

"What about you," the man demanded, pointing towards my friend.

"Oh, yes, I love rock and roll, especially Elvis and Buddy Holly."
"No, no, no!" the man screamed. Rock and Roll is short for dole," he yelled.
"Oh I see," I smiled back, but also telling our newly acquired acquaintance that my friend had never been on the dole.
"Oh but I have," I proudly boasted.
"How long," the craggy faced Welshman asked?
"Come to think of it, it must be all of five years now."
"Well done boyo," the Welshman replied back with a look of delirious excitement.
"Look, let me introduce myself, my name is Elwyn-Dia-Jones, but most people call me Taffy.
"Well, it's great to make your acquaintance Taffy," we both replied.
Having got the introductions out of the way, we settled back to the hectic activities of the Jobcentre. Giving a nervous cough Taffy decided to fill us in about his life's precarious journey, leading up to the present. Taffy told us he originated from the Tiger Bay area of Cardiff. Then, upon reaching the age of ten, he had the terrible misfortune of losing both his parents, and for the better part of his childhood he was taken into care by the local authorities and brought up in an orphanage.
From what Taffy was telling us I gathered he hadn't had much luck in his life from the word go. No dought, the poor fellow had suffered tremendous hardship, but it may be said of him, he seemed a true warrior.
"Here's where I come to the most difficult part of my story so I hope you'll bear with me," Taffy continued in a subdued voice. "Now pay attention you boyos!" Taffy demanded. "I would like to point out that I have no parents, brothers or sisters, not even an auntie or uncle," Taffy sadly said. "Once I had reached the age of sixteen I was forcibly removed from the care home and thus thrown out to an unforgiving world, forcing me to survive on state handouts. I'd usually end up travelling round from town to town, dossing about in some derelict building. When necessary, I'd take any old job just to keep my head above water. My last job was dustbin-man," Taffy proudly boasted, "working for the local council in the Huddersfield

area, and you know what the buggers gave me the bullet just because I took a couple of old rubbish bags home. That was way back in 1975 and ever since then I've been on the Rock and Roll."

"Why that's well over forty years ago, how the hell have you managed to stay on the dole for so long," we queried?

"Take a closer look at me you guys. Who in their right mind would employ a guy like me? Any sensible employer would take one look at me and say: no way Jose."

Having taken in the Welshman's heartbreaking story we both thought Taffy was an extremely sad case of neglect and misfortune.

"You see, it's like this chaps," Taffy smiled, "unless you put a brave face on in life you'd otherwise fold up with grief."

I got up from where we were sitting and gave Taffy a good old regimental salute. My right arm was firmly fixed to my forehead, my left foot banging the floor and then bringing myself to attention.

"Taffy," I said. "Here's to your beloved regiment, the Department of Health and Social Security, better known as the Nabs, to which we have served with many many years of distinguished service - seen action with sorties in a variety of different towns and grotty offices and battled your way against all the odds and under great stress."

Taffy's face lit up with an expression of sheer elation.

"Why, you're a couple of ruddy tofts, you two are, here put it there boyo." Taffy beamed, shoving his hand into ours.

"Hey, how about us going out or a drink together, Taffy pleaded?"

I pointed out that this was not the sort of place to have any form of intelligent conversation. "But yes, we do seem to share a common ground of interest."

Our heads nodded with approval at Taffy's proposal and thus shaking hands on the deal, thus departing our separate ways. The rain had now stopped so we continued on with the more serious business of shopping - all in all a most invigorating day.